# The EU's Crisis Decade

Chih-Mei Luo

# The EU's Crisis Decade

## Reflecting on EU Capitalism and Governance

Chih-Mei Luo
Public Administration and Policy
National Taipei University
New Taipei City, Taiwan

ISBN 978-981-13-6567-6 ISBN 978-981-13-6565-2 (eBook)
https://doi.org/10.1007/978-981-13-6565-2



This Palgrave Macmillan imprint is published by the registered company Springer Nature Singapore Pte Ltd.
The registered company address is: 152 Beach Road, #21-01/04 Gateway East, Singapore 189721, Singapore

# Acknowledgements

This research is co-funded by the European Commission. The European Commission support for the production of this publication does not constitute an endorsement of the contents which reflects the views only of the author. The Commission cannot be held responsible for any use which may be made of the information contained therein.

# Contents

# Contents

# List of Figures

# List of Figures

# List of Tables

CHAPTER 1

# Introduction: A Crisis Decade for the EU

When the sovereign debt crisis first broke out in Greece in 2008, very few people, if any, in the world anticipated that it was only the beginning of a crisis decade for the EU. The sovereign debt crisis soon evolved from a one-off case to a wider eurozone crisis and, unexpectedly, dragged over several years. While the EU has been occupied with containing the first crisis since the eurozone was established, populist right parties (PRPs) won significant victories in the European Parliament election in 2014 in a number of non-euro crisis countries. Since then, PRPs were on a continuing rise from one general election to another, from the Netherlands, France, Austria, Germany, to Italy and Sweden. What was more shocking for EU leadership, however, was the unexpected Brexit result of the UK referendum in 2016. It was the first time that a member state was exiting from the EU since European integration was initiated more than 60 years ago.

Why has 2008–2018 become a crisis decade for the EU? Were these crisis events isolated from each other or were they interrelated? In terms of event sequencing, why did the rise of PRPs and Brexit appear after the euro crisis, and not the other way around? More importantly, did the EU manage these crises in a way that would ensure that such a painful crisis decade would not repeat in the future? These are the questions this book aims to answer and explore. It attempts to investigate each crisis individually and then to observe whether there was a causal relationship between them. A political economy perspective will be employed to explain this eventful decade for the EU, surrounding its economic governance.



C.-M. Luo, *The EU's Crisis Decade*,
https://doi.org/10.1007/978-981-13-6565-2_1

This book is a collection of papers that the author has published in academic journals in the past few years and brings together her research on these crises that the EU has been experiencing in the last decade. They are arranged in chronological order. They will first start from the European sovereign debt crisis, then proceed to labour market reforms that euro crisis members have been engaging in as part of their post-crisis management, then to the 2014 European Parliament election—resulting in the rise of populist right parties—and finally to the Brexit referendum in 2016. The book will propose its own answer to the EU's future—inclusive capitalism with reference to the Danish practices in Chap. 6. A brief introduction to each chapter is illustrated as follows.

Chapter 2 investigates why European sovereign debt crisis broke out under the existing fiscal regulation of the Economic and Monetary Union (EMU) and identifies the causes and nature of the crisis. A broad and complete survey to trace the course of the crisis was conducted in order to fully unfold the complexity of the European sovereign debt crisis. After re-establishing the whole picture, certain characteristics of the crisis were observed and were used further to dialogue with mainstream theories of European integration. After identifying the causes, natures, and characteristics of the crisis, the chapter goes on to discuss and evaluate the EU's crisis management, mainly in the form of bailouts, fiscal compact, and austerity policies. This chapter found that the European sovereign debt crisis, with a few euro members being stuck with high deficits and high indebtedness, was oversimplified to be referred to as the euro crisis. In fact, it consisted of several individual crises with different causes. Without recognizing their differentiations in respective crises, EU leadership managed this compound crisis with one uniform policy answer—restoring fiscal discipline through austerity policies. This chapter argues that EU leadership's mismanagement of the euro crisis would not only prolong the crisis but also worsen economic inequality within the EU.

Chapter 3 follows to discuss the other major policy that some euro crisis members resorted to in their post-euro crisis management—labour market reforms. Labour market reforms, following austerity and fiscal discipline, became another, if not the last, resort for unemployment-stricken euro crisis members to resume their growth and employment. Germany, with its record high employment rate in the EU, especially with its conspicuous employment stability during the global financial crisis and the European sovereign debt crises, stood out and its labour market reforms during 2003–2005, the so-called Hartz reforms, became the model that some EU countries looked up to. Chapter 3 is an attempt to clarify the effects of the Hartz reforms from competing arguments and identify their welfare implications for the German society and economy, so as to explore whether these kinds of reforms were suitable for the post-euro crisis management and whether they could be applicable to other EU members or not. The chapter identifies that, while effectively reducing German unemployment, the Hartz reforms have brought the German economy an increase in the size of the low-paid sector, negative wage growth, and increasing income inequality. The reforms, thus, were not qualified as welfare-enhancing because poverty levels in both the employed and unemployed increased. The chapter therefore argues that the Hartz-style reforms are neither a desirable model for other EU countries nor the answer to the EU's post-euro crisis management in a time of fiscal austerity and negative interest rates. It warns that the mishandling of labour market reforms could result in the collapse of the already fragile public confidence in EU leadership.

After comprehending the EU's economic governance during and following the euro crisis, Chap. 4 looks into the result of the 2014 European Parliament (EP) election. It was the first post-euro crisis election at the European level and was seen as 'an important test of faith in the European project'. The election outcome was that anti-EU, anti-immigration populist right parties (PRPs) gained significantly and became the third largest political force in EU politics. This chapter asks three interrelated questions: firstly, why were PRPs able to rise in the 2014 EP election? Secondly, what messages were delivered from the election result to the EU leadership? Thirdly, did they read the messages correctly with right policy responses? After examining the competing interpretations, this chapter argues that deep disillusion and mistrust of EU leadership, deriving from their long neglect of deteriorating distributional justice and fairness of European integration, which became acute after the euro crisis mismanagement, explain more comprehensively the 2014 EP election results. After assessing policy responses of EU leadership, economic Europe was expected to revive, but a social Europe that could address economic inequality remained absent.

The rise of PRPs in the EU politics culminated in the Brexit result of the UK referendum in 2016. Chapter 5 looks into the issue of Brexit and its implications for European integration and beyond. In order to clarify the interrelationship between the two, it was necessary to identify whether

Brexit was the outcome of a UK-specific issue or the result of more structural and general factors. This chapter identifies that Brexit and its development into a referendum issue were out of a specific national issue in UK politics. Nevertheless, the characteristics and divisions of voting behaviours revealed in the referendum—in regions, generations, educational levels, and social classes—demonstrate that it was a class divisive vote based on different economic rationales. Brexit voters and non-Brexit voters were divided along the lines between the winners and losers of market liberalization during the process of European integration. This telling fact therefore highlights a deeper structural issue—economic inequality and distributive injustice—which has been neglected since the economic liberalism has triumphed ideologically in the 1990s and has been aggravated by the mismanagement of the euro crisis. Reflections among EU leadership on Brexit, however, failed to produce any consensus on reforms or policy changes to the EU's economic governance. Neither of the competing visions—'more Europe' versus 'less Europe'—as a response to Brexit, rightly recognized the nature of the Brexit result. Again, EU leadership missed an opportunity to correct its faulty governance, and the public's disillusion and trust crisis with EU leadership remained unsolved.

After criticizing the EU's economic mismanagement in the previous chapters and recognizing that trade protectionism and populist nationalism became the answers from those left behind and economically disadvantaged voters to ever-growing economic inequality, this book proposes its own answer to the EU's economic governance in Chap. 6 with a case study on Denmark's inclusive capitalism. In order to provide a holistic, systematic, concrete policy combination, Inclusive Development Index (IDI) was employed to investigate seven policy pillars. This chapter demonstrates that Denmark has been performing well in areas surrounding acquired equal opportunities: quality public education, health, and active labour market policies for developing personal capability from childhood to adulthood on the one hand; uncorrupted public services and business-friendly legal and tax regimes for facilitating market competition from business creation and operation, especially for small business on the other. Governance played a key role in the functioning of this self-producing policy eco-system, staging at the centre as big investor and enabler for both labour and capital. The distinctive thinking underpinning this policy eco-system—treating economic policies also as social policies and vice versa—reconciled economic growth and justice simultaneously, resulting in inclusive capitalism in day-to-day realities. The chapter thus contends that the prevailing liberalist orthodoxy that guided EU economic governance was in desperate need of overhaul.

This book concludes in Chap. 7 with an overview on the EU's crisis decade. It believes that the origins of this crisis decade derived from the misperceptions of EU leadership regarding market capitalism. The solution to this crisis decade is an ideational revolution to EU leadership's neo-liberalist economic ideology. Without that, the crisis decade that the EU has been experiencing from 2008 to 2018 may not be a one-off. The future of European integration is dependent on EU leadership's thinking.

CHAPTER 2

# Unfolding the European Sovereign Debt Crisis

## 1 Introduction[1]

In early 2010, the so-called Greek sovereign debt crisis broke out as a result of Greece's national debt reaching 125% of its GDP (€340 billion) and its budget deficit 13.6% of the GDP, causing concerns in the international financial market over the ability of the Greek government to repay its huge debts. In the meantime, small eurozone economies such as Ireland and Portugal also sought financial assistance from the EU because of their worsening budget deficit and public debt to GDP ratios. As the Greek crisis persists, the ten-year government bond yield of Italy and Spain, the eurozone's third and fourth largest economies, rose in 2011 to above 7%, which is a criterion for judging whether a country is facing a fiscal crisis. With the unfolding of these events, there have been worries about the debt-paying ability of the eurozone as a whole, the prospect of an effective resolution to the fiscal problems, and the recurrence of similar events in other members of the euro area, thereby resulting in a sovereign debt crisis on a pan-eurozone scale.

The European sovereign debt crisis raises worldwide concern. Decision-makers in both public and private sectors not only worry that the European financial crisis may harm the vulnerable global economy that has not fully recovered from the collapse of the US subprime mortgage market in

[1]This chapter was first published by *Asia-Pacific Journal of EU Studies* (2013), 11(2): 1–34.



C.-M. Luo, *The EU's Crisis Decade*,
https://doi.org/10.1007/978-981-13-6565-2_2

2008/2009 but also question whether the lingering of the European crisis will lead to a second global financial meltdown. As UK chancellor George Osborne indicated, the crisis is a specific case in that problems in the periphery cause 'shock waves across the whole European economy and the world economy'.[2] For the EU, the sovereign debt crisis is the first crisis since the establishment of the Economic and Monetary Union (EMU) in 1999, and the deepening of the crisis further makes the project of European integration 'facing the greatest challenge', as José Manuel Barroso, president of the European Commission, suggested.[3] The crisis hence generates heated debates among the EU and the member states on how it may be dealt with, as well as on a more fundamental issue regarding the sustainability of the single currency.

The crisis, however, is not simply a European matter. The eurozone accounts for more than one-fifth of world gross domestic product (GDP), ranking second after the US, and is the world's most important exporter and importer of goods and services.[4] Because of the important role of the euro in global economy, its stability—or collapse—will necessarily have huge impacts on both the eurozone and the outside world. A study of the crisis not only contributes to the field of European studies but also brings implications to such subjects as regional integration, global political economy, globalization, and global governance.

This chapter discusses the causes and nature of the European sovereign debt crisis under the existing fiscal regulation of the EMU. The second section conducts a broad survey to trace the course of the crisis, as the complexity of the European sovereign debt crisis has not yet been fully captured and commentators offer their insights only to explain part of the picture.[5] After re-establishing the whole picture, the third section identifies certain features or particularities of the crisis from the perspectives of

[2] 'Davos 2012: IMF Issues Austerity Warning', *BBC News*, January 28, 2012, www.bbc.co.uk/news/business-16771939.

[3] 'EU "Faces Its Greatest Challenge" - José Manuel Barroso', *BBC News*, September 28, 2011, www.bbc.co.uk/news/world-europe-15087683.

[4] The European Central Bank, 'The Euro Area and the Global Economy', http://www.ecb.europa.eu/ecb/tasks/international/globaleconomy/html/index.en.html.

[5] This is the primary approach to discussing the European sovereign debt crisis in the current Anglo-American world. The author observes that in the literature few would adopt a specific theory to analyse the crisis; even commentators such as Robert Mundell, the 'Father' of euro and the pioneer of the optimal currency area theory, and Andrew Moravcsik, the founder of liberal intergovernmentalism, offer their insights on the basis of the events themselves rather than applying the theory that each is known for to the crisis.

intergovernmentalism and neofunctionalism, the two most prominent theories in the study of European integration. The fourth section then discusses and evaluates the solutions being put forth so far. The fifth section provides conclusions.

## 2 Reconstructing the European Sovereign Debt Crisis

The European sovereign debt crisis began with the Greek debt crisis in the end of 2009. Despite the fact that both the EU and the International Monetary Fund (IMF) have offered several bailout funds and the EU summit has been held dozens of times, over the first two years of the crisis, the problem has not been solved but indeed worsened. The crisis spread to the core eurozone countries and reached a critical stage when bond yields soared in Italy and Spain in August 2011. It was not until the two EU summits in October and December 2011, respectively, that decision-makers in the eurozone came up with concrete action plans.

### *2.1 The Origin and Propagation of the European Sovereign Debt Crisis: Greece, Ireland, and Portugal Seeking for Financial Support*

In December 2009, Greek Deputy finance minister Philippos Sachinidis revealed that the government's debt reached a historical high of €300 billion and amounted to 115% of its GDP, which was almost twice the limit of 60% imposed by EU rules; Greece's budget deficit, on the other hand, was 13.6% of its GDP, way beyond the EU 3% ceiling.[6] Although the Greek government pledged to make spending cuts and take austerity measures, they were proved to be ineffective. In May 2010, Greece sought assistance from the EU and IMF. Germany, once reluctant to rescue Greece, shifted its position out of a concern for maintaining the stability of the eurozone, and with a condition of the IMF participation. There hence was a first bailout package for Greece in that eurozone members,

[6] The reasons behind include the following: first, the government's overspending in the past decade and the doubling of wages in the public sector; second, a loss of tax income due to widespread tax evasion; and, third, the impacts of the 2008 global financial downturn. See 'Q&A: Greece's Economic Woes', *BBC News*, March 26, 2010, http://news.bbc.co.uk/go/pr/fr/-/2/hi/business/8508136.stm.

and the IMF agreed to offer Greece a €110 billion three-year loan in return for the latter's taking major austerity cuts that involved 'great sacrifices'.[7] In addition, to safeguard financial stability in the eurozone, the member states also agreed to found a European Financial Stability Facility (EFSF) with a scale of €440 billion,[8] which would provide financial assistance to member states running into trouble.

In November 2010, Ireland applied for bailout funds from the EU and the IMF as the government's efforts to save its banks resulted in a budget deficit of 32% of the GDP. European leaders responded promptly and approved an €85 billion rescue package.[9] In return, the Irish government proposed a four-year austerity plan with tough steps.[10] However, it was held in the financial market that the fiscal measures undertaken by the Irish government would hinder the country's economic growth. Hence the yield on ten-year Irish bonds hit more than 8.9%, and Standard & Poor's also cut Ireland's long-term debt rating from AA-minus to A.[11]

The increase in Ireland's borrowing costs led to a loss of confidence in holding bonds issued by the Portuguese and Spanish governments, with the Portuguese ten-year government bond yield rising to a record high of 7.23%, exceeding the 7% threshold for seeking financial aid.[12] The Portuguese parliament passed the deepest budget cuts in three decades in response, while José Manuel Barroso, president of European Commission, warned EU leaders for the first time. He urged that as the crisis deepened,

[7] 'Huge Greece Bail-out Deal Agreed', *BBC News*, May 2, 2010, http://news.bbc.co.uk/go/pr/fr/-/2/hi/business/8656649.stm.

[8] The EFSF was replaced by a permanent European Stability Mechanism (ESM), which was inaugurated on 8 October 2012.

[9] Joe Brennan & Stephanie Bodoni, 'Ireland Seeks Bailout as "Outsized" Problem Overwhelms Nation', *Bloomberg*, November 21, 2010, http://www.bloomberg.com/news/2010-11-21/lenihan-says-he-will-recommend-ireland-should-formally-ask-for-eu-bailout.html; James G. Neuger & Simon Kennedy, 'Ireland Gets $113 Billion Bailout as EU Ministers Seek to Halt Debt Crisis', *Bloomberg*, November 29, 2010, http://www.bloomberg.com/news/2010-11-28/ireland-wins-eu85-billion-aid-germany-drops-threat-on-bonds.html.

[10] Gabriele Steinhauser & Shawn Pogatchnik, 'Ireland Second European Nation to Seek Bailout', *NBC News*, November 21, 2010, http://www.msnbc.msn.com/id/40299184/ns/business-world_business/t/ireland-second-european-nation-seek-bailout/.

[11] Jill Treanor, 'Fears Irish Contagion Will Spread across Europe', *The Guardian*, November 24, 2010, http://www.guardian.co.uk/business/2010/nov/24/european-debt-crisis-spain-portugal-bailout-fears/print.

[12] James G. Neuger & Simon Kennedy, 'Ireland Gets $113 Billion Bailout as EU Ministers Seek to Halt Debt Crisis'.

EU leaders must 'deal with it in the most responsible way'. Germany, on the other hand, insisted that the private investor bond holders should also bear the losses.[13]

After January 2011, the difference between European Commission and Germany of how to deal with the crisis went public. Barroso proposed that the EFSF should be reinforced, while Merkel and her finance minister, Wolfgang Schäuble, described Barroso's intervention as 'unnecessary'. The chancellor's office was even reported to tell Barroso to shut up, as the €440 billion guaranteed by eurozone governments was 'none of his business' and 'not his money'. Olli Rehn, EU commissioner for monetary affairs, criticized Germany for hindering the increase of the rescue fund.[14]

As the disagreement between the Commission and Germany continued, Portugal's ten-year government bond yield climbed to 7.63%, the highest level since the country joined the euro, and its budget deficit also reached 7% of its GDP.[15] In April 2011, the international credit rating agency Moody's downgraded the government debt of Portugal,[16] and one month later the Portuguese government turned to the EU and the IMF for bailout. Eurozone finance ministers quickly endorsed a three-year loan of €78 billion; in return, Portugal agreed to a number of measures to increase tax revenue and reduce spending.[17]

In the meantime, the Greek crisis has not been effectively resolved by the EU's aid, and a second bailout was called for. Eurozone finance ministers were not in agreement with the conditions for the bailout, and this resulted in public criticism from the IMF. In its annual assessment of the eurozone, the IMF pointed out that the failure of European leaders to undertake decisive actions would bring the Greek crisis to the core of the eurozone, thereby harming the global economy. John Lipsky, the then

[13] Jill Treanor, 'Fears Irish Contagion Will Spread across Europe'.

[14] Ian Traynor, 'Eurozone Tensions Rise amid Bailouts', *The Guardian*, January 18, 2011, http://www.guardian.co.uk/business/2011/jan/18/eurozone-crisis-over-bailout-response/print.

[15] Larry Elliott, 'European Debt Crisis Threatens Portugal', *The Guardian*, February 10, 2011, http://www.guardian.co.uk/business/2011/feb/10/european-debt-crisis-threatens-portugal/print.

[16] Graeme Wearden, 'Portugal Edges Closer to Bailout after Debt Downgrade', *The Guardian*, April 5, 2011, http://www.guardian.co.uk/business/2011/apr/05/portugal-edge-bailout-debt-downgraded/print.

[17] James G. Neuger & Anabela Reis, 'Portugal's $111 Billion Bailout Approved as EU Prods Greece to Sell Assets', *Bloomberg*, May 17, 2011, http://www.bloomberg.com/news/2011-05-16/portugal-bailout-approved-as-eu-prods-greece-to-sell-assets.html.

IMF's acting head, criticized that Europe's attempts to deal with the crisis over the past 18 months had been 'disjointed, indecisive, and unproductive', and this was interpreted as targeting Germany.[18]

### 2.2 *Critical Stage After August 2011: Financial Difficulties in Italy and Spain*

The European sovereign debt crisis spread from the periphery to the core of the eurozone in August 2011. With bond yields in Italy and Spain, the eurozone's third and fourth largest economies, soaring, and with the Italian government bond market being the third largest in the world, the European sovereign debt crisis entered a critical stage. After an emergency conference, the European Central Bank (ECB) announced that it would buy government bonds from Italy and Spain[19] and showed the financial market the bank's will to support the two states by affirming the austerity measures already taken by the two.[20] Borrowing costs for both Italy and Spain fell as a result of the ECB's intervention. Spain then passed a constitutional amendment to add in the 'golden rule' of keeping limited budget deficits, while the Italian parliament passed a €50 billion austerity budget to achieve budget balance by 2013.[21]

[18] Ian Traynor & Larry Elliott, 'Greek Crisis: EU Leaders Must Act Decisively or Face Disaster, Say IMF', *The Guardian*, June 21, 2011, http://www.guardian.co.uk/world/2011/jun/20/greece-europe-act-fast-disaster-imf/print.

[19] There has been a debate about whether the ECB is entitled to buy the government bond of a member state both in European politics and academia. The opponents argue that according to Article 104 of the Maastricht Treaty, there would be no bail-out for member states in fiscal difficulty, while the supporters contend that the Treaty, as indicated in Article 103, Section 2, allows the Council to grant financial assistance to a member state that is in difficulties caused by natural disasters or 'exceptional occurrences'. The controversy has led two members of the ECB governing council to quit. See Kevin Featherstone, 'The Greek Sovereign Debt Crisis and EMU: A Failing State in a Skewed Regime', *Journal of Common Market Studies*, Vol. 49, No. 2 (2011), p. 202; Georgios P. Kouretas and Prodromos Vlamis, 'The Greek Crisis: Causes and Implications', *PanoEconomicus*, Vol. 4 (2010), p. 396; Heather Stewart, 'Greece: We Could Exit Euro in Three Months', *The Guardian*, January 3, 2012, http://www.guardian.co.uk/business/2012/jan/03/greece-warns-over-euro-exit.

[20] 'ECB "to Act" over Eurozone Debt Crisis', *BBC News*, August 8, 2011, http://www.bbc.co.uk/news/business-14439224.

[21] Alex Hawkes, 'ECB Intervention Brings Short-Term in Volatile Day for Markets', *The Guardian*, August 8, 2011, http://www.guardian.co.uk/business/2011/aug/08/ecb-intervention-european-stock-markets; 'Timeline: the Unfolding Eurozone Crisis', *BBC News*, February 13, 2012, http://www.bbc.co.uk/news/business-13856580.

After the crises in Italy and Spain, European Commission President José Manuel Barroso called for a 'community method' to deal with the crisis. He proposed the introduction of 'eurobonds' issued by the 17 euro members, so that they could borrow money collectively. The idea was backed by the Italian government and investor George Soros, but was opposed by Germany on the basis that at the current stage individual member states conduct their own economic policies and that the introduction of such bonds could reduce the will of those in trouble to carry out reform and austerity policies.[22]

Between September and the end of October 2011, when the EU summit was held in Brussels, was the period in which the European sovereign debt crisis appeared to be most chaotic. On the one hand, the crisis has spread to the core of the eurozone, but the original problem—the Greek crisis—remained. Eurozone finance ministers have postponed the Greek aid payment for several times as Greece had failed to implement the austerity measures promised. There hence has been speculation about a Greek default or exit from the eurozone.[23] In addition, the eurozone has not been short of bad news, as Standard & Poor's downgraded Italy's debt rating in September, and data from the EU indicated growth in the eurozone's private sector shrinking for the first time in two years.[24]

On the other hand, France and Germany were not able to reach a consensus on how to deal with the crisis. Of particular importance was the issue of boosting the EFSF. France urged to increase the firepower of the EFSF in case large economies such as Italy or Spain may need rescuing. German chancellor Angela Merkel, however, has promised German taxpayers that Germany's contribution would not go above €211 billion to increase their liabilities, while Wolfgang Schäuble, finance minister as well as an important partner of the coalition government, repudiated the idea of boosting the EFSF. Similarly, the French proposal to turn the EFSF into a bank so that it could borrow from the ECB was ruled out by

[22] 'Commission President Barroso to Put forward Eurobonds', *BBC News*, September 14, 2011, http://www.bbc.co.uk/news/business-14913517; 'Q&A: Bonds and Eurobonds', *BBC News*, September 14, 2011, http://www.bbc.co.uk/news/business-11743952.

[23] 'Greece "Integral" to the Eurozone, Say European Leaders', *BBC News*, September 15, 2011, http://www.bbc.co.uk/news/business-14924089; Phillip Inman, 'Greece under Pressure as Finance Ministers Put Brakes on Bailout', *The Guardian*, September 16, 2011, http://www.guardian.co.uk/business/2011/sep/16/greece-finance-ministers-bailout-payment.

[24] 'Timeline: the Unfolding Eurozone Crisis', *BBC News*, February 13, 2012.

Germany, as this move might compromise the ECB's impartiality and go against the rule that the ECB may not finance member states. On the contrary, Germany's push for the private sector to take steeper losses was opposed by France and the ECB on the ground that a heavy loss in the banking sector would result in a credit crunch. The deep divisions between France and Germany have led an EU summit on the debt crisis to be delayed by a week in order for both sides to have more time to negotiate.[25]

As the situation worsened while exchanges between Germany and France remained deadlocked, rumours of eurozone disintegration have been circulating. The IMF warned in September 2011 that global economy has entered 'dangerous new phase',[26] and IMF chief Christine Lagarde later called for countries to 'act now and act together'.[27] The US president, Barack Obama, also urged publicly that the big countries in Europe must meet and take a decision on how to deal with the crisis.[28] Mounting international pressure finally led Germany and France to reach an agreement in the end of October. The deal agreed at the October summit was a vital step for solving the European debt crisis.[29]

After marathon talks in Brussels, European leaders reached a 'three-pronged' agreement on 27 October 2011. The main points include, first, banks holding Greek debt accepted a 50% loss; second, the firepower of the EFSF would be boosted from €440 billion to €1 trillion; and, third, weak European banks were required to recapitalize by the middle of 2012 so they can withstand their losses on the holdings of government debt.[30] These three items were the first concrete and long-term solutions European

[25] 'Angela Merkel Faces Big Test in Germany EU Bailout Vote', *BBC News*, September 29, 2011, http://www.bbc.co.uk/news/world-europe-15103052; 'Eurozone Ministers Approve 8bn Euro Greek Bailout Aid', *BBC News*, October 21, 2011, http://www.bbc.co.uk/news/business-15401280; 'Deadlock in the Eurozone', *BBC News*, October 21, 2011, http://www.bbc.co.uk/news/world-europe-15400806.

[26] 'IMF: Global Economy Has Entered "Dangerous New Phase"', *BBC News*, September 20, 2011, http://www.bbc.co.uk/news/business-14984087.

[27] 'IMF: Global Economy Needs Collective Action Now', *BBC News*, September 23, 2011, http://www.bbc.co.uk/news/business-15041674.

[28] Dominic Rushe, 'Tim Geithner Urges Europe to Act Decisively on Debt Crisis', *The Guardian*, September 14, 2011, www.guardian.co.uk/business/2011/sep/14/geithner-europe-debt-crisis/print.

[29] 'Leaders Agree Eurozone Debt Deal after Late-Night Talks', *BBC News*, October 27, 2011, http://www.bbc.co.uk/news/world-europe-15472547.

[30] 'Leaders Agree Eurozone Debt Deal after Late-Night Talks', *BBC News*, October 27, 2011.

leaders brought forth in the two years since the crisis broke out, and were largely a compromise between Germany and France.

### 2.3 *The 'Make-or-Break' Summit in December 2011*

The summit in October did bring the Euro crisis some signs of easing. After mid-November 2011, however, the yields on Italy's and Spain's ten-year government bonds rose close to the 7% threshold. With respect to Italy, the financial market did not believe that the austerity measures could be fully implemented, as growth in Italy was weak and vested interests in Berlusconi's cabinet hindered the fiscal reform. As for Spain, the government's borrowing cost rose because the 23% of unemployment and the regional spending problems led investors to doubt Spain's long-term repay capability. It was suggested that if Italy and Spain required a rescue, the EFSF would need to provide at least €2 trillion. In this sense the summit in October did not solve the problem 'once and for all'. As a result, the escalating crisis further put France under pressure as yields on French bonds were also rising.[31]

The worsening of the crisis led eurozone banks to act cautiously in lending to each other. The figures from the ECB in November 2011 showed that just within two weeks the amount of money eurozone banks deposited with the ECB increased by €100 billion. This indicated a risk of interbank loan and hence a potential if not yet an actual credit crunch. European Council President Herman Van Rompuy warned that 'The trouble has become systemic'.[32]

In facing the escalating crisis, member states of the euro had different opinions. On the one hand, France proposed to enhance the role of the ECB, rendering it to become the 'lender of last resort'. This idea was supported by countries such as Austria, Finland, and the Netherlands, but was opposed by Germany, as it believed that eurozone member states should

[31] Rachel Donadio and Elisabetta Povoledo, 'Facing Crisis, Technocrats Take Charge in Italy', *The New York Times*, November 16, 2011, http://www.nytimes.com/2011/11/17/world/europe/monti-forms-new-italian-government.html; Sonya Dowsett and Martin Roberts, 'Spain's New Government Faces First Test', *Reuters*, November 22, 2011, http://www.reuters.com/article/2011/11/22/us-spain-election-idUSTRE7AL0LF20111122; 'Is This the Man to Save Spain?', *The Economist*, December 22, 2011, http://www.economist.com/blogs/newsbook/2011/12/spain-new-government.

[32] 'EU Entering "Critical Period" to Solve Debt Crisis', *BBC News*, November 30, 2011, http://www.bbc.co.uk/news/business-15958461.

copy Germany's economic governance to restore the fiscal stability.[33] Opponents such as Olli Rehn, EU economic and monetary affairs commissioner, contended that Germany alone could not determine the fate of the eurozone.[34] On the other hand, there were people arguing that the solution of the crisis lies in Germany as it is the largest economy in the eurozone. Poland's foreign minister Radoslaw Sikorski for one urged Germany to take a stronger lead, because 'You know full well nobody else can do it'.[35]

A sense of urgency heightened in the end of November. The credit rating agency Standard & Poor's issued a warning that eurozone countries, including Germany and France, would risk a downgrade of credit rating because of systemic stress.[36] In the meantime, US president Barack Obama called for bold action.[37] Facing mounting pressure, an agreement between Germany and France finally was reached and presented at the EU summit on 9 December 2011. Because the summit was held by many as key to the survival of the euro, it was also called the 'make-or-break' summit.[38]

[33] David Gow and Giles Tremlett, 'Eurozone Looks to International Monetary Fund as Contagion Spreads', *The Guardian*, November 25, 2011, http://www.guardian.co.uk/business/2011/nov/25/eurozone-crisis-ecb-imf-bonds.

[34] 'Will the Euro Survive', *BBC News*, November 28, 2011, http://www.bbc.co.uk/news/world-europe-15917175.

[35] 'Eurozone Finance Ministers Likely to Miss Rescue Target', *BBC News*, November 30, 2011, http://www.bbc.co.uk/news/business-15933685.

[36] Mark Deen & Ben Livesey, 'S&P Puts 15 Euro Nations on Watch for Downgrade amid Sovereign-Debt Crisis', *Bloomberg*, December 6, 2011, http://www.bloomberg.com/news/2011-12-05/s-p-said-to-place-all-17-euro-nations-on-downgrade-watch-over-debt-crisis.html. The reports of credit rating agencies help banks and investors determine their lending rates, and hence the acts of these agencies to adjust the credit rating of the eurozone countries tend to affect the development of the eurozone crisis. On the role of the credit rating agencies on market and economy, see Rabah Arezki, Bertrand Candelon, and Amadou N.R. Sy, 'Sovereign Rating News and Financial Markets Spillovers: Evidence from the European Debt Crisis', *IMF Working Paper*, WP/11/68 (2011), pp. 3–5; Manfred Gartner, Bjorn Griesbach, and Florian Jung, 'PIGS or Lambs? The European Sovereign Debt Crisis and the Role of Rating Agencies', *International Advances in Economic Research*, Vol. 17, No. 3 (2011), pp. 288–99; Robert Mundell, 'The European Fiscal Reform and the Plight of the Euro', *Poznan University of Economic Review*, Vol. 11, No. 1 (2011), p. 14; Georgios P. Kouretas and Prodromos Vlamis, 'The Greek Crisis: Causes and Implications', p. 393; Kevin Featherstone, 'The Greek Sovereign Debt Crisis and EMU', p. 200.

[37] 'Eurozone Finance Ministers Likely to Miss Rescue Target', *BBC News*, November 30, 2011.

[38] 'Merkel Urges Euro Fiscal Union to Tackle Debt Crisis', *BBC News*, December 2, 2011, http://www.bbc.co.uk/news/world-europe-15997784.

France and Germany proposed two approaches to tackling the crisis. First, EU member states agreed to move towards a 'fiscal stability union' and sign a fiscal compact, under the latter of which there would be an automatic correction mechanism to carry out fiscal discipline of individual member states. Second, the European Stability Mechanism (ESM), a permanent rescue facility, was agreed to be accelerated and brought into force in July 2012.[39] These were the second critical step in dealing with the crisis after the summit in October.

The market's reaction varied as to whether the December summit did solve the crisis and prevent the eurozone from falling apart. On the one hand, credit rating agencies generally held a negative view, as Moody's stated that the summit lacked 'decisive policy measures', while Standard & Poor's downgraded nine eurozone countries including France in January 2012.[40] On the other hand, bond yields in Spain and Italy fall sharply in the same month, indicating a sign of relief.[41] This was mainly because in the end of 2011, the ECB decided for the first time to provide European banks with cheap three-year loans to solve the liquidity issue. European banks ended up borrowing €489 billion from the ECB, and this has helped to reduce stress in the credit markets.[42]

To the extent that the summit 'solved' the crisis, the effects only lasted for half a year. In June 2012, Spain's borrowing costs rose to the highest rate since the launch of the euro. Spain asked for a partial bailout for its

[39] European Council, 'Statement by the Euro Area Heads of State or Government', December 9, 2011, http://www.consilium.europa.eu/uedocs/cms_data/docs/pressdata/en/ec/126658.pdf; 'Euro Crisis: Eurozone Deal Reached without UK', *BBC News*, December 9, 2011, http://www.bbc.co.uk/news/world-16104089.

[40] 'Shares Fall as Moody's Warns on EU Policy Measures', *BBC News*, December 12, 2011, http://www.bbc.co.uk/news/business-16137947; Larry Elliott and Phillip Inman, 'Eurozone in New Crisis as Ratings Agency Downgrades Nine Countries', *The Guardian*, January 14, 2012, http://www.guardian.co.uk/business/2012/jan/13/eurozone-crisis-france-credit-rating-aaa.

[41] Raphael Minder and David Jolly, 'Borrowing Costs Fall for Italy and Spain in Debt Auctions', *The New York Times*, January 12, 2012, http://www.nytimes.com/2012/01/13/business/global/strong-debt-auctions-held-in-spain-and-italy.html; 'Spain and Italy's Borrowing Costs Fall', *BBC News*, January 12, 2012, http://www.bbc.co.uk/news/business-16527374.

[42] 'Huge Demand for ECB's Three-Year Loans', *BBC News*, December 21, 2011, http://www.bbc.co.uk/news/business-16282206; Raphael Minder and David Jolly, 'Borrowing Costs Fall for Italy and Spain in Debt Auctions'.

banking sector and secured €100 billion in July.[43] Cyprus became the fifth eurozone country that asked for a rescue from the EU, because its banking system has been severely hit by the Greek crisis and the associated debt-restructuring deal.[44] The credit rating agency Moody's also downgraded Italy's debt rating on the basis of a contagion risk from Spain and Greece.[45]

After a lengthy internal discussion, the ECB changed its official stance from non-intervention to 'Outright Monetary Transactions', that is, an 'unlimited' bond-buying programme once governments apply for eurozone financial assistance, on 6 September.[46] This has been called the 'eurozone D-Day'[47] and had an immediate effect on lowering the borrowing cost in Italy and Spain. The German Federal Constitutional Court also ruled that the there are no grounds to block ratification of the European Stability Mechanism, the permanent euro bailout fund.[48] These developments effectively prevented the sovereign debt crisis from escalating. By the end of 2012, German finance minister Wolfgang Schäuble stated publicly that 'the worst [of euro crisis] is behind us'.[49] In August of 2018, the EU formally announced Greece, the last crisis country, to exit from bailout programmes. After eight years since it broke out, the European sovereign debt crisis was finally put to an end.

[43] 'Spain Borrowing Costs Hit Euro-Era Record High', *BBC News*, June 12, 2012, http://www.bbc.co.uk/news/business-18405729; Valentina Pop, 'ECB Chief Indicates Upcoming Help for Spain', *EU Observer*, July 27, 2012, http://euobserver.com/economic/117077.

[44] Valentina Pop, 'Cyprus Becomes Fifth Eurozone Country to Seek Bailout', *EU Observer*, June 26, 2012, http://euobserver.com/economic/116753.

[45] Honor Mahony, 'Italy Debt Rating Downgraded', *EU Observer*, September 13, 2012, http://euobserver.com/economic/116964.

[46] Valentina Pop, 'ECB to Buy Spanish Bonds, but with Strings Attached', *EU Observer*, September 6, 2012, http://euobserver.com/economic/117461.

[47] Valentina Pop, 'Eurozone D-Day: Central Bank to Announce Bond-Buying Scheme', *EU Observer*, September 6, 2012, http://euobserver.com/economic/117446.

[48] 'Green Light for ESM: German High Court OKs Permanent Bailout Fund with Reservations', *Der Spiegel*, September 12, 2012, http://www.spiegel.de/international/germany/german-high-court-oks-permanent-bailout-fund-with-reservations-a-855338.html; Valentina Pop, 'Sighs of Relief as German Court Approves Bailout Fund', *EU Observer*, September 12, 2012, http://euobserver.com/institutional/117520.

[49] Valentina Pop, 'Worst of Euro Crisis over, Says German Minister', *EU Observer*, December 28, 2012, http://euobserver.com/economic/118613.

## 3 The Characteristics of the European Sovereign Debt Crisis

After re-establishing the trajectories of the crisis, this section will highlight certain issues or characteristics. As there is no observation without theory, the perspectives adopted here are intergovernmentalism and neofunctionalism, the two prominent theories in the study of European integration. Running the risk of oversimplification, the core of various branches of intergovernmentalism generally maintains that the states—or national governments—are the most important actors in international relations, and integration comes from the convergence of governmental preferences. On the contrary, neofunctionalism holds that once states initiate the programme of regional integration, the course of integration is no longer in the hands of governments. The state is neither a unitary nor the only actor in the integration process; interest groups and non-governmental organizations within and without the state will participate in the process. Hence integration is the result of 'spillover', that is, integration in one sector will generate pressure for integration in other sectors.[50] As the following will show, the European sovereign debt crisis provides factual evidence to support both theories (except the case of Greece, which is mainly a matter of domestic politics).

### 3.1 *The Key Role of German and French (In)Action*

The break of fiscal discipline in the eurozone was mainly due to the 2003 decision of Germany and France to suspend the enforcement mechanism of the Stability and Growth Pact (SGP), as the vacuum in fiscal governance indirectly encouraged such member states lacking a tradition of fiscal discipline as Greece for lax governance.[51] As Peter Doukas, Greek deputy minister of economy and finance in 2003, pointed out, the fact that Germany and France violated the rules of the SGP without any sanctions being imposed sent a message to others that fiscal discipline need not be adhered and the enforcement of the Treaty would be more relaxed.[52]

[50] On the history and development of intergovernmentalism, see Ben Rosamond, *Theories of European Integration* (New York: St. Martin's Press, 2000), pp. 75–81, 130–47. On the part of neofunctionalism, see Ben Rosamond, *Theories of European Integration*, pp. 50–73.

[51] The issue of the dysfunction of the SGP will be further discussed in section 4.2.

[52] Allan Little, 'Did Germany Sow the Seeds of the Eurozone Debt Crisis?', *BBC News*, January 29, 2012, http://www.bbc.co.uk/news/world-europe-16761087.

Dietrich von Kyaw, German ambassador to the EU in the 1990s, also admitted that Germany's government 'really sinned' in that when big countries broke the rules they had insisted on for everyone else, the EU could hardly require smaller countries such as Greece to obey.[53]

Furthermore, the deepening of the crisis is in a sense a result of Germany and France's slow response. First, the debt crisis has been lasting for more than three years, with such eurozone member states as Greece, Ireland, Portugal, Italy, and Spain being caught in. As early as in November 2010, when Ireland became the second member state seeking a bailout, European Commission president Barroso warned Germany and France of the need to take responsible measures, but no actions on the part of the latter were taken. When the third country, Portugal, demanded a rescue in May 2011, Germany and France showed no sign of acknowledging the worsening of the crisis in the summit being held. Even if subsequently the crisis spread from the periphery to the core of the eurozone in August 2011, there was only the intervention of the ECB but no active response from the two. As Kouretas and Vlamis argue, a part of blame for the worsening of the crisis has to do with the failure of eurozone countries—and Germany in particular—to show the markets their will to provide immediate political and financial support to countries in need.[54]

Second, the two summits that are vital to the handling of the crisis were held in the context of mounting international pressure, not a result of Germany and France's active leadership. Moravscik for one points out that it was not until October 2011 and, at the insistence of the IMF, that Chancellor Merkel shifted her stance and began to trim Greek sovereign debt.[55] This indicates that the ways in which Germany and France responded to the crisis were passive and reactive. As the largest economy in the eurozone as well as the biggest contributor to the bailout funds, Germany was held to be the key to resolving the crisis. For this reason, criticism that Germany's passive action has led to the deepening of the crisis surfaced every now and then. Germany's inaction also partially explains why, in the midst of the crisis, member states such as France,

[53] Allan Little, 'How "magic" Made Greek Debt Disappear before It Joined the Euro', *BBC News*, February 3, 2012, http://www.bbc.co.uk/news/world-europe-16834815.

[54] George P. Kouretas and Prodromos Vlamis, 'The Greek Crisis: Causes and Implications', p. 393.

[55] Andrew Moravcsik, 'Europe after the Crisis', *Foreign Affairs*, Vol. 91, Issue 3 (2012), p. 58.

Finland, the Netherlands, and Austria would opt for empowering the ECB to tackle the problems.

Why was Germany reluctant to play a more active role? There are different explanations at hand. First, in terms of domestic political constraints, the German public opposed the Greek bailout, while the German Constitutional Court ruled that the parliament has to be consulted on policies regarding the EMU. This domestic constraint explains why, when French President Sarkozy put pressure on Chancellor Merkel to agree to expand the scale of the EFSF, the latter responded by 'we live in democracies and have to operate according to fundamental rules'.[56] Second, in terms of historical constraint, the shadow of Nazi Germany still exerts some influence in that Germany in general hesitates to become a leading power in Europe. Facing the worsening situation, Polish foreign minister Radoslaw Sikorski called for Germany to act in public. Describing himself as probably the first Polish foreign minister to say so, he stated that 'I fear German power less than I am beginning to fear German inactivity',[57] expressing a view that Germany should leave behind its historical burden.

While both factors may account for the German passivity to some extent, they have their limits. Compared with the Germany in the 1990s when the EMU was established, Chancellor Helmut Kohl was facing stronger opposition from the public than Chancellor Merkel was now.[58] In addition, historical constraint cannot explain how the Franco-German axis has come to play a key role in the process of European integration. Instead, this chapter suggests that the main reason may be the leadership factor, that is, contemporary German and French leaders lack a sense of responsibility and strategic thinking on the significance of European integration for European peace and security.

[56] 'Deadlock in the Eurozone', *BBC News*, October 21, 2011.

[57] Allan Little, 'Did Germany Sow the Seeds of the Eurozone Debt Crisis?'

[58] The German public took deutschmark as a symbol of post-war German economic miracle, and therefore the idea of Germany's participation in the EMU was unpopular, as it was understood as abandonment of one crucial achievement and a negation of identity. In addition, the coalition government formed by the Christian Democrats (CDU) only had a marginal majority in Bundestag, while Bundesrat was controlled by the opposition. Chancellor Kohl eventually persuaded the opposition within his party and the society by the argument that the EMU was the necessary cost as well as foundation of German unification. See Malcolm Levitt and Christopher Lord, *The Political Economy of Monetary Union* (Basingstoke: Palgrave Macmillan, 2000), pp. 52–3, 68–9; Mathieu Segers and Femke Van Esch, 'Behind the Veil of Budgetary Discipline: the Political Logic of the Budgetary Rules in EMU and the SGP', *Journal of Common Market Studies*, Vol. 45, No. 5 (2007), pp. 1089–109.

In this regard, Young and Semmler present a view of 'generational change' to explain why the attitude of contemporary German and French leaders towards European integration differs from that of their predecessors. Past leaders, such as Helmut Kohl, Hans-Dietrich Genscher, and Helmut Schmidt in Germany and Jacques Chirac, François Mitterrand, and Valery Giscard d'Estaing in France, because of their wartime memories, tend to see integration as the way to prevent the horrors of World War II from re-emerging and are therefore more pro-Europe. In contrast, later leaders—especially Gerhard Schröder and Angela Merkel—do not share the same vision and incline to prioritize the notion of 'national interests'.[59] One commentator even goes so far to suggest that 'Angela Merkel having grown up in the East does not appear to have the slightest understanding of the essence of the EU and the costs that are associated with its neglect'.[60] Without a leader like Kohl, who acknowledged well the historical and strategic importance of the EMU, contemporary German government only sees the euro and the sovereign debt crisis from a narrow perspective of 'economic interests'.[61]

If the widespread of the crisis was partially related to the German and French passivity, the solution to it also relied on the leadership of the two. The fact that the agreement on the fiscal compact could be reached by 25 member states and in two months suggests that as long as the leaders—specifically German and French ones—have the political will, an international agreement could be concluded in a short time-span.[62] President of the European Central Bank Mario Draghi also indicated that the fiscal compact is a 'major political event', 'a sign of commitment by all states, especially large ones, to the euro'.[63] This suggests that although the EU has become a vast international organization covering 28 member states, and the eurozone also has as many as 17 members, the nature of European integration to a great extent remains a German-Franco union. Speaking of the solution to the crisis, French finance minister François Baroin hence

[59] Brigitte Young and Willi Semmler, 'The European Sovereign Debt Crisis: Is Germany to Blame?' *German Politics and Society*, Vol. 29, No. 1 (2011), pp. 18–9.

[60] Cited in Brigitte Young and Willi Semmler, 'The European Sovereign Debt Crisis: Is Germany to Blame?' p. 19.

[61] Kevin Featherstone, 'The Greek Sovereign Debt Crisis and EMU', pp. 201 & 211.

[62] 'The EU Summit: A Deal, but to What End?' *The Economist*, January 31, 2012, http://www.economist.com/blogs/charlemagne/2012/01/eu-summit.

[63] 'The Euro Crisis: Modest Mario', *The Economist*, February 9, 2012, http://www.economist.com/blogs/freeexchange/2012/02/euro-crisis-5.

stated that 'no agreement between the two [France and Germany] means no engine'.[64]

### 3.2 *The Particularities of Greece in the Crisis*

Among the countries running into trouble in the crisis, the case of Greece is unique. The financial crisis was triggered by debt problems in Greece, the first country asking for a rescue. In addition, Greece is also the country whose problems remain unsolved after having been bailed out two times, its debt halved, and receiving the largest amount of aid (€289 billion). The Greek crisis was also the longest crisis in the eurozone. It took the country eight years to formally exit bailout programmes. During the bailout periods, the EU has postponed or split into instalments the aid to Greece several times because of the latter's lagging efforts to implement the reforms required. This not only changed the course of the crisis, but has made speculation about a Greek default or exit from the eurozone circulating in international financial markets. That the crisis has not been over also relates to the inability for Greece to address its problems effectively.

The longevity and severity of the Greek crisis indicate that the problems not only lie in the country's debt burden but also in the effectiveness and credibility of its governance. With respect to the former, the debt problem of Greece had been quite severe even before the country joined the euro. The statistical agency of Greece produced misguided financial figures in order to meet the criteria of having low deficit and debt levels for joining the euro. After the political turnover in 2004, the huge gap between the published debt and the real one was revealed, but under the consideration that the Olympics was approaching, the succeeding government decided to cover the truth and borrowed more to meet the deficit.[65] As a result, Greece's public debt reached 160% of its GDP in 2011, a decade after joining the common currency.

With respect to the latter, it was the lack of effectiveness and credibility in Greek governance that made the bailout funds unable to be used to address the debt problems effectively. The main issue here is the Greek government's difficulty in carrying out the austerity measures promised by Athens, thereby rendering the continuation of fiscal deficits. This was

[64] John Irish, 'France, German Leaders Meet amid Euro, Syria Crises', *Reuters*, February 6, 2012, http://www.reuters.com/assets/print?aid=USTRE81502A20120206.

[65] Allan Little, 'How "Magic" Made Greek Debt Disappear before It Joined the Euro'.

most evident in the then Greek prime minister George Papandreou's proposal in October 2011 to hold a referendum to decide whether Greece should accept the EU's debt deal, as the government could not guarantee its implementation.[66] Although the idea of referendum was eventually cancelled under the pressure of Germany and France, and a new government was formed, the successive coalition government remained unable to regain the trust of the Troika—the EU, the ECB, and the IMF—regarding its governance. Germany even proposed to have an EU budget commissioner to veto Greek budgetary measures if they were not in line with the bailout programmes, but the idea was rejected by the Greek government on the ground of violating its financial sovereignty.[67] However, the fact that some eurozone finance ministers insisted the troika to stay in Greece permanently to monitor its progress reflected a deep-seated distrust of Greece's governance.[68]

Among the countries that were in trouble, why was it that only Greece ran into governance difficulties? While domestic protests and the holding of general elections may explain the pressure on political leaders and their attempts to please the public, these however were not unique to Greece but were common phenomena in countries caught in the crisis. The concern of public opinion as well as the outcome of the elections hence cannot be the main cause of Greece's ineffective governance. Rather, Greece's problem had much to do with the country's long-term government incompetence and the problem of rule of law.

Many have pointed out that the failure of governance in Greece is a main reason for the eruption of the European sovereign debt crisis. The failure was an outcome of factors such as the weakness of the bureaucratic system, the lack of coordination and control within the government, and a political culture of corruption, which together rendered public expenditure unable to be managed and monitored effectively. Both major parties have been accused of scandals and corruption, and there has also been a severe problem of tax evasion. For these reasons, data provided by the

[66] Rachel Donadio and Niki Kitsantonis, 'Greek Leader Calls off Referendum on Bailout Plan', *The New York Times*, November 3, 2011, http://www.nytimes.com/2011/11/04/world/europe/greek-leaders-split-on-euro-referendum.html?pagewanted=all&_r=0.

[67] 'Greeks Rejects "Impossible" German Plan for Budget Veto', *BBC News*, January 29, 2012, http://www.bbc.co.uk/news/business-16780448.

[68] Fred Pals, 'De Jager Backs "Permanent Troika" in Athens to Monitor Economy', *Bloomberg*, January 20, 2012, http://www.bloomberg.com/news/2012-02-20/de-jager-backs-permanent-troika-in-athens-to-monitor-economy.html.

Greek government has been treated as unreliable by the EU and international investors after the break out of the crisis.[69] These long-term and systematic problems endogenous to Greek governance are what made the case of Greece different from others.

### 3.3 *Intergovernmentalism Over Supranationalism*

The third dimension observed in the development of the crisis is the struggle and interaction between member states—especially the leading ones—on the one hand and the EU as a supranational organization on the other. The European Commission has shown attempts to play an active role in various stages of the crisis. Before the crisis, and when France and Germany violated the Stable and Growth Pact deliberately in 2003, the Commission reported to the ECOFIN Council and suggested to impose sanctions on the two and brought the case to the European Court of Justice after the Council determined to suspend the excessive deficit procedure. After the eruption of the crisis, Commission president Barroso has tried to bring forward some policy initiatives such as increasing the firepower of ESM bailout funds and issuing eurobonds. Retrospectively speaking, however, the efforts of the supranational organization clearly could not determine the course of the crisis, which remained dominated by the leading member states. As Romano Prodi, the president of the Commission in 2003, pointed out, although the institutions of the EU have often been criticized as having too much power, the truth nevertheless was that when France and Germany violated the SGP, he did not have the power to fine them.[70] Similarly, although Barroso has tried to enhance the role of the Commission in order to solve the problems, he tended to be ignored by the member states as he is a political appointee but not an elected leader.[71] This suggests that, before the democratic legitimacy of the EU is improved, the EU remains a club of the member states. It is the

[69] Kevin Featherstone, 'The Greek Sovereign Debt Crisis and EMU', pp. 195–9. See also George P. Kouretas and Prodromos Vlamis, 'The Greek Crisis: Causes and Implications', p. 393; Heather Gibson, Stephen G. Hall, and George S. Tavlas, 'The Greek Financial Crisis: Growing Imbalances and Sovereign Spreads', *Journal of International Money and Finance*, Vol. 31 (2012), p. 515.

[70] Allan Little, 'Did Germany Sow the Seeds of the Eurozone Debt Crisis?'

[71] Laurence Knight, 'Europe's Four Big Dilemmas', *BBC News*, October 27, 2011, http://www.bbc.co.uk/news/business-14934728.

preferences and wills of the member states—but not that of the EU—that determine the development of European integration.

This also applies to the role and function of the ECB. Among the EU institutions, the ECB is the most resourceful one given its independent status and the power to make monetary policy. When Portugal, Italy, and Spain were facing fiscal problems, the ECB reacted promptly by buying their government bonds. Its successive actions such as providing eurozone banks with low-interest loans and exchanging its holding of Greek bonds also to a great extent prevented the crisis from escalating. The swift and effective actions of the ECB may explain why some eurozone member states proposed to empower the ECB and make it the 'last resort' when Germany and France could not reach an agreement on how to deal with the problems. This proposal, however, was not accepted by most member states. In addition, while the intervention of the ECB did show some effects, the solution for the crisis could not simply be buying government bonds or offering extra finance, but requires comprehensive, systematic, and more fundamental measures such as the establishment of the EFSF/ESM and the signing and implementation of the fiscal compact. The making of these non-monetary policies remains at the hand of the member states.

It might be argued that the fiscal compact and the automatic sanctions mechanism can be seen as the practices of supranationalism as well as a 'spillover' of the monetary union. Indeed, the realization of the monetary union does reveal the necessity for a fiscal union, as the sovereign debt crisis has shown clearly. Yet, the effectiveness of any fiscal union depends ultimately on the willingness of the member states to abide by the norms and rules. The origin of the European sovereign debt crisis is not the lack of rules about fiscal discipline, but the problem that the rules were not strictly followed. Judging from the failure of the SGP, the key to the success of the fiscal compact in keeping fiscal discipline in the eurozone hinges on the action of the leading states. When asked if she will take France to the ECJ should it violate the rules in the compact, Chancellor Merkel said, 'I cannot imagine taking legal action against France because I cannot imagine that France will not institute a golden rule'.[72] This in a sense indicates that both the SGP and the fiscal compact are meaningful as long as the major member states are willing to follow the rules and show the leadership.

[72] 'The EU Summit: A Deal, but to What End?' *The Economist*.

### 3.4 *The Convergence of EU Economic Governance to German Standards*

In the course of the crisis, the role of Germany in European economic governance has been strengthened. Although the Franco-German axis has been the driving force in European integration, Germany has come to exert more influence than has France, because it is the largest economy in the EU, the biggest contributor to the bailout funds, and more industrially competitive. In contrast, France seems to become a junior partner in dealing with the crisis.

In terms of the measures adopted to solve the crisis, they mostly reflect German policy preferences and governance style. France had proposed increasing the capacity of the EFSF and strengthening the role and function of the ECB and was against the idea that private creditors should take losses, but, except the case of the EFSF, many of these were not accepted because of German opposition. On the contrary, German preferences such as the autonomy and independence of the ECB, the private creditors of an insolvent country having to take losses, the establishment of a fiscal union, and monitoring Greece's fiscal governance have all been realized. In addition, under Germany's demand, the fiscal compact requires member states to write the 'balanced budget rule' (the golden rule) into their national legal systems, preferably constitutions. After the Economic and Monetary Union, the establishment of the fiscal union reflects once again the German style of governance.[73] Economic governance in the EU, both monetary and fiscal, hence moves towards German standards.[74]

That Germany has become a leader in the eurozone is also evident in its influence over individual countries. Although it has been criticized for inaction from time to time, this by no means implies that German influence has been absent. For instance, it was reported that José Sócrates, then prime minister of Portugal, once phoned Chancellor Merkel for help before seeking a bailout from the EU, although the news was denied by the prime minister's office.[75] It was also reported that Chancellor Merkel

[73] The institutional set-up of the ECB and its objectives already took into consideration certain German preferences in order to ensure Germany would become a founding member of the EMU. See Malcolm Levitt and Christopher Lord, *The Political Economy of Monetary Union*, p. 45 and Chapter 12.

[74] 'Germany's Debt Brake: Tie Your Hands, Please', *The Economist*, December 10, 2011, http://www.economist.com/node/21541459.

[75] Ian Traynor, 'Eurozone Tensions Rise amid Bailouts', *The Guardian*, January 18, 2011, http://www.guardian.co.uk/business/2011/jan/18/eurozone-crisis-over-bailout-response/print.

had intervened in Italian domestic politics by asking the Italian president to change the prime minister, as the incumbent Silvio Berlusconi was believed to fail to deal with the crisis properly, but Merkel's alleged demand was denied by the president's office.[76] While the factuality of the news is difficult to examine, they nevertheless indicate the central role of Germany in the eurozone.

Interestingly, one of the purposes of the EMU was to 'Europeanize' Germany, that is, to constrain German leadership in economic policy-making by binding Germany in the monetary union.[77] The course of the sovereign debt crisis shows, however, that instead of Germany being Europeanized, it is Europe that is Germanized.[78] The EMU has not changed but rather strengthened the dominant role of Germany in European affairs.

### *3.5 International and Structural Factors Beyond Fiscal Discipline*

The European sovereign debt crisis is a crisis in which several member states of the eurozone ran into problems of excessive deficit and debt. While the lack of fiscal discipline is the main factor contributing to the Greek crisis, it is not what caused the problems in Ireland, Portugal, Spain, and Italy. There are factors other than fiscal discipline that account for these cases.

In the Irish case, the deficit was mainly a result of the government's attempt to save the country's banking sector. After Ireland joined the euro, its banks were able to borrow cheap money and invested heavily on property markets in the US, the UK, and Ireland. Following the US sub-prime mortgage crisis in 2008, the Irish banks suffered heavy losses and were on the edge of bankruptcy. The Irish government announced that it would insure all deposits against any default, thereby resulting in an

[76] 'Europe Will Fix the Euro, Insists Germany's Finance Minister', *The Guardian*, December 30, 2011, http://www.guardian.co.uk/business/2011/dec/30/euro-wolfgang-schauble-stabilise-handelsblatt.

[77] Malcolm Levitt & Christopher Lord, *The Political Economy of Monetary Union*, pp. 55–7.

[78] David Marsh, *The Euro: The Battle for the New Global Currency* (New Haven: Yale University Press, 2011), p. 293.

unprecedented budget deficit.[79] Spain's fiscal problems were also a continuation of the US subprime mortgage crisis to some extent. The access to cheap loans gained after joining the euro has made a boom underpinned by a housing bubble. When the bubble burst in 2008, the construction sector collapsed and households cut their spending, making the unemployment rate rising rapidly, to 21.5% in the third quarter of 2011. Apart from the problems in the property market, the Spanish government also had to finance its banking sector to prevent the banks from bankruptcy as a result of the mortgages they have lent. Together, the increase in unemployment benefits, the decrease in tax revenue, and the need to rescue the banking sector propelled the Spanish government to borrow heavily, thereby causing a serious deficit problem.[80]

The cases of Portugal and Italy tell a different story. With respect to Portugal, although a budget deficit had made it the first country to violate the regulations of the SGP, in order to meet the rules of the EU, the Portuguese government has since 2006 implemented a series of projects such as cutting public sector jobs by 10%, pension reform, freeing up labour markets, and cutting red tape, making its budget deficit dropping from 6.1% of GDP in 2005 to 2.8% by 2008. The real issue for Portugal hence was not fiscal discipline, but huge national debts resulting from the lack of competitiveness. The average real GDP growth in the past decade or so is below 1%,[81] thereby making the country short of tax revenue.

Italy's problem also relates a weak economy. At the end of 2010, the ratio of government debt to GDP in Italy was 119%, almost twice the EU limit (60%).[82] This high level of debt, however, was not due to the government's failure of fiscal governance, but a result of excessive public debt accumulation in the 1970s and 1980s. Hence, while the government is financially prudent in that it has spent less than it has earned in taxes virtu-

[79] Joe Brennan & Stephanie Bodoni, 'Ireland Seeks Bailout as "Outsized" Problem Overwhelms Nation'; Gabriele Steinhauser & Shawn Pogatchnik, 'Ireland Second European Nation to Seek Bailout'.

[80] 'What's the Matter with Spain?', *BBC News*, December 7, 2011, http://www.bbc.co.uk/news/business-15734280.

[81] 'Fear Spreads: A Big Rescue Package for Greece Has Not Protected Other Countries such as Portugal', *The Economist*, May 6, 2010, http://www.economist.com/node/16060961; James G. Neuger & Simon Kennedy, 'Ireland Gets $113 Billion Bailout as EU Ministers Seek to Halt Debt Crisis'.

[82] 'News Release: Euro Indicators', *Eurostat*, April 26, 2011, http://epp.eurostat.ec.europa.eu/cache/ITY_PUBLIC/2-26042011-AP/EN/2-26042011-AP-EN.PDF.

ally since 1992, the country's poor economic performance—0.75% of average economic growth rate over the past 15 years—nevertheless requires the government to borrow to meet the principal and interest payments on its existing debts. In a time of crisis, low growth further makes the government's debt load seemingly unsustainable, despite the fact that relatively speaking, Italy's government budget deficit has not been very serious, and ordinary Italians generally have very little debt.[83]

These four cases indicate that the solutions to the European sovereign debt crisis and the long-term sustainability of the EMU have to take into consideration international and structural factors along with the fiscal ones. Ireland's and Spain's problems are a continuation of the US financial crisis, while Portugal's and Italy's are mainly a result of low economic growth. The trouble of these countries cannot be attributed to the failure of fiscal governance and cannot be corrected simply by taking austerity measures and establishing a fiscal union.

On the basis of these characteristics of the crisis, this chapter will analyse the solutions drawn up by the EU summits to discuss whether they are able to address the issues effectively.

## 4 Seeking Solutions to the Crisis

Leaders in the eurozone responded to the sovereign debt crisis by establishing the European Stability Mechanism (ESM) and signing the fiscal compact. The former is a reparative instrument that provides firewall measures to limit contagion once a debt crisis erupts, while the latter is preventive in that it aims to set up a framework for fiscal governance in the eurozone to prevent similar crisis from recurring. After the German Federal Constitutional Court's decision to back the ESM, those countries in trouble could gain financial support, and the debt crisis was temporarily relieved. With respect to the effectiveness of the fiscal compact, it is necessary to determine first the relationship between the nature of the crisis and fiscal discipline, as well as the conditions for the function of the fiscal union. This is where this section turns to.

[83] 'What's the Matter with Italy?', *BBC News*, December 28, 2011, http://www.bbc.co.uk/news/business-15429057; 'What's the matter with Spain', *BBC News*.

### 4.1 *The Nature of the Crisis and the Fiscal Compact*

In appearance, the occurrence of the European sovereign debt crisis was associated with excessive deficit and government debts of several member states of the eurozone, it therefore seems reasonable for the eurozone to opt for re-establishing a sound fiscal order as the main solution. As discussed before, however, countries except Greece ran into trouble not because of the lack of fiscal discipline, but because of systematic and structural factors. To be sure, the worsening of fiscal conditions is an issue that has to be tackled, because otherwise fiscal problems in some countries may escalate and become a systematic risk to the entire eurozone. Yet, if the fiscal runaway is caused by other deep-seated factors, resorting to a fiscal compact or union can never address the root of the problem. This is evident in that while the EU summit had decided to establish a fiscal union as early as by the end of 2011, the sovereign debt crisis has not been resolved but worsened in 2012.

In terms of fiscal discipline in the eurozone, it has been lax since the sanctions procedures of the SGP were suspended in 2003. All eurozone member states except Estonia and Luxembourg broke the regulations of the SGP in different times and with different intensity.[84] Between 2003 and 2008, however, neither the problem of fiscal discipline in the eurozone turned into a sovereign debt, nor did countries violating the SGP penalized by the markets.[85] While the lack of fiscal discipline may explain the emergence of the Greek crisis, it is insufficient to account for the debt crises in other eurozone member states.

Robert Mundell hence argues that although the euro has usually been taken as the main cause of the European sovereign debt crisis, the crisis is in fact a continuation of the US subprime mortgage banking crisis in 2007, the global financial crisis in 2008, and the US and global recession of 2008–2009. In other words, it is the fourth phase of one crisis, and for this reason the European debt crisis is not, and should not be called, a crisis of the euro.[86] Another study by three ECB officials suggests that

[84] European Commission, *EMU@10: Successes and Challenges after Ten Years of Economic and Monetary Union* (Brussels: European Commission, 2008), p. 135; European Commission, *Public Finances in EMU-2011* (Brussels: European Commission, 2011), p. 2.

[85] Kathryn M. E. Dominguez, 'The European Central Bank, the Euro, and Global Financial Markets', *Journal of Economic Perspectives*, Vol. 20, No. 4 (2006), p. 85.

[86] Robert Mundell, 'The European Fiscal Reform and the Plight of the Euro', pp. 10–14. Moeller also suggests that the crisis in the eurozone is part of the global debt problem. See

some member states' announcements of bank rescue packages in response to the global financial crisis led investors to expect higher government debt ratios and contributed to higher government bond yield, which consequently developed into a sovereign debt crisis.[87] As such, the European debt crisis may be understood as the European part of the global financial crisis.

According to this perspective, the European debt crisis reveals the problem that apart from the single currency, the eurozone does not have a single financial regulatory mechanism to deal with pan-systematic issues. The Commission's proposal to set up a single supervision mechanism around the ECB to oversee 6000 banks in the eurozone should address the regulatory issues more effectively.[88] The ECB's decision of unlimited bond-buying programme through Outright Monetary Transactions (OMTs) in September 2012 is also better than the fiscal compact in enhancing the reaction ability of the eurozone.[89] The idea put forth by Gros and Mayer is also worth considering that a European Monetary Fund (EMF) should be created to keep fiscal discipline in the eurozone and to set up a sovereign bankruptcy procedure.[90]

To deal with cases such as the crises in Italy and Portugal, it is necessary to address the problem of low economic growth, which is more structural and fundamental. According to the optimum currency area theory, the problem of uneven economic development, although is common for economies in a monetary union to have differing economic structures, can be tackled through means such as the transfer of fiscal/budget resources from boom regions to recessionary ones, labour mobility and wage flexibility.[91] Amongst these means, labour mobility cannot be fully realized in the eurozone because of the differences of language, culture, and social

Joergen Oerstroem Moeller, 'Europe after the Debt Crisis', *Asia Europe Journal*, Vol. 9, No. 1 (2011), pp. 67–72.

[87] Maria-Grazia Attinasi, Cristina Checherita, and Christiane Nickel, 'What Explains the Surge in Euro Area Sovereign Spreads during the Financial Crisis of 2007–2009?', *Public Finance and Management*, Vol. 10, No. 4 (2010), pp. 595–645.

[88] Valentina Pop, 'Banking Union to Put 6,000 Banks under ECB Supervision', *EU Observer*, August 31, 2012, http://euobserver.com/economic/117388.

[89] Valentina Pop, 'ECB to Buy Spanish Bonds, but with Strings Attached', *EU Observer.*

[90] Daniel Gros and Thomas Mayer, 'How to Deal with the Threat of Sovereign Default in Europe: Towards a Euro(pean) Monetary Fund', *Intereconomics*, Vol. 45, No. 2 (2010), pp. 64–8.

[91] Malcom Levitt and Christopher Lord, *The Political Economy of Monetary Union*, pp. 20–1.

security policies, while wage flexibility is constrained by the laws. A fiscal union that is able to transfer fiscal resources across the eurozone hence becomes a possible and desirable solution. Mundell indicates that the solution to the crisis not only lies in enforceable fiscal rules but also in a fiscal union that removes the member states' fiscal sovereignty.[92] Moeller also holds that the European sovereign debt crisis reveals a built-in problem of the eurozone that there is no fiscal union along with the monetary one. The necessity of having a fiscal union was generally acknowledged but deemed politically unripe or 'a step too far' when the Maastricht Treaty was written. The debt crisis signifies, according to the author, that 'that time has come'.[93]

This line of reasoning suggests that the fiscal compact can only partially address the problem. A fiscal union that emphasizes fiscal discipline but does not involve the transfer of fiscal resources cannot bridge the gap of uneven growth and development between the member states. Before the growth problem in Italy and Portugal is relieved, the European debt crisis cannot be settled.

Even if the necessity of a full fiscal union is widely acknowledged and accepted, it remains to be seen whether the political conditions are ripe for a fiscal union to which member states will transfer their fiscal sovereignty. The main difficulty is that fiscal governance involves taxation and public spending, both of which have the effect of wealth redistribution and are highly sensitive political matters. This is why, in contrast to their supranational approach to the monetary union, the member states in the eurozone opted for an intergovernmental approach to economic and fiscal policy-making, as a supranational organization only has limited accountability, whereas national governments must take pressure from the public. As such, to establish a fiscal union requires confronting the long-term problem of democratic deficit, which involves the institutional design of the EU and is therefore constitutional.[94]

It is not clear yet whether the debt crisis makes the fiscal union easier to be established or generates more controversies that eventually lead to the suspension of the idea yet again. It depends on decision-makers' creativity

[92] Robert Mundell, 'The European Fiscal Reform and the Plight of the Euro', p. 14.

[93] Joergen Oerstroem Moeller, 'Europe after the Debt Crisis', p. 72.

[94] Barry Eichengreen, 'Europe, the Euro and the ECB: Monetary Success, Fiscal Failure', *Journal of Policy Modeling*, Vol. 27, No. 4 (2005), p. 435; Stefan Collignon, 'The End of the Stability and Growth Pact?', *International Economics and Economic Policy*, Vol. 1, No. 1 (2004), p. 19.

to overcome the challenge of democratic deficit or to establish a certain form of fiscal union that is substantial enough to transfer limited budgetary resources while able to avoid the issue of fiscal sovereignty. It is worth observing, for instance, whether Van Rompuy's proposal of a common budget was accepted by the EU summit as a means to 'deal with asymmetric shocks and help prevent contagion'.[95]

### 4.2 *How the Fiscal Union/Compact May Be Enforced?*

Although it is suggested that the fiscal compact can only partially address the issues revealed by the debt crisis, it is still vital for the eurozone to re-establish fiscal discipline that has been lacking. After the sanctions mechanism of the SGP was terminated in 2003, there has been a vacuum at the core of economic governance in the eurozone, making fiscal discipline a matter of national self-responsibility.[96] The extreme outcome of this moral laxity was the Greek crisis. Restoring fiscal discipline hence is the first step to regulate the member states as well as to regain market confidence in eurozone economic governance. The fact that most EU states agreed to put the fiscal compact into force reflects the urgency of this matter. What is important here therefore is not whether there should be fiscal discipline, but how it can be enforced effectively. As mentioned, there has been an SGP that provides the eurozone with regulations of fiscal and budgetary measures. The problem lies in that the rules were not followed, and not followed by Germany and France, the leading states in the eurozone.

In 1995, German proposed to sign a Stability and Growth Pact to limit government deficit and debts of the member states in the eurozone, so that the difference of fiscal policy among the member states may not hinder the task of the ECB to maintain price stability. The treaty requires the member states to keep a government deficit of below 3% of GDP and a government debt of below 60% of GDP. If a member state does not comply and the violation continues, the Economic and Financial Affairs Council (ECOFIN) may vote and impose fines of an appropriate size on the state under concerned.[97]

[95] Valentina Pop, 'Van Rompuy Paper Floats Eurozone Budget, Parliament', *EU Observer*, September 13, 2012, http://euobserver.com/institutional/117527.

[96] Kevin Featherstone, 'The Greek Sovereign Debt Crisis and EMU: A Falling State in a Skewed Regime', p. 211.

[97] European Central Bank, 'The Implementation of the Stability and Growth Pact', *European Central Bank Monthly Bulletin*, May 1999, pp. 45–72.

The SGP encountered difficulties in enforcing in the early stage of the euro. In 2002, the European Commission confirmed that Germany would run an excessive fiscal deficit for the year, and ECOFIN then issued a recommendation to Germany, asking the latter to take actions. As Germany's economic growth continued to decline, the government was not able to improve the deficit situation and ran an excessive deficit in 2003 again. In the meantime, France also received an early warning in 2003, as the newly elected government insisted to fulfil President Chirac's electoral promises, thereby generating an excessive deficit. Yet the French government decided to defy the warnings and recommendations issued by the Council. Given the two countries' apparent breach of the SGP and no sign of improvement, the Commission issued recommendations in the end of 2003 calling for ECOFIN to give notice to the two. Council Regulation (EC) No. 1467/97 states that a member state failing to comply with the Council's decisions shall be sanctioned within two months after notice has been sent. With the support of Italy and Portugal, however, Germany and France were able to block a vote in favour of the Commission's recommendations in the ECOFIN meeting, and instead passed a resolution of the 'temporary' suspension of the SGP's excessive deficit procedure.[98] Even if the Commission brought the case to the European Court of Justice and the latter ruled that the Council did not have the right to suspend the enforcement of the SGP, this did not cause any member state violating the SGP to be sanctioned.[99] As a result, the SGP exists in name only, and it becomes the EU convention with the least compliance rate.[100]

The SGP case indicates that there is a gap between a member state's willingness and its ability to keep fiscal discipline. Germany first proposed to have the SGP, but was not able to follow the rules for domestic economic reasons, and eventually led to suspend the core of the SGP, its sanctions mechanism. This suggests that enforcing fiscal discipline is more

[98] Patrick Leblond, 'The Political Stability and Growth Pact Is Dead: Long Life the Economic Stability and Growth Pact', *Journal of Common Market Studies*, Vol. 44, No. 5 (2006), pp. 971–3.

[99] Martin Feldstein, 'The Euro and the Stability Pact', *Journal of Policy Modeling*, Vol. 27, No. 4 (2005), pp. 423–24.

[100] After these events, the European Council decided in 2005 to retain the basic rules of a government deficit of below 3% of GDP and a government debt of below 60% of GDP, but to give greater flexibility to the calculation of government debt and deficit as well as the enforcement of the treaty. See Martin Feldstein, 'The Euro and the Stability Pact', pp. 424–25; Barry Eichengreen, 'Europe, the Euro and the ECB', pp. 429–30.

difficult and complicated than conducting a treaty, as the latter involves political leaders' subjective willingness as well as the objective economic conditions facing the state in question. As in the case of Germany and France in 2002–2003, the unfavourable macroeconomic conditions also pose a serious challenge to the implementation of the current fiscal compact.

Indeed, a report from the European Commission in 2012 indicated that there were around 8 million young people jobless in the EU, and for Greece, Ireland, Portugal, and Spain that were already in debt trouble, the overall unemployment rate ranged between 15% and 25%.[101] Another survey further shows that 72% of the respondents prioritize employment to austerity.[102] Under the constraints of high unemployment level and public pressure, the fiscal compact, which takes austerity and discipline as the main targets, is likely to be breached as the SGP was, or to cause public opposition and dissatisfaction in those member states putting the rules in force. The European sovereign debt crisis was triggered by the problems in the banking system and the real estate sector, but those who suffered most have been the poor and the disadvantaged relying on social welfare and public spending, for whom austerity measures without substantial economic growth would mean joblessness and difficulty in maintaining life. A sense of relative deprivation would thereby be generated, undermining democratic legitimacy for European economic governance. Moravcsik further argues that no austerity measure would succeed without domestic support, as an electoral mandate is necessary for any government.[103] As such, the current emphasis on austerity is only partially correct. In order to gain support from the public, those countries in crisis will have to present a vision of growth and job creation. In the meantime, the austerity measures taken should be based on the principles of fairness and justice, that is, to take as the objects of reform both the public and private sectors, especially the financial system. It is only in so doing that electorates may be persuaded to endure short-term losses in exchange for long-term gains, thereby granting legitimacy to fiscal governance. In this line of reasoning, Steinberg and de Cienfuegos warn that the German-dominated

[101] Honor Mahony, 'EU Faces "Lost Generation" of almost 8 Million Young People', *EU Observer*, September 7, 2012, http://euobserver.com/economic/117458.

[102] Benjamin Fox, 'Euroscepticism in Decline, Poll Indicates', *EU Observer*, September 7, 2012, http://euobserver.com/news/117473.

[103] Andrew Moravcsik, 'Europe after the Crisis', p. 67.

austerity policies and fiscal compact may not resolve the European debt crisis but lose legitimacy as a result of low economic growth and high unemployment rate in the eurozone. Consequently, the euro may collapse.[104]

This warning is not without justification. In countries that ran into debt trouble and had to take austerity measures in return for EU bailouts such as Greece, an anti-EU sentiment has been growing and become a significant political force, which is expressed in the rise of nationalist and/or populist parties.[105] What is more worth noticing, though, is the phenomenon that populist political parties have also been gaining support in countries not having sovereign debt issues such as France and the Netherlands.[106] Even in countries such as Ireland and Italy, which generally support the austerity policies, there is a demand for the EU to introduce initiatives to stimulate economic growth, as austerity can only be economically and politically sustainable with the dynamic of economic growth. In so far as the fiscal compact is concerned, therefore, its enforcement will run into serious difficulties without the complement of growth and employment.

The goal of economic growth and employment, however, cannot be achieved by those countries in debt crisis alone, as these countries have lost their monetary sovereignty, and their fiscal sovereignty is now constrained by the fiscal compact. The task thus will depend on the collective effort of the EU. In this respect, although the EU has tried to boost growth and jobs through the single market in the 1980s, the EMU/euro in the 1990s, and the Lisbon Strategy in 2000, these efforts of 'supply management' did not come with significant results. To stimulate growth through 'demand management' is therefore a sensible idea. The Commission's proposal in 2012 is worth trying that the European Investment Bank (EIB) may finance interstate infrastructure projects, as a modest sum of €230 m was estimated to be able to generate €4.6 billion worth of projects. Such proposal was also backed by French president

[104] Federico Steinberg and Ignacio Molina Álvarez de Cienfuegos, 'The New Government of the Euro Zone: German Ideas, Divergent Interests and Common Institutions', *Revista de Economia Mundial*, Issue 30 (2012), pp. 59–81.

[105] 'The Greek Run', *The Economist*, May 19, 2012, http://www.economist.com/node/21555572.

[106] 'Kicking against austerity', *The Economist*, April 28, 2012, http://www.economist.com/node/21553464; Nikolaj Nielsen, 'Dutch Pro-Europe Parties Win Heated Election', *EU Observer*, September 13, 2012, http://euobserver.com/political/117531.

François Hollande, who held that austerity and discipline alone are not sufficient to bring growth and employment.[107] On the part of Germany and other surplus countries, Moravcsik suggests that they must increase public spending, wages, and consumption to help bridge the competitiveness gap between surplus and deficit countries, as well as to encourage the deficit countries to grow and export more.[108]

To create demand by increasing investment and consumption is indeed a viable approach, but this does not seem to be supported by the Merkel government. Bound by the domestic impression that the European debt crisis is a result of some individual countries' irresponsible fiscal behaviour, the government's attitude towards the crisis is conservative, focusing on preventive initiatives such as the fiscal compact. This vein of understanding and practice, however, is both short-sighted and double standard.

First, as some commentators point out, the European sovereign debt crisis is the result of three problems—a banking crisis, a sovereign debt crisis, and a growth crisis. Dealing with one will make the others worse.[109] In fact, the deficit and debt problems of the US, the UK, and Japan are more serious than that of the eurozone countries in crisis, but the markets do not see the former countries having a sovereign debt crisis.[110] This reflects that the eurozone's current austerity programmes and the fiscal compact cannot convince international investors that these practices can address the problems of growth and employment.

Second, Germany violated the SGP twice in 2002–2003 mainly because of its weak economic growth and high unemployment rate. This experience should have made it clear that fiscal discipline requires the complement of growth and employment to be politically and economically enforceable. In a time when the macroeconomic conditions are even worse than before, however, Germany's insistence on imposing fiscal discipline on all the EU member states indicates a double standard and the fact that it has not learnt the lesson. The question thus is: how can the fiscal compact not repeat the failure of the SGP, both of which have been dominated by Germany? The German leaders should notice the importance of growth

[107] 'Add Hollandaise sauce', *The Economist*, May 8, 2012, http://www.economist.com/blogs/charlemagne/2012/05/austerity-and-euro-crisis.

[108] Andrew Moravcsik, 'Europe after the Crisis', p. 65.

[109] 'Still Sickly', *The Economist*, May 31, 2012, http://www.economist.com/node/21551495.

[110] Carlo Cottarelli, 'Sovereign Debt Crisis: Why in Europe and Not Elsewhere?', *Intereconomics*, Vol. 47, No. 2 (2012), pp. 74–5.

and employment in solving the sovereign debt crisis, as well as the consequences of austerity for social and political cohesion within the EU. Only in so doing can the eurozone break the circle of fiscal regulation violation, governance breakdown, and crisis reoccurrence.

After Germany rejected the Commission's proposal of creating demands, an EU-wide directive on growth and employment is not likely to be made in the short term. It is suggested that individual member states in the eurozone should maintain a certain degree of fiscal autonomy to meet the challenges of growth. The OECD's suggestion is worth considering that the eurozone may learn from 'the Danish policy of expanding and contracting government spending automatically to reflect ups and downs in the economic cycle'.[111] In response to France's inability to meet the EU target of 3% budget deficit by the end of 2013, the Commission's decision to grant France extra time to correct its excessive deficit instead of imposing sanctions seems to be moving towards the direction proposed.[112] This policy may gain, or at least maintain, public support for the fiscal compact.

## 5 Conclusion

It took the EU eight years to formally end the European sovereign debt crisis. It is the first crisis after the establishment of the EMU and also the longest in the history of European integration. Its endurance indicates the complexity of the problem as well as the difficulty in finding a solution. Although usually called a European sovereign debt because of serious sovereign debt problems in several member states in the eurozone, the crisis is in fact the result of various factors. At the core of the Greek crisis is a failure of governance resulted from the lack of fiscal discipline and accountability. The main issues confronting Ireland and Spain are the burst of the housing bubble and the ensuing financial exposure of the banking sector, which are also related to the US subprime mortgage crisis. As for Italy and Portugal, both suffer from a structural and long-term problem of economic growth. The European sovereign debt crisis hence involves effective governance in the public sector as well as the regulation of the private sector. Furthermore, it is not only a continuation of the global financial

[111] Honor Mahony, 'EU Faces "Lost Generation" of almost 8 Million Young People'.

[112] Andrew Rettman, 'EU Unlikely to Punish France for Budget Lapse', *EU Observer*, February 14, 2013, http://euobserver.com/economic/119068.

downturn but also a symptom of weak growth and high unemployment rate the EU has been facing.

As such, the austerity measures and the fiscal compact that Germany has been promoting can only partially address the problems, because they only focus on reforming the public sector and restoring fiscal discipline. While the financial disorder in Greece has largely been settled after the intervention of the Troika, and the problems of the banking sector in Ireland and Spain may also be corrected after the role of the ECB in financial regulation is strengthened, the lack of sufficient economic growth in Italy and Portugal is not likely to be addressed in the short term, as it requires the support of a fiscal union in the eurozone, which is nevertheless hampered by the question of democratic deficit. Given the complexity of the issues these countries have been facing, it is not difficult to grasp the fact that although Germany and France have been taking a more active stance, the European debt crisis is only controlled but not entirely solved.

Although individual countries have their own problems and require different approaches, each—including those not in a debt trouble—nevertheless needs growth and employment to be the conditions for maintaining fiscal discipline, following the fiscal compact, and avoiding the failure of the SGP. The members in the eurozone, especially Germany, nevertheless have not been able to reach a consensus on how to stimulate growth and support job creation. So far, the eurozone has come up with a fiscal 'discipline' union but not a fiscal 'resource-sharing' one, and this has made expansionary fiscal policies at the EU level highly unlikely. Under such constraint, it seems necessary to allow the member states of the eurozone (perhaps except Greece) more room to expand or cut their public spending according to the domestic economic conditions, so that the quest for growth and employment may be met.

The making of the euro has been a point of debate between intergovernmentalism and neofunctionalism. For the former, the euro is the result of power struggle between Germany and France after the end of the Cold War, reflecting how the two reached a compromise on the arrangement of European political and security order. For the latter, the euro is the spillover effect of the 1986 single market. In so far as the European sovereign debt crisis is concerned, the case cannot settle the debate between the two. On the one hand, those characteristics shown in the course of the crisis that support the arguments of intergovernmentalism include the key role of German and French (in)action, individual member states over the supranational institutions, and the convergence of EU economic governance to German standards. On the other hand, the neofunctionalist concept of the spillover effect is reflected in the solutions put forth such as the German-led fiscal compact/union and the French proposal for growth and employment. Yet neither can explain how the governance problem in Greece would have such a great impact on European integration. The Greek crisis, indeed, is a particular case, this nevertheless suggests that the complexity of integration cannot be captured by a single theory, while also indicates the importance of governance.

## References

Alves, Henrique Rui, and Oscar Afonso, "The 'New' Stability and Growth Pact: more flexible, less stupid?," *Intereconomics*, Vol. 42, No. 4 (2007), pp. 218–25.

Arezki, Rabah, Bertrand Candelon, and Amadou N.R. Sy, "Sovereign rating news and financial markets spillovers: evidence from the European debt crisis," *IMF Working Paper*, WP/11/68 (2011), pp. 1–27.

Attinasi, Maria-Grazia, Cristina Checherita, and Nickel, Christiane, "What explains the surge in euro area sovereign spreads during the financial crisis of 2007–2009?," *Public Finance and Management*, Vol. 10, No. 4 (2010), pp. 595–645.

Avellaneda, D. Sebastian and Niamh Hardiman, "The European context of Ireland's economic crisis," *The Economic and Social Review*, Vol. 41, No. 4 (2010), pp. 473–500.

Bohn, Frank and Eelke de Jong, "The 2010 euro crisis stand-off between France and Germany: Leadership styles and political culture," *International Economics and Economic Policy*, Vol. 8, Issue 1 (2011), pp. 7–14.

Carlo, Cottarelli, "Sovereign debt crisis: Why in Europe and not elsewhere," *Intereconomics*, Vol. 47, Issue 2 (2012), pp. 74–5.

Collignon, Stefan, "The end of the Stability and Growth Pact?," *International Economics and Economic Policy*, Vol. 1, No. 1 (2004), p. 15.

Commission of the European Communities, "One Market, One Money," *European Economy*, Vol. 44 (1990).

de Haan, Jakob, Helge Berger, and Jansen, David-Jan, "Why has the Stability and Growth Pact failed?," *International Finance*, Vol. 7, No. 2 (2004), p. 236.

Dyson, Kenneth and Kevin Featherstone, *The Road to Maastricht: Negotiating Economic and Monetary Union* (Oxford: Oxford University Press, 1999), pp. 2–5.

Eichengreen, Barry, "Europe, the euro and the ECB: Monetary success, fiscal failure," *Journal of Policy Modeling*, Vol. 27, No. 4 (2005), pp. 427–8.

European Central Bank (ECB), "The implementation of the Stability and Growth Pact," *European Central Bank Monthly Bulletin*, May (1999), pp. 45–72.

European Commission, *EMU@10: Successes and Challenges after Ten Years of Economic and Monetary Union* (Brussels: European Commission, 2008), p. 135.

European Commission, *Public Finances in EMU-2011* (Brussels: European Commission, 2011), p. 2.

*European Council*, "Statement by the Euro Area Heads of State or Government," December 9, 2011. http://www.consilium.europa.eu/uedocs/cms_data/docs/pressdata/en/ec/126658.pdf, last viewed 23 February 2012.

*Eurostat*, "News release: Euro indicators," April 26, 2011. http://epp.eurostat.ec.europa.eu/cache/ITY_PUBLIC/2-26042011-AP/EN/2-26042011-AP-EN.PDF, last viewed 27 February 2012.

Featherstone, Kevin, "The Greek sovereign debt crisis and EMU: A falling state in a skewed regime," *Journal of Common Market Studies*, Vol. 49, No. 2 (2011), pp. 193–217.

Feldstein, Martin, "The euro and the stability pact," *Journal of Policy Modeling*, Vol. 27, No. 4 (2005), pp. 423–4.

Fourcans, Andre and Thierry Warin, "Stability and Growth Pact II: Incentives and Moral Hazard," *Journal of Economic Policy Reform*, Vol. 10, No. 1 (2007), pp. 55–61.

Goodhart, A.E. Charles, "Replacing the Stability and Growth Pact?," *Atlantic Economic Journal*, Vol. 34, No. 3 (2006), pp. 243–57.

Gartner, Manfred, Bjorn Griesbach, and Jung, Florian, "PIGS or lambs? The European sovereign debt crisis and the role of rating agencies," *International Advances in Economic Research*, Vol. 17, No. 3 (2011), pp. 288–99.

George, Stephen and Ian Bache, *Politics in the European Union* (Oxford: Oxford University Press, 2001), p. 51.

Gibson, D. Heather, Stephen G. Hall, and Tavlas, George S., "The Greek crisis: Growing imbalances and sovereign spreads," *Journal of International Money and Finance*, Vol. 31 (2012), pp. 498–516.

Gilpin, Robert, Global Political Economy: Understanding the International Economic Order (Princeton and Oxford: Princeton University Press, 2001), pp. 86–98.

Grieco, Joseph, "The Maastricht Treaty, Economic and Monetary Union, and the neo-realist research program," *Review of International Studies*, Vol. 21, No. 1 (1995), p. 34.

Gros, Daniel and Thomas Mayer, "How to deal with the threat of sovereign default in Europe: Towards a Euro(pean) Monetary Fund," *Intereconomics*, Vol. 45, No. 2 (2010), pp. 64–8.

Heijman, J.M.W., "The need for a European fiscal policy," *Intereconomics*, Vol. 44, No. 2 (2006), p. 101.

Jenkins, Charles "Commentary: Can the euro zone find a democratic way out of the crisis," *European Policy Analyst*, October 2011, Issue 4, pp. 3–6.

Kouretas, P. George and Prodromos Vlamis, "The Greek crisis: Causes and implications," *PanoEconomicus*, Vol. 4 (2010), pp. 391–404.
Lachman, Desmond, "Greece's threat to the euro," *Intereconomics*, Vol. 45, No. 2 (2010), pp. 93–5.
Leblond, Patrick, "The political Stability and Growth Pact is dead: Long life the economic Stability and Growth Pact," *Journal of Common Market Studies*, Vol. 44, No. 5 (2006), p. 971.
Levitt, Malcolm and Christopher Lord, *The Political Economy of Monetary Union* (Basingstoke: Palgrave Macmillan, 2000), pp. 16–20, 52–7, 162–4.
Luttwak, Edward, "The politics of eurozone crisis," *International Economy*, Vol. 26, Issue 1 (2012), pp. 28–33.
Dominguez, M.E. Kathryn, "The European Central Bank, the euro, and global financial markets," *Journal of Economic Perspectives*, Vol. 20, No. 4 (2006), pp. 67–88.
Marsh, David, *The Euro: The Battle for the New Global Currency* (New Haven and London: Yale University Press, 2011).
Moeller, Joergen Oerstroem, "Europe after the debt crisis," *Asia Europe Journal*, Vol. 9 (2011), pp. 67–72.
Moravcsik, Andrew, "Europe after the crisis," *Foreign Affairs*, Vol. 91, Issue 3 (2012), pp. 54–68.
Mundell, Robert, "The European fiscal reform and the plight of the euro," *Poznan University of Economics Review*, Vol. 11, No. 1 (2011), pp. 7–22.
Padoa-Schioppa, Thomasso, *The Road to Monetary Union in Europe* (Oxford: Clarendon Press, 1994), p. 4.
Prokopijevic, Miroslav, "Euro crisis," *PanoEconomicus*, Vol. 3 (2010), pp. 369–84.
Savage, D. James and Amy Verdun, "Reforming Europe's stability and growth pact: Lessons from the American experience in macrobudgeting," *Review of International Political Economy*, Vol. 14, No. 5 (2007), p. 844.
Schuknecht, Ludger, "Stability and Growth Pact: Issues and lessons from political economy," *International Economics and Economic Policy*, Vol. 2, No. 1 (2005), pp. 65–6.
Segers, Mathieu and Femke Van Esch, "Behind the veil of budgetary discipline: The political logic of the budgetary rules in EMU and the SGP," *Journal of Common Market Studies*, Vol. 45, No. 5 (2007), pp. 1089–109.
Shore, Cris, "The euro crisis and European citizenship: The euro 2001–2012-celebration or commemoration," *Anthropology Today*, Vol. 28, Issue 2 (2012), pp. 5–9.
Steinberg, Federico and IMA de Cienfuegos, "The new government of the euro zone: German ideas, divergent interests and common institutions," *Revista de Economia Mundial*, 30 (2012), pp. 59–81 (in Spanish with English summary).
Young, Brigitte and Willi Semmler, "The European sovereign debt crisis: Is Germany to blame," *German Politics and Society*, Vol. 29, No. 1 (2011), pp. 1–24.

Zervoyianni, Athina, George Argiros, and Agiomirgianakis, George, European Integration (Basingstoke: Palgrave Macmillan, 2006), pp. 220–1.

## Media Websites Consulted

*BBC*, http://www.bbc.co.uk.
*Bloomberg*, http://www.bloomberg.com.
*CBN.com*, http://www.cbn.com.
*EU Observer*, http://euobserver.com.
*Financial Times*, http://www.ft.com.
*MSNBC*, http://www.msnbc.msn.com.
*Reuters.com*, http://www.reuters.com.
*The Economist*, http://www.economist.com.
*The Guardian*, http://www.guardian.co.uk.
*The Independent*, http://www.independent.co.uk.
*The New York Times*, http://www.nytimes.com.
*The Wall Street Journal*, http://online.wsj.com.

CHAPTER 3

# Are Labour Market Reforms the Answer to Post-Euro Crisis Management? Reflections on Germany's Hartz Reforms

## 1 Introduction

In its 2015 official report on growth and employment, the European Commission indicates that the EU economy would be characterized by slow growth and high but stable unemployment. The Commission therefore suggests that reforms supporting well-functioning labour markets must take and continue in order to effectively reduce unemployment. Labour market reforms, following austerity and fiscal discipline, seemingly become another recipe for recovering the eurozone economy in the EU's post-euro crisis management. With both monetary and fiscal policies reaching their limits and unemployment still at high levels in some EU members, labour market reforms are expected to be the major, if not the last, resort that policy-makers can turn to. As the European Central Bank (ECB) indicates in its report (2012: 10), a comprehensive strategy of labour market reforms is key to solid economic recovery.

Against this backdrop, Germany stands out with its record high employment and low unemployment since the mid-2000s, especially with its conspicuous employment stability during the global financial crisis and the European sovereign debt crises. Indeed, Germany was the only advanced OECD economy that did not experience the rise of unemployment during the financial crisis (OECD, 2009: 20, Table 3.1). Following

This chapter was first published by *European Review* (2018), 26(4): 738–4.



C.-M. Luo, *The EU's Crisis Decade*,
https://doi.org/10.1007/978-981-13-6565-2_3

Table 3.1 Main contents of the Hartz reforms

| *Reforms* | *Implementation* | *Main features* | *Likely effects* |
|---|---|---|---|
| Hartz I | January 2003 | – Enlist private firms to help jobless find work<br>– Tighten conditions for job acceptance and introduce sanctions for refusal of job offer<br>– Liberalize temporary agency work | Improving job search efficiency and enhancing incentives to take up employment |
| Hartz II | January 2003 | – Reform mini-jobs and midi-jobs with no or limited social contributions<br>– New subsidy for unemployed who become self-employed (Me-inc) | Raising incentives to take up employment |
| Hartz III | January 2004 | – Reorganize Federal Employment Agency and local Employment agencies<br>– Simplify active and passive labour market policies<br>– Case management for the long-term unemployed | Improving job search efficiency |
| Hartz IV | January 2005 | – Merge long-term unemployment assistance and social assistance into a (lower) means-tested unemployment benefit II<br>– Benefit type I: 60% (with children 67%) of the last wage for 6–12 months<br>– Benefit type II: flat-rate and means-tested benefit<br>– Workfare measures in the public sector, so-called 1-euro jobs | Raising incentives to welfare recipients by lowering reservation wages |

Source: Extracted from OECD, 2012: 14 and Klinger & Rothe, 2010: 9

fiscal governance, Germany, again, becomes a reference model for some unemployment-stricken EU members to look up to. Why and how the German economy could be transformed from what *The Economist* terms as 'the sick man of Europe' (17 November 2004) in the early 2000s to an 'economic superstar', described by Dustmann et al. (2014: 167) after the mid-2000s has been an issue of debate among both academics and policy-makers. The conventional wisdom is that serial structural reforms introduced by the German Schröder government on the labour market a decade ago, the so-called Hartz reforms (also known as Agenda 2010), are the main explanation, as following these reforms, the German unemployment rate has been in a steady decline from a peak of 11% in 2005 to 5% by the end of 2014. For example, the European Commission recognizes in its official report that the robust labour market and sound public finance are the solid underpinnings for the German economy (European Commission, 2016: 3). OECD also points out that Germany has witnessed the lowest increase in unemployment during the global financial crisis in OECD countries, and labour market reforms in the past decade are the main factor contributing to this 'labour market miracle' (Hufner and Klein, 2012: 5–6).

In contrast to international interests in the German experience and the compliments from the EU and international authorities on the Hartz reforms, scientific evidence of its effectiveness remains under debate, and reflections on its policy effects emerged after a decade of its implementation. Debates have further developed on whether or not this German model is applicable to other EU members. Despite a number of research studies that have analysed the effects of these reforms, a consensus has not yet been reached. This chapter is an attempt to clarify the reforms' effects from competing arguments and to identify its welfare implications for the German society and economy so as to explore why or why not labour market reforms can be another German answer, following fiscal discipline, to the EU's post-euro crisis management.

The rest of this chapter is arranged as follows. The first section briefly introduces the policy contents of Hartz reforms. The second section discusses its overall policy effects. The third section analyses whether the German model can or cannot be the recipe for reviving the weak eurozone economy.

## 2 Background of the Hartz Reforms and Its Contents

In order to have thorough discussions on the effects of the Hartz reforms, it is essential to have an understanding on its background and contents first.

### *2.1 Policy Background*

At the turn of the twenty-first century, Germany demonstrated the typical symptoms of Eurosclerosis—a stagnant economy with increasing unemployment since the 1970s. The high unemployment issue was further aggravated by the German reunification in 1990. By 2003, the German unemployment rate exceeded that in most advanced OECD countries. The labour market scenario, expressed by the deteriorating Beveridge curve which combines data on the number of the unemployed and companies looking for workers, was regular employment on the decline and long-term unemployment on the rise (Rinne and Zimmermann, 2012: 7; Bonin, 2012: 788–9). On the other hand, with the heavy burden of generous unemployment benefits, Germany had breached the Stability and Growth Pact (SGP), the EU's regulation on public finance, for four consecutive years by running excessive budget deficits of the 3% ceiling. A majority of economists believe that the crux of the issue was the rigidity of the German labour market, which was in desperate need of reform (Sinn, 2006: 1157; Geishecker, 2001: 581).[1]

A few reforms, such as the Employment Promotion Act and the new Social Code, were tried out since the 1990s, but they failed to lower unemployment to satisfactory levels. A scandal involving the German Federal Labour Office fabricating employment statistics finally ushered in what the then German chancellor Gerhard Schröder called as the 'biggest package of changes in post-war German history'—the Hartz reforms (*The Economist*, 17 November 2004).

### 2.2 *Policy Contents*

The Hartz reforms, on their principle of supporting and demanding (fördern und fordern), were composed of four laws and implemented gradually from January 2003 to January 2005. The first three measures, Hartz I–III, aimed at improving job search efficiency and employment flexibility, including restructuring the Federal Labour Agency, deregulating temporary work sector, and exempting social security taxes for

[1] During the time of the reform debate in 2003, there were as many as 300 German economists issuing a public declaration to call for labour market reforms. However, Carlin and Soskice (2009: 79) disagree with this common view by arguing that Germany's labour market reforms began in the mid-1990s and it ranked fourth highest of OECD countries in the measure of reform effort for 1994–2004 period. These reforms did not lower unemployment as expected but rather increased it by 1.4% from 1993 to 2003. Therefore, they argue that it is the persistent weakness of domestic aggregate demand rather than the failure to reform the labour market accounts for Germany's low growth and high unemployment.

low-paid jobs, the so-called mini-jobs and midi-jobs.[2] As Germany's long-term unemployment benefits were extremely generous due to its unlimited duration, which resulted in the long-term unemployment rate higher than that of any OECD country, the final and crucial component of the reforms, the Hartz IV, was an overhaul of Germany's long-term unemployment benefit systems by reducing the amount and duration of unemployment benefits and by tightening the rules and conditions of job search and acceptance for unemployment benefit receipts (see Table 3.1 for details) (Engbom et al., 2015: 7–9; Jacobi and Kluve, 2007: 46–7).

Unlike previous reforms, the Hartz reforms addressed all stakeholders of the labour market—services providers (job agencies), the demand side of the workforce (employers), and the supply side of the potential workforce (the unemployed). They emphasized on improving the efficiency of services providers by reorganizing them, increasing flexibility for employers by introducing various work arrangements, and putting pressure and obligations for the unemployed to return to work by cutting the scale and duration of their benefits. In short, policy-makers believed that, with better services provision, lower barriers to create new jobs, and fewer incentives to stay unemployed, Germany's high and persistent unemployment rate, especially in the long term, could be reduced effectively. It is noteworthy that although the Hartz reforms were extensive in its width and depth, they left the core labour market untouched and only picked on marginal employment, the so-called 'atypical' jobs, and the unemployed to be the reforming targets.

## 3 Debating Policy Effects

It has been more than a decade since the Hartz reforms were implemented. It is now appropriate to evaluate its overall effects on the German economy and society.

[2] Mini-jobs are referred to works that are exempt from social security contribution. Before the Hartz reforms, income threshold of mini-jobs were €325 per month. The Hartz II reform raised this threshold to €400. The Hartz reform further introduced midi-jobs, a type of employment with reduced social security contribution for the income range of €400.01 to €800 per month.

### *3.1 Are the Hartz Reforms Effective in Reducing Unemployment?*

Going by the significant decrease in the German unemployment rate after the reforms (see Fig. 3.1), most economists agree that the Hartz reforms successfully reduced unemployment, although they disagree on the causes and estimates of the policy effects because of their different approaches and simulations.

In its own official evaluation, the German Federal Employment Agency indicates that, within three years, from 2006–2008, after the reforms were implemented, unemployment reduced by one-third. Long-term unemployment dropped more significantly by 40%. These positive results were explained to be achieved by the improvement of matching efficiency, which was 10–20% more efficient than before. The report believes the long-term unemployed was the group that benefited the most from the

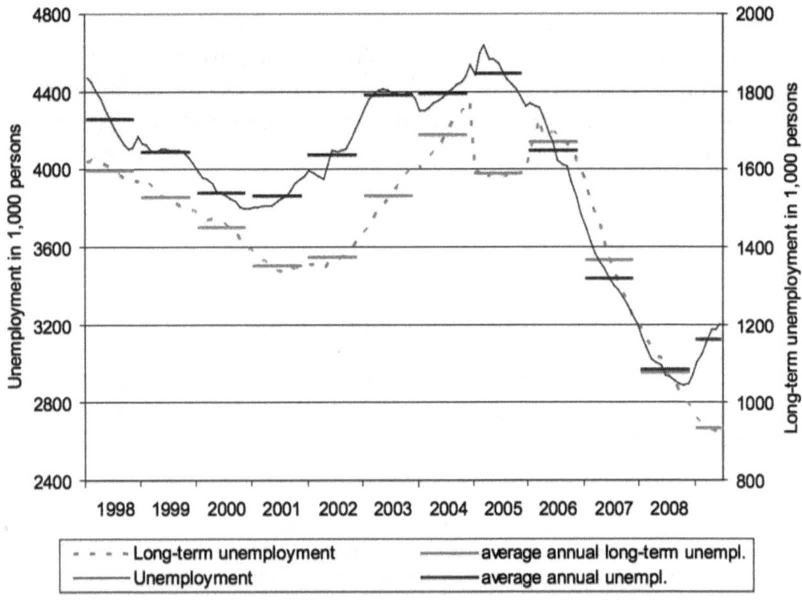


**Fig. 3.1** The stocks of unemployment and long-term unemployment in Germany, 1998m1 to 2009m6. Remarks: Monthly data, seasonally adjusted. Source: German Federal Employment Agency

reforms, with up to 6% more benefiting than the short-term unemployed (Klinger and Rothe, 2010: 5 & 29–30).

Rinne and Zimmermann (2013: 5), the second author and the policy advisor to the then Schröder government on the reforms, contend that the reforms accelerated the matching process between the unemployed and job vacancies and thus the labour market witnessed a significant increase in employment of female workers, low-skilled workers, older workers, and young workers.

OECD economists agree with the German official views that the Hartz reforms reduced structural unemployment by increasing work incentives for low-income and older workers and by improved matching efficiency. Employment rate for older workers of 55–64 years increased by 19% and was almost five times that of the OECD average. These altogether resulted in a decrease of NAIRU (non-accelerating inflation rate of unemployment) by 0.5% (Hufner and Klein, 2012: 7–9).

Other economists follow a similar line, albeit with their individual explanations and estimates. For example, Krebs and Scheffel (2013: 689 & 695) estimate that Hartz I–III reduced structural unemployment rate by 1.5% and Hartz IV reduced it by 1.4%. Together, the four reforms contributed to half of unemployment reduction in the period of 2005–2012. Giannelli et al. (2013: 3) suggest that the reforms reduced unemployment by one-third in three years, accompanied by a similar rise in employment. Kirkegaard (2014: 4) asserts that the reforms created more than 3 million jobs since 2005 and reduced the recorded unemployed by more than 2 million in the same period. Busl and Seymen (2013: 2 & 40) estimate that the Hartz reforms reduced unemployment by 3.3% due to improving matching efficiency and lower unemployment benefits, and these positive policy effects contributed to a quarter of Germany's GDP growth between 2003 and 2010. Krause and Uhlig (2012: 75) obtain similar estimates that the reforms reduced the unemployment rate by about 3.45%.

While having consensus on the Hartz reforms' effects on reducing unemployment, economists disagree on which parts of the reforms were more effective in reducing unemployment. For example, Krebs and Scheffel (2013: 689 & 695) and Moller (2010: 328) identify the reforms for the long-term unemployed were more effective than for the short-term unemployed. On the contrary, Bonin (2012: 792) and Jacobi and Kluve (2007: 59–61) assert that the reforms were more effective in reducing the short-term unemployed becoming long-term unemployed and had little or no effect on the long-term unemployed.

Explanations for the causes of policy effectiveness vary, too. For example, Fahr and Sunde (2009: 284), Hertweck and Sigrist (2013: 20), and Caliendo and Hogenacker (2012: 12) all argue that it was effectively the improved matching efficiency that reduced unemployment. Hertweck and Sigrist (2013: 20) suggest that a 23% increase in the matching efficiency would result in a 20% decrease in unemployment rate and the effects of Hartz reforms in matching efficiency (Hartz I–III) lie between 12% and 31%. Meanwhile, Engbom et al. (2015: 21–2) contend that both improved matching efficiency and strengthened incentives to return to work accounted for reducing unemployment. On the contrary, Dlugosz et al. (2014: 330) emphasizes the role of reforming the unemployment benefit system (Hartz IV) in reducing unemployment.

Only a handful of economists are the exceptions to the mainstream viewpoint, casting doubts on the reforms' effects. Launov and Walde (2013: 1161 & 1185) argue that the reforms produced only a negligible effect, 0.07%, on reducing unemployment. For the group of low-skilled labour, unemployment actually went up. In their simulations, productivity growth explains, about 80% more than the reforms, the entire unemployment reduction. Fertig et al. (2006: 399) also found no significant effects of the reforms on inflow and outflow of the German unemployment. Beissinger et al. (2016: 317 & 326–8) and Bornhorst and Mody (2012: 19–20) remind that the evidence to confirm the reforms' effects on reducing unemployment was 'still preliminary' and 'inconclusive'. The former believe that without these reforms, unemployment would have dropped anyway, while the latter indicate that similar reforms were undertaken in other European countries in the mid-1990s, but they did not produce the same magnitude of policy results as in the German case.

However, such doubts cannot conceal the fact that the sharp fall of the German unemployment started only from 2005, coinciding with the implementation of the Hartz reforms, as Fig. 3.1 shows. Nor can they explain, if productivity growth was the driver for this unemployment reduction, then why the fall did not appear a decade earlier as productivity growth started from the mid-1990s (Dustmann et al., 2014: 169–76), not the mid-2000s. It is hard to deny the effectiveness of the Hartz reforms on unemployment reduction. What should be noteworthy, however, is its waning and stagnating effects over time. The reforms considerably reduced the long-term unemployment from 1.8 million to 1 million between 2005 and 2011. But the number has remained largely unchanged since then, and neither more carrots nor sticks from the reforms could reduce it further. So far, Germany's long-term unemployment rate was still 10% higher than the OECD average (Spermann, 2015: 2–3 & 8). That is to say, the Hartz reforms were effective to reduce unemployment to a certain extent, but they did not fundamentally solve the problem.

### 3.2 *Explanations for Germany's Jobs Miracle in the Financial Crisis?*

The Nobel Prize winner, Paul Krugman, describes in his column of the *New York Times* that the very modest increase in the German unemployment during the global financial crisis was 'Germany's jobs miracle'. Indeed, it was Germany's high and stable employment during the recession that brought the Hartz reforms into the international spotlight. As Hufner and Klein (2012: 5) indicate, during the global financial crisis, Germany's GDP declined by over 5%, compared to the OECD average of 3.8%, and its export fell more sharply by 14%. Its unemployment, however, increased only slightly by 0.2%, compared to the OECD average of 2.2%. It is at this point that economists are divided on the effects of the Hartz reforms.

Some government-related economists attribute Germany's exceptional performance during the world recession to the Hartz reforms. For example, Rinne and Zimmermann (2012: 2 & 9–16, 2013: 7) argue that the reforms were implemented before the crisis so as to allow the improved German labour market putting in a strong position to weather the financial crisis more effectively and efficiently. They admit that internal flexibility within the German industry, such as working-time accounts and short-time work, exercised in the crisis-hit-most exporting manufacturing sector, saved many jobs from redundancy. However, they insist that such internal flexibility of labour hoarding could not be sustained without an effective and efficient labour market which was delivered by the reforms.

Klinger and Rothe (2010: 30), who evaluate the effects of the Hartz reforms for the German Federal Employment Agency, hold the similar views that the good performance of the German labour market during the global financial crisis was attributed at least partially to the Hartz reforms. Hufner and Klein (2012: 9), OECD economists, also suggest that the impact of these reforms continued over time and kept lowering unemployment even during the crisis. Krebs and Scheffel (2013: 668) agree that the steady decline in unemployment induced by the Hartz reforms dampened the unemployment effects of cyclical factors such as the global crisis. Without the reforms, they estimate, the German economy would have experienced a cyclical increase in the unemployment rate by 2%.

But the official report of the French government (Bouvard et al., 2013: 7) disagrees with such arguments. It points out that adjustment mechanisms, such as short-time work, time-saving accounts, job-preservation agreements, and so on, account for the resilience of the German jobs market during the crisis. Other economists also exclude the Hartz reforms as a plausible explanation.

For example, Moller (2010: 335) indicates that labour hoarding used by the German industry was the explanation for Germany's employment stability during the crisis. Krause and Uhlig (2012: 77–8) emphasize on the government's role in explaining by arguing that it was government subsidies to short-time work that restrained unemployment during the recession from rising. Without such supporting policies, they estimate, Germany would experience the same magnitude of unemployment increase as in other G7 countries by about 2–2.5%. Burda and Hunt (2011: 30–1) and Eichhorst (2012: 12–3) suggest that both government-subsidized short-time work arrangements and employer' needs to hoard skilled workers in the forms of negotiated working-time accounts contributed to this remarkable employment stability during the crisis. Bonin (2012: 801–5) explains from the nature of the crisis and the responses of the German government and industry. First, the German financial system was featured with a large number of small and semi-public local banks that mostly were disconnected from international capital markets and Germany did not have the problem of housing market bubbles. Second, what was hit most by the crisis was the German export-oriented manufacturing sector. But most firms were willing to hoard workers through working-time flexibility because they learnt from the previous experiences of the shortage of skilled workers before the crisis. Helped by government-sponsored short-time subsidies, most firms were able to avoid large-scale redundancy. He estimates that a decline in productivity per hour by 1% could buffer 1.1 million job losses and a decline in working time by 4% could buffer 1.4 million job losses.

The following facts would help us to clarify the role of the Hartz reforms from these divided arguments. The first evidence comes from

Germany itself. It was the temporary work sector that suffered most from job losses during the global financial crisis, declining by 20% compared to a 4% decline of the manufacturing sector during the same period. Other vulnerable groups that faced greater risks than the average in losing earnings were low-skilled and non-standard workers (Rinne and Zimmermann, 2012: 15). That is to say, marginal jobs that the Hartz reforms targeted were the ones that were lost most during the financial crisis. The core and skilled workforces of the manufacturing sector, which were hoarded during the crisis, contributed to the employment stability during this period. They were the ones that the Hartz reforms did not target. In short, Germany's jobs miracle during the financial crisis derived from labour hoarding of the core workforce in the manufacturing sector, not from the Hartz reform effects on continuing unemployment reduction. Quite the contrary, the above-average losses of temporary, low-paid, and non-standard jobs in the recession indicate that the Hartz reforms increased Germany's unemployment during this period in an unexpected way. The second evidence comes from other European countries. The Netherlands and Austria did not have similar labour market reforms prior to the financial crisis. The two countries resorted to the same strategy of short-time work to retain qualified workforce during the crisis and there was not witnessed a significant rise in unemployment in these countries (Rinne and Zimmermann, 2012: 16). The fact simply demonstrates that short-time work, rather than labour market reforms, can explain the job market performance during this period more convincingly.

### 3.3 By What Quality and at What Costs of Job Creation?

With the Hartz reforms' effects on increasing employment being clarified, further questions were raised: what kinds of jobs were created then and what types of jobs were taken up? And more importantly, at what and whose costs?

In terms of job quality, the reforms failed to create standard (full-time), high-quality jobs as much as they did for non-standard, low-quality ones. According to the official report of the French government (Bouvard et al., 2013: 3), from 2004 to the first half of 2012, the Hartz reforms had created 2.5 million jobs, but most of them were marginal, non-standard jobs. Temporary (agency) work increased 2.7 times from 331,000 persons in 2003 to 882,000 in 2011. Standard and full-time jobs increased only very slightly by 2.4% between 2004 and 2011, while part-time jobs increased by 33%.[3] After the reforms, Germany part-time employment rate became the second highest in the eurozone. The report accordingly criticizes that most macroeconomic evaluations on the Hartz reforms failed to measure the quality and duration of jobs created by the reforms.

Other atypical jobs that were seen in fast increase were mini-jobs and midi-jobs. As Jacobi and Kluve (2007: 58–9) point out, the Hartz reforms increased midi-jobs by about 125,000 in number and expanded mini-jobs much more by 1.8 million in number in just two years. Looking in a longer timeframe, mini-jobs were increased from 4 million in 2003 to 7.5 million in 2014 (Kirkegaard, 2014: 4–5). A total of 4.9 million of mini-jobs was held as main jobs, and 75% of them earned less than €10 per hour. The huge increase in mini-jobs also replaced regular jobs, especially in smaller firms (Beissinger et al., 2016: 316–7).

Mini-jobs and midi-jobs have existed in Germany long before the Hartz reforms, but why did they grow so rapidly after the reforms? Eichhorst (2012: 17–9) explains from the 'carrot' side that the reforms liberalized non-standard jobs, combined with minimum income support by Hartz IV, and they together provided strong incentives for benefit recipients to take up these jobs to maximize the benefits. This can explain an unexpected rise in taking up low-pay and non-standard works in low- and medium-skilled services sectors. After the reforms, around 1.3 million workers were identified as 'working unemployed', half of them in marginal part-time work.

Bonin (2012: 792 & 805), on the other hand, explains from the 'stick' side that the unemployed felt the 'demanding' part of the reforms and had to prove their efforts in job search or even had to take up the so-called 1-euro jobs, a form of public employment rewarded with a symbolic wage, but the 'supporting' part of the reforms, such as good quality counselling and training, did not reach many of the long-term unemployed. Therefore, the rapid decline in the German unemployment rate was because the reforms put pressure on people who were at risk to become long-term unemployed to accept low-wage works.

Non-standard jobs do not necessarily mean low-pay jobs, but the atypical jobs that the reforms induced were, indeed, paid lower. Engbom et al. (2015: 21) estimate that the reforms lowered post re-entry earnings by 10% in relation to similar workers who remained employed. Beissinger

[3] Figures from Beissinger et al. (2016: 316–7) were even alarming. They indicate that, from 2003 to 2012, part-time jobs increased by 72%, reaching 7.4 million in 2012. By contrast, full-time jobs declined by 3% over the same period.

et al. (2016: 316–7) further argues that temporary jobs that the reforms liberalized were paid 20–40% lower than the normal level. Engbom et al. (2015: 22) therefore comment that the reform was successful in reducing unemployment; however, it came at the cost of unemployed workers not only in terms of benefit cuts but also in lowering re-entry earnings post unemployment.

The direct consequences from the growing low-paid sector in the German economy were the emerging two worlds of the job market, wage restraint, and increasing income inequality. As Carlin and Soskice (2009: 77) and Kirkegaard (2014: 6) indicate, the reforms liberalized low-wage workforce and increased part-time jobs in Germany, but did little to reform the regular employment. They aggravated the 'insider-outsider' labour market (those with secure jobs and those outside job protection). More women, young people and elder ones participated in the labour market after the reforms, but most of their jobs lacked employment protection as insider workers have enjoyed. Eichhorst (2012: 17–9) also agreed that the reforms led to the growing dualization of the German employment system—'good' and 'insider' jobs and 'bad' and 'outsider' jobs. Although the employment stability and pay level of 'insider jobs' were not affected so far, he predicts that the marginal workforce would put pressure on the core workforce as the latter can be replaced by the former in the long run.

That day came earlier than he assumes. As Engbom et al. (2015: 6) point out, the period of the Hartz reforms coincided with a prolonged period of negative growth in average wages. Krebs and Scheffel (2013) even directly assert that it was the reforms that reduced real wages. Wage was reduced, as Krebs and Scheffel (2013: 685) and Caliendo and Hogenacker (2012: 12) explain, because the reforms forced unemployed people to take up less-paid jobs by cutting benefits and therefore increased labour supply. This development in the 'outsider' job market further lent wage pressure for 'insider workers' in collective negotiations and thus lowered down unit labour costs in Germany. Bonin (2012: 798–9) specifies that unit labour costs dropped particularly evident in the post-reform period 2005–2007 by more than 4%. 'Additional wage restraint is a rational answer to the reforms'.

However, Rinne and Zimmermann (2012: 10) do not accept the phenomenon of wage restraint as the outcome of the reforms, but attributed to the behaviour of social partners in order to make firms more internationally competitive.

It is true that wage restraint cannot be explained by only one single factor, as the declining power of trade unions driven by globalization and less companies following collective bargaining agreements than before all contributed to this outcome to various extents. However, the changing behaviour of social partners cannot explain why real wage actually fell for the first time, not just stagnated, only after the reforms appeared. According to the OECD report (Hufner and Klein, 2012: 10), wage moderation in Germany during the 2000s was especially remarkable by both international and historical standards. Internationally, compared to an increase of 22% in the average OECD country, Germany's unit labour cost fell by 2% from 2000 to 2007. Historically, this figure increased by 15% in the 1990s, 20% in the 1980s, and 69% in the 1970s. The report explains the negative growth of wage to be associated with the Hartz reforms as they led the unemployed to accept lower-paid jobs.

A natural development of the growing low-pay sector is the rising income inequality. Kirkegaard (2014: 4–5) indicates that income inequality in Germany increased after the reforms and the share, 22%, of Germans earning two-thirds or less of the national median gross hourly earnings was higher than any other Western euro members. The report of the French government (Bouvard et al., 2013: 6) points out that income inequality in Germany has increased markedly during the time when the Hartz reforms were deployed as the Gini coefficient[4] rose by 3 points from 26.2 in 2000 to 29.2 in 2008. This brought Germany into one of the few OECD countries where median income stagnated between the mid-1990s and mid-2000s. Real income for lowest quintile of households actually fell at an average annual rate of 0.3% during this period.

However, Biewen and Juhasz (2012: 645) argue that it is a change in employment patterns such as the growth of part-time and marginal part-time work, not the Hartz reforms, contributed to the increase in income inequality and poverty. Such arguments cannot stand by empirical examination. Giannelli et al. (2013: 4–6 & 22–4) investigate the quality of new jobs, measured in job duration and wages, created by the Hartz reforms. They found that the disadvantaged groups—temporary, unskilled, and unemployed workers—actually faced wage losses more than others as their re-entry wage reduced significantly after the reforms. Although the

[4] The Gini index measures income distribution from 0 to 100, the higher the score, the more unequal in income distribution.

reforms were not found to affect labour turnover rates, it was not because of high satisfaction with new jobs, but because of higher costs of being unemployed and lower entry wages after the reforms. As a result, the reforms reinforced an already existing tendency towards lower wages and greater income inequality.

In sum, the reforms were effective for reducing unemployment by creating non-standard, low-quality, low-pay jobs, taken up by the unemployed with lower re-entry wage and no job protection, at the cost of the negative growth of wage for the general German workers for the first time since the 1970s, accompanied by rising income inequality for the society.

### 3.4 *After All, Are the Hartz Reforms a Worthy Trade-Off and Welfare-Enhancing?*

If these adverse effects are inevitable price paying for the reforms' effectiveness on reducing unemployment, a question needs to be asked further: are they a worthy trade-off and welfare-enhancing on balance for the entire German economy after all?

For Kirkegaard (2014: 4), a large increase in job creation in return for a modest increase in inequality is a positive trade-off and worth embracing. Krebs and Scheffel (2013: 667 & 686) suggest that the reforms produced winners and losers. Winners were employed household as the reforms reduced their tax burden, which was equivalent to an increase of 0.4% of lifetime consumption. Losers were the unemployed and low-skilled workers, as the reforms raised the cost of being unemployed for the long-term unemployed and pressured the short-term unemployed to accept low-paid and usually precarious jobs. The welfare loss of the long-term unemployed was estimated around 1% of lifetime consumption. Overall, they believe, the reforms increased the long-term growth for the German economy by 0.1%.

On the contrary, Poilly and Wesselbaum (2014: 157 & 169) do not accept labour market reforms necessarily welfare-enhancing, depending on what types of reforms are put in place. Launov and Walde (2013: 1159 & 1184–7) suggest that the Hartz-style reforms reduced welfare for most workers, 76%, because the value of being employed falls and this is why there were public demonstrations against the reforms because they were seen as only beneficial to firms and would be 'the direct road to poverty'.

In their explanations, productivity growth was more important than the reforms to explain Germany's economic growth.[5]

Busl and Seymen (2013: 40), Bornhorst and Mody (2012: 24), and Carlin and Soskice (2009: 89) all suggest that the rise of low-pay and temporary jobs after the Hartz reforms constrained the consumption growth of the German economy in the medium term, as the consumption of low-skilled workers was restrained by low wage and precautionary savings in core workforce was unexpectedly raised. In the long term, the weak demand for consumption would be detrimental to Germany's much-needed economic transformation from a heavy dependence on manufacturing and exporting to a domestically driven growth economy.

In the French government's assessment, the Hartz reforms were not seen as a desirable trade-off because of rising poverty in both employment and unemployment. It indicates that by increasing the supply of low-paid jobs, the Hartz reforms increased the poverty rate of employed workers from 4.8% in 2004 to 7.5% in 2006. The largest increase in the poverty rate was found among the unemployed, rising from 41% in 2004 to 68% in 2010. Two-thirds of unemployment benefit recipients found a job after the reforms, but the hours and wages of temporary and part-time jobs were too low to raise them from the poverty line (Bouvard et al., 2013: 6).

Beissinger et al. (2016: 327–8) also contend that the reforms show that low pay is the price for low unemployment. However, such inequality-unemployment trade-off may be damaging, as a policy that fosters inequality by impoverishing low-skilled workers could be counter-productive in the long term. The evidences show that the reforms reduced unemployment by creating cheap jobs in the non-tradable sector and this came with a decrease in exports/production ratio.

There are many different ways for policy-makers and academics to measure economically whether the Hartz reforms are a worthy trade-off or not. For the general public, however, there is only one way to measure it—the effects on their real income and living standard which they feel most personally. Any reform that cannot raise real wage and living standard for the general public can hardly be said a welfare-enhancing policy. The

[5] Similar views were held by Dustmann et al. (2014: 184), Reisenbichler and Morgan (2012: 550–1), and Hassel (2014: 57) that it was productivity growth and innovations, combined with business-labour's consensus on wage restraint, not the Hartz reforms, accounted for the German economic revival.

fact of the negative growth of wage and living standard illustrates a simple reality that the general public were invisible losers of these reforms, not the winners as Krebs and Scheffel (2013: 686) claim, along with the visible losers of the unemployed, and thus made the whole society, in effect, welfare-deteriorating. Unemployment, indeed, reduced in Germany, but it came with the rise of low-pay employment, which is not only economically counter-productive for the growth of domestic consumption but also socially destabilizing because of rising income inequality. The political and social costs of public riots and terroristic attacks associated with these reforms explain clearly the public perceptions of the welfare effects of these reforms. The revisions taken by the succeeding Merkel government to the reforms as a response to the strong public opposition by reinstating some benefits back further illustrate the unsustainability of these reforms in realpolitik whatever effective they were. After all, the ways that the Hartz reforms resorted to, as Whyte (2010: 8) describes, were 'perspiration', not 'inspiration', and therefore by no means a politically and economically desirable trade-off.

## 4 Can/Can't It Be Another German Answer to the Post-Euro Crisis Management?

With the overall effects of the Hartz reforms being clarified, this leads to the key question of this paper—can the Hartz reforms be another German model, following fiscal governance, for other unemployment-stricken EU members? Before answering this question, two issues have to be clarified first. First, why can the Hartz reforms work and what are the main factors for its effectiveness? Second, what is the nature of the German unemployment issue before the reforms and that in unemployment-suffering EU members mainly from the euro crisis? That is to say, are the nature of unemployment and contextual environments between Germany and these countries comparable?

### *4.1 Can the German Model Fit All?*

If the Hartz reforms can shed light on reducing unemployment per se, then what are the conditions underpinning its success? And more importantly, are these required conditions existing in the present national and international contexts?

The favourable international context, viewed by *The Economist* (2004), was the most important, if not the only, factor to explain the Hartz reforms' success. It contends that the reforms would not be successful if the German export did not grow and the export was able to grow thanks to the increasing demand from emerging markets such as China at that time. This factor drove the German economy to expand by 2%. 'None of this (Hartz reforms) will help … if growth doesn't return'.

Other commentators place emphases on the German national contexts from the competitiveness of the German industry to macroeconomic policies. Sinn (2006: 1163) and Bornhorst and Mody (2012: 12 & 20) suggest that Germany's unique competitiveness in exporting capital goods, of which 450 small- and medium-sized enterprises (SMEs) are world leaders in their respective niche markets, was the main factor to explain the success of the Hartz reforms. Bonin (2012: 797–8) further explains that Germany's international competitiveness was restored before the Hartz reforms through a long period of wage growth lagging behind productivity growth.[6] In other words, if international competitiveness was not restored before the reforms, it would be very doubtful that the reforms could reduce unemployment in a favourable international context.

Rinne and Zimmermann (2013: 17–8), on the other hand, comment that the reforms were successful because of the absence of fiscal austerity. Germany's public debt increased by 40% between 2000 and 2010, and public resources were used to foster growth when the Hartz reforms were implemented.

In short, the Hartz reforms were effective in a growing economic context, may it be an expanding international market or an expanding national economy from either/both the competitive exporting sector or/and the public spending. Without favourable national and international contexts, the fortunes of the Hartz reforms would be quite reverse.

Do such expanding economic contexts, national and international, exist in the current eurozone? Internationally, the low and negative inter-

[6]Bonin (2012) explains that this remarkable wage restraint for such a long period was achieved through the cooperation between trade unions and employer organizations, and their mutual agreement on maintaining employment stability as a response to the German unification and the pressure of offshoring to central and eastern European countries. Similar views are also held by Dustmann et al. (2014) and Carlin and Soskice (2009).

est rates taken by central banks of major economies since 2015 highlight the weakness of the aggregate demand of the global market. Nationally, with the fiscal compact in operation, austerity became the norms of fiscal governance for euro members. As for the exporting competitiveness, different euro members perform differently from one another. As Beissinger et al. (2016: 328) point out, the scale of unskilled workers is higher in other euro countries; therefore, the Hartz-style reforms, which produced inequality-unemployment trade-off in Germany, would be more painful in such countries.

Furthermore, the nature of unemployment was not identical between Germany and other European countries. As Krebs and Scheffel (2013: 693–4) contend, for countries where long-term unemployment benefits were already very low, such as France and Spain, the Hartz-style reforms would have only very modest effects. Similarly, for other unemployment-stricken EU countries, such as Ireland, Portugal, and Italy where high unemployment was brought up by the breakout of the euro crisis, not from the generous unemployment benefits for low- and unskilled workers, the Hartz-style reforms certainly could not address to the problems. This very different nature of unemployment between Germany and other EU countries explains why the Hartz-style reforms were already undertaken throughout much of Europe in the mid-1990s and similar strategies of government-subsidized short-time work during the global financial crisis were also adopted in other European countries, but they failed to produce similar effects as in the German case, as Bornhorst and Mody (2012: 12 & 20) indicate.

With both national and international economic contexts very different from then, and the nature of the unemployment issue very different between Germany and other European countries, the German model of labour market reforms cannot fit to other European countries this time, as it did for fiscal governance. In sum, the Hartz reforms were effective in a very German-specific context for a very German-specific problem. Without favourable national and international conditions mentioned above, an increase in labour supply resulted from the Hartz reforms would not be translated into an increase in employment. Equally, without reforms addressing to the German-specific crux, an increase in labour demand from national and international conditions would not be translated into a decrease in unemployment, either.

### 4.2 *The Real Danger of European Integration: The German Complacency of One-Size-Fit-All Thinking and Its Double-Standard Approaches*

The performance of the Hartz reforms in reducing unemployment intrigues Kirkegaard (2014: 9) to suggest that all euro countries without exchange rate flexibility should learn from Germany. The true believers come from German policy-makers themselves. The German chancellor, Angela Merkel, urged EU countries suffering from the euro crisis to carry out labour market reforms as Germany did on the Hartz reforms so as to better compete in the global market (*Bloomberg Business*, 19 February 2013). Rinne and Zimmermann, the policy advisor on the Hartz reforms, praises the reforms as the 'North Star of labour policy' (2013: 18) in his commemorating paper with Rinne at the reforms' tenth anniversary and can serve as a role model for other countries (Rinne and Zimmermann, 2012: 16).

Such remarks, however, neglect the fact that it was the Merkel government that revised the reforms in 2006 by extending the duration of unemployment benefits up to 24 months because the reforms were too unpopular, as Dlugosz et al. (2014: 333) point out. It also neglect the fact that the adverse political repercussions of the Hartz reforms were so strong and persisted over time that no major political party were willing to openly identify itself with these reforms, as Rinne and Zimmermann (2013: 4) criticize. Such remarks, therefore, reflect not only the danger of an over-simplified one-size-fit-all thinking of German policy-makers towards EU governance but also their ignorance of both the very different nature of unemployment issue between Germany and other EU countries and different national and international economic contexts between now and then. The realities of the Merkel government's revisions to the reforms out of the strong public opposition but the German chancellor's opposite demands on other EU government to push through labour market reforms, regardless the strong public opposition they encountered, as the French government did,[7] show not only Germany's double standard on its own and European affairs but also how politically unjustifiable and unsustainable such demands were.

[7] The labour market reforms presented by the French government caused a nationwide protest movement, the so-called Nuit Debout Movement, that spread out to more than 60 towns and cities in March 2016. See *EU Observer*, 'The French protest that wants to redefine politics', 11 April 2016, available at https://euobserver.com/beyond-brussels/132993 for more details.

Economically, the Hartz-style labour market reforms were not a welfare-enhancing project, not to mention their effects would wane over time, as mentioned above. German policy-makers may believe that a eurozone that turns into a larger version of Germany, with fiscal disciplines and labour market reforms, would be the best scenario for the eurozone's economic governance. However, as Whyte (2010: 9–10) rightly reminds, 'a eurozone that becomes "too German" could be as crisis-ridden as one that remains too "Greek"'. This is because if the domestic consumption of core euro countries such as Germany continued contracting on the scale they used to be, one of the adverse consequences of the Hartz reforms, then the eurozone would lack sufficient demand to prop up the growth and would further worsen the situations of indebted countries.

On the other hand, other EU countries without experiencing similar labour market reforms, such as Denmark, Austria, Sweden, and the Netherlands, were proved to be more resilient to the financial crisis than others, as indicated in the official report of the European Commission (*EU Observer*, 15 January 2015). For example, Denmark was a good example of balance between labour market flexibility and job security and investment in working conditions (*EU Observer*, 11 April 2016). That is to say, there is more than one way, other than just the German model, to answering the unemployment question that some indebted euro countries were facing. What should be worried about more for European integration is not the unemployment challenge that these indebted euro countries faced. It is, indeed, serious, but not intractable. Rather, it is Germany's complacency of one-size-fit-all thinking and, being the leading country of the eurozone, its double standards on and ignorance of European affairs that pose the real danger to European integration.

## 5 Conclusion

Since 2005, there has been a steady decline in the German unemployment rate, from the record peak of 11% in 2005 to the historic low of 5.3% in 2013. It is no doubt that the Hartz reforms implemented in 2003–2005 played a key role in this impressive unemployment reduction. In terms of their primary policy goal—reducing unemployment—the reforms achieved it successfully. However, their effectiveness waned over time. Furthermore, such effects were fulfilled at the cost of the rise of low-pay sector, negative wage growth, and increasing income inequality. For individuals, the successful Hartz reforms were by no means welfare-enhancing because the poverty in employment and unemployment both increased. For the German economy and society as a whole, the reforms imply a counter-productive risk because of the contraction of domestic consumption, and potential social instability because of rising inequality and deteriorating living standards. This can explain why the successive Merkel government re-reformed the reforms to a considerable extent. Therefore, the Hartz-style reforms were not a desirable model for other EU countries to refer to. Neither can they be the answer to the post-euro crisis management in an age of fiscal austerity and negative interest rates, as some commentators and German policy-makers assume. As Allan Pall (2015), the secretary-general of the European Youth Forum, reminds, labour market reforms should focus on both quantity and quality of jobs—jobs that can offer career and investment possibilities, jobs that are stepping stones rather than dead ends.

It is at this point that this chapter views the real danger to European integration not from the unemployment challenge faced by some indebted euro countries, but from Germany's complacency of one-size-fit-all thinking and, being the leading country of the eurozone, its double standards on its own domestic and European affairs and its ignorance of the differential nature and contexts of the European unemployment issue from the German one. Germany's mismanagement of the European sovereign debt crisis already helped the rise of extremist populism in the EU politics as can be seen in the results of the 2014 European Parliament election. A further mishandling of labour market reforms as a convenient way out of unemployment predicament could cost the collapse of the already fragile public confidence in European integration and guarantee the continuing success of extremist populism in the EU politics. The latter, as the EU Commissioner Guenther Oettinger fears, puts the EU in the real danger of falling apart (*EU Business*, 1 January 2016). The effective way to secure the future of European integration and confront extremist populism is not focusing seemingly on reducing unemployment, but on a clear-cut solution to improving wage growth and living standards. The German-style labour market reforms, as the Hartz reforms demonstrated, address none of these challenges for the EU economy and society.

## References

Beissinger, Thomas, Nathalie Chusseau and Joel Hellier (2016), 'Offshoring and labour market reforms in Germany: Assessment and policy implications', *Economic Modelling*, 53: 314–33.

Biewen, Martin and Andos Juhasz (2012), 'Understanding rising income inequality in Germany', *The Review of Income and Wealth*, 58(4): 622–47.

*Bloomberg Business* (2013), 'Merkel cites East Germany lessons for EU's problem states', 19 February 2013, available at http://www.bloomberg.com/news/articles/2013-02-18/merkel-cites-east-german-lessons-for-crisis-wracked-euro-states, accessed 10 March 2016.

Bonin, Holger (2012), 'The two German labour market miracles: Blueprints for tacking the unemployment crisis', *Comparative Economic Studies*, 54:787–807.

Bornhorst, Fabian and Ashoka Mody (2012), 'Tests of German resilience', *IMF Working Paper*, No. WP/12/239, Washington, DC: IMF.

Bouvard, Flore, Laurence Rambert, Lucile Romanello, and Nicolas Studer (2013), 'How have the Hartz reforms shaped the German labour market?', *Tresor-Economics*, No. 110, Paris: The Ministry of Economy and Finance and the Ministry of Foreign Trade of the French Government.

Burda, Michael C. and Jennifer Hunt (2011), 'What explains the German labour market miracle in the Great Recession?', *NBER Working Paper Series, Working Paper 17187*, Cambridge, MA: National Bureau of Economic Research.

Busl, Claudia and Atilim Seymen (2013), 'The German labour market reforms in a European context: A DSGE analysis', *ZEW Discussion Paper No. 13-097*, Mannheim, Germany: Centre for European Economic Research (ZEW).

Caliendo, Marco and Jens Hogenacker (2012), 'The German labour market after the Great Recession: Successful reforms and future challenges', *IZA Discussion Paper Series*, IZA DP No. 6810, Bonn: The Institute for the Study of labour (IZA).

Carlin, Wendy and David Soskice (2009), 'German economic performance: Disentangling the role of supply-side reforms, macroeconomic policy and coordinated economy institutions', *Socio-Economic Review*, 7(1): 67–99.

Dlugosz, Stephan, Gesine Stephan, and Ralf A. Wilke (2014), 'Fixing the leak: Unemployment incidence before and after a major reform of unemployment benefits in Germany', *German Economic Review*, 15(3): 329–52.

Dustmann, Christian, Bernd Fitzenberger, Uta Schonberg, and Alexandra Spitz-Oener (2014), 'From sick man of Europe to economic superstar: Germany's resurgent economy', *Journal of Economic Perspectives* 28(1): 167–88.

Eichhorst, Werner (2012), 'The unexpected appearance of a new German model', *IZA Discussion Paper Series*, IZA DP No. 6625, Bonn: The Institute for the Study of Labor (IZA).

Engbom, Niklas, Enrica Detragiache and Faezeh Raei (2015), *IMF Working Paper: The German Labor market Reforms and Post-unemployment Earnings*, Washington, DC: IMF.

*EU Business* (2016), 'German Commissioner Oettinger voices fears of EU "collapse"', 1 January 2016, available at http://www.eubusiness.com/news-eu/politics-oettinger.15q1, accessed 14 March 2016.

*EU Observer* (2015), 'EU unemployment and social problems will take years to fix', 15 January 2015, available at https://euobserver.com/social/127221, accessed 10 March 2016.

——— (2016), Junker urged to revive "social Europe" model', "The French protest that wants to redefine politics", 11 April 2016, available at https://euobserver.com/beyond-brussels/132993, accessed 11 April 2016.

European Central Bank (2012), *Euro Area Labour Markets and the Crisis*, Occasional Paper Series No 138, Frankfurt: ECB.

European Commission (2016), *Commission Staff Working Document: Country Report Germany 2016*, Brussels: European Commission.

Fahr Rene and Uwe Sunde (2009), 'Did the Hartz reforms speed-up the matching process? A macro-evaluation using empirical matching functions', *German Economic Review*, 10(3): 284–316.

Fertig, Michael, and Christoph M. Schmidt, and Hilmar Schneider (2006), 'Active labor market policy in Germany—Is there a successful policy strategy?' *Regional Science and Urban Economics* 36 (3): 399–430.

Geishecker, Ingo (2001), 'Does outsourcing to Central and Easter Europe really threaten manual workers' jobs in Germany?', *The World Economy*, 29 (5): 559–83.

Giannelli, Gianna C., Ursula Jaenichen and Thomas Rothe (2013), 'Doing well in reforming the labour market? Recent trends in job stability and wages in Germany', *IZA Discussion Paper Series*, IZA DP No. 7580, Bonn: The Institute for the Study of Labor (IZA).

Hassel, Anke (2014), 'The paradox of liberalization—Understanding dualism and the recovery of the German political economy', *British Journal of Industrial Relations* 52(1): 57–81.

Hertweck, Matthias and Oliver Sigrist (2013), 'The aggregate effects of the Hartz reforms in Germany', *SOEP Papers on Multidisciplinary Panel Data Research*, Berlin: German Socio-Economic Panel Study (SOEP).

Hufner, Felix, and Caroline Klein (2012), 'The German labour market', *OECD Economics Department Working Papers No. 983*, Paris: OECD.

Jacobi, Lena and Jochen Kluve (2007), 'Before and after the Hartz reforms: The performance of active labour market policy', *Journal for Labor Market Research*, 40 (1): 45–64.

Kirkegaard (2014), 'Making labor market reforms work for everyone: Lesson from Germany', *Policy Brief*, Number PB14-1. Washington, DC: Peterson Institute for International Economics.

Klinger, Sabine and Thomas Rothe (2010), 'The impact of labour market reforms and economic performance on the matching of short-term and long-term unemployed', *IAB Discussion Paper 13/2010*, Berlin: The Research Institute of the Federal Employment Agency (IAB).

Krause, Michael and Harald Uhlig (2012), 'Transitions in the German labor market: Structure and crisis', *Journal of Monetary Economics* 59: 64–79.

Krebs, Tom and Martin Scheffel (2013), 'Macroeconomic evaluation of labor market reform in Germany', *IMF Economic Review*, Washington, DC: IMF.

Launov, Audrey and Klaus Walde (2013), 'Estimating incentive and welfare effects of nonstationary unemployment benefits', *International Economic Review* 54(4): 1159–98.

Moller, Joachim (2010), 'The German labor market response in the world recession-de-mystifying a miracle', *Journal of Labour Market Research*, 42(4): 325–36.

OECD (2009), *Tackling the Job Crisis: The Labour Market and Social Policy Response*, Paris: OECD.

——— (2012), *Economic Survey of Germany*, Paris: OECD.

Pall, Alan (2015), 'Youth worst affected by labour market gaps', published on *EU Observer*, 29 May 2015, available at https://euobserver.com/opinion/128896, accessed 6 April 2016.

Poilly, Celine and Dennis Wesselbaum (2014), 'Evaluating labor market reforms: A normative analysis', *Journal of Macroeconomics*, 39: 156–70.

Reisenbichler, Alexander and Kimberly J. Morgan (2012), 'From "sickman" to "miracle": Explaining the robustness of the German labor market during and after the financial crisis 2008–09', *Politics and Society* 40(4): 549–79.

Rinne, Ulf and Klaus F. Zimmermann (2012), 'Another economic miracle? The German labor market and the Great Recession', *IZA Journal of Labor Policy*, 1 (3): 1–21.

——— (2013), 'Is Germany the North Star of labor market policy?', *IZA Discussion Paper No. 7260*, Bonn: Institute for the Study of Labor (IZA).

Sinn, Hans-Werner (2006), 'The pathological export boom and bazaar effect: How to solve the German puzzle', *The World Economy*, 29 (9): 1157–75.

Spermann, Alexander (2015), 'How to fight long-term unemployment: Lessons from Germany', *IZA Journal of Labor Policy*, 4:1–15.

*The Economist* (2004), 'Europe: Germany on the mend', 17 November 2004, available at http://www.economist.com/node/3352024, accessed 20 October 2015.

Whyte, Philip (2010), 'Why Germany is not a model for the eurozone', *Centre for European Reform Essays*, London: Centre for European Reform.

CHAPTER 4

# The Rise of Populist Right Parties in the 2014 European Parliament Election and Implications for European Integration

## 1 Introduction

The eighth European Parliament (EP) election was held in May 2014 across 28 members of European Union (EU). It was widely regarded as the most important election to date for the following reasons. First, it was the first post-euro crisis election at the European level and thus was described as 'an important test of faith in the European project' (*The Economist*, 18 November 2013). The renewal, or retake, of the electorate's mandate to further European integration would be demonstrated. Second, it was the first post-Lisbon Treaty election. Under the Lisbon Treaty, the newly elected European Parliament is endowed with new powers of legislation, the so-called co-decision powers with the European Commission. As Hix (2013: 1) describes, 'the next European Parliament will have legislative powers to change the way the single market is regulated, …, to reform the Common Agricultural Policy, to ratify or reject an EU-US free trade agreement, and to scrutinise the implementation of the "fiscal compact" treaty'. Furthermore, the new Parliament will, for the first time, formally 'elect' the next Commission president. As the Lisbon Treaty stipulates, the European Council, which will propose a candidate for the Commission president, has to 'take into account the elections to

This chapter was first published by *European Review* (2017), 25(3): 406–22.



C.-M. Luo, *The EU's Crisis Decade*,
https://doi.org/10.1007/978-981-13-6565-2_4

the European Parliament' (Ibid.: 1–2).[1] That is to say, the new Parliament co-decides not only the EU's policies but also its chief executive officer (CEO).

The election outcome reveals that anti-EU, anti-immigration populist right parties (PRPs) fared considerably well in a number of EU members, especially in France and the UK where PRPs have become the largest party. All together, they have become the third largest political force in EU politics. *The Economist* comments such an election result as 'The Eurosceptic Union', and the rise of such parties presents an 'anti-European question' to the EU to answer. It points out a reality that the EU's political fault line has been shifting from the conventional left versus right to pro-EU versus anti-EU (26 May 2014a & 18 November 2013). The then French prime minister, Manuel Valls, described this outcome as a 'political earthquake', while the then president of the European Council, Herman Van Rompuy, viewed the rise of PRPs in EU politics as the big danger to European integration (*BBC*, 26 May 2014a; Mudde, 2013: 2).[2]

Some do not agree the 2014 EP election outcome as a PRP earthquake. For example, Mudde argues that, quantitatively speaking, only 10 of 28 EU members elected PRP members of European Parliament (MEPs), and such parties gained additional seats in six countries while losing seats in seven others (*The Washington Post*, 30 May 2014). Goodwin also argues that some PRPs, indeed, were more established after the 2014 EP election, but others remained on the margins (*New Statesman*, 2 January 2014).

It is true that some PRPs performed badly, for example, they did not perform well as expected in Italy, the Netherlands, and Finland. However, it cannot be ignored that such parties have greatly raised in number. As *Financial Times* points out, the number and breadth of their gains in the

[1] Because of these new powers that are endowed to the new European Parliament and the new change to the production of the Commission president, Simon Hix argues that the 2014 EP elections is 'a genuinely "European" election' and could significantly reduce the EU's democratic deficits consequently. See Simon Hix (2013), 'Why the 2014 European elections matter: The key votes in the 2009–2013 European Parliament', *European Policy Analysis*, Issue 15, p. 11, for more details.

[2] The other group that also gained significantly in the election was the anti-austerity, anti-EU radical left parties in the euro crisis-hit countries such as Greece, Spain, and Portugal. Interestingly, the electoral gains of radical left parties received much less criticism and concerns than radical right ones.

2014 EP election were unexpected (26 May 2014a). Moreover, beyond these actual voters, 'there is a greater pool of potential supporters who are also receptive to' PRPs' appeals (Goodwin, 2011: 4). Secondly, as some critics argue, the point is not how many seats they can acquire in the European Parliament, but rather how much pressure they put on to their national governments. National governments, especially in France and the UK, encounter an acute dilemma of how to respond to policy issues that these parties have great appeals to voters, for example, in immigration and EU-related issues (European Policy Centre, 2014: 3; Gunduz, 2010: 43–4; Fligstein et al., 2012: 116; Howard, 2010: 735; Gunduz, 2010: 43–4; *The Economist*, 26 May 2014a, 4 January 2014b, 18 November 2013).[3] Thirdly, some election experts explain the 2014 EP election result that minority parties tend to perform better in European elections because the electorate feel freer to vote with their heart. If that is the case, then the 2014 EP election result vividly reflects the true feelings of the electorate towards the EU and European integration. Provided that scenario, the sharp rise of PRPs in France and the UK in the 2014 EP election is more worrying than some would comprehend.[4] It is not only because France and the UK are the EU's second and third largest members, respectively, and their domestic politics interact with their EU polices closely, but also because Franco-German axis is the locomotive of European integration, and the likelihood of the UK's departure from the EU in a referendum is increasing as a result. The developments of Euroscepticism in major EU members thus produce political instability to European integration.

[3]For example, the UK Cameron government's increasingly hardline stances on immigration from the EU and on open borders were seen as a response to the rise of the UK independence party (UKIP). See *The Economist*, 'Europe's populist insurgents: Turning right', 4 January 2014, available at http://www.economist.com/news/briefing/21592666-parties-nationalist-right-are-changing-terms-european-political-debate-does, for more details.

[4]T. Bale, C. Green-Pederson, A. Krouwel, K.R. Luther, and N. Sitter (2010) argue that the rise of PRPs challenges mainstream parties on both the centre-right and centre-left. To centre-right parties, PRPs have been pushing centre-right parties to adopt increasingly restrictive policies on immigration and integration, the so-called contagion from the right. To centre-left parties, they presented a 'triple challenge' by forming coalitions with centre-right, by highlighting the salience of social and cultural issues in domestic politics that tend to favour the right, by attracting support from manual workers who traditionally supported the left. See Bale, Green-Pederson, Krouwel, Luther, and Sitter (2010), 'If you can't beat them, join them? Explaining social democratic responses to the challenge from the populist radical right in Western Europe', *Political Studies*, Vol. 58, pp. 410–26, for more details.

This chapter aims to answer three related questions: first, why can PRPs rise in the 2014 EP election, where tolerance and multiculturalism are the core values of European integration? Second, what kind of messages delivered from their rise in the EU politics to European integration? Third, can European integration, which encountered serious setbacks by anti-European populism in the 2014 EP election, still be a role model for regional integration?

The rest of the chapter is arranged as follows. The first section will review the theoretical accounts of the rise of PRPs. It will follow the discussions of identifying causes of the 2014 EP election results from the competing interpretations in the second section. With causes being identified, the third section will clarify what the election result implies for European integration and whether or not EU policy-makers read them rightly. The conclusion summarizes the findings of this chapter with comments on whether or not the EU can still be a role model of regional integration.

Before entering into the discussions, some definition issues have to be clarified first. To define what populist right parties are is both academically and practically difficult.[5] Academically, there lacks a consensus on terminology, as PRPs appear similar in some respects, but different in others. For example, some PRPs are rooted in fascist and anti-democratic grounds, others demand more democracy and the protection of individual rights; some support the free market, others call for more intervention in the economy and nationalization (Arzheimer, 2009: 259; Goodwin, 2011: 12). Practically, they vary significantly on issues according to their local preferences, traditions, and political circumstances. For example, PRPs in France and in the Netherlands hold different views on issues of Israel: gay

[5]These difficulties demonstrate in a fact that there is no consensus among scholars and media on the use of terminology. Terms like extreme right, far right, radical right, radical right-wing populism, right-wing populism, national populism, new populism, new populism, neopopulism, exclusionary populism, xenophobic populism, etho-nationalism, anti-immigrant, nativism, racism, racist extremism, fascism, neofascism, postfascism, reactionary tribalism, integralism, and antipartyism are all different languages referring to the same subject. This terminological chaos, as Mudde (2007: 11–2) points out, 'is largely the consequence of a lack of clear definitions'. However, it does not prevent academics from discussing this issue, because 'we know *who* they are, even though we do not know exactly *what* they are' (Mudde, 1996: 233). According to Mudde's observations, nativism, authoritarianism, and populism are reoccurring features of PRPs and constitute the 'three pillars' of such parties (2007: 294). See Cas Mudde (2007), *Populist Radical Right Parties in Europe*, Cambridge: Cambridge University Press, pp. 11–2; (1996), 'The war of words: Defining the extreme right party family', *West European Politics*, Vol. 19, No. 2, pp. 225–48, for more details.

marriage and Islam. The former, National Front (FN), is anti-Semitic, anti-gay marriage, but not anti-Islam as a religion in principle, while the latter, Freedom Party (PVV), is supportive of Israel, gay marriage, but against Islam. Some PRPs, for example, Belgium's Vlaams Belang and Italy's Northern League, support regional autonomy within the EU, while others, the UK's UKIP and Finland's Finns Party, reject EU membership entirely (*The Economist*, 4 January 2014b; Mudde, *The Washington Post*, 30 May 2014).

Despite these differences and different criteria to divide PRPs, these parties do share core features: that is, they are all populist, nationalistic, anti-EU, and anti-immigration (Mudde, 2013: 3; *The Economist*, 4 January 2014b). One cross-country study even points out that 'the appeal on immigration is the only issue that unites all successful populist right parties' (Ivarsflaten, 2010: 3), and this striking feature leads to some analysts even defining such parties simply as 'anti-immigrant/immigration parties' (Van der Brug and Fennema, 2007: 474). This chapter, however, defines PRPs based on their sharing commonalities, which refers to those parties that are populist (as they are anti-establishment) and right (as they emphasize on ethno-nationalism) with anti-immigration, anti-EU attitudes (for their cultural identity ideology) (Rydgren, 2007: 242–6).

## 2 Theoretical Accounts for Explaining the Rise of PRPs

PRPs emerged in three distinct waves in the post-war years. The first wave began right after the end of the war and was composed of openly fascist and neo-Nazi parties that remained committed to political ideas that flourished in the interwar years. These parties were either banned or received only marginal support. The second wave rose in the 1970s and was mainly anti-tax populist movements. Again, they only attracted to only a handful of support. The third wave developed from the mid-1980s, following a new phase of immigration of 30 million people moving into Europe, and has been seen more sustainable than previous two waves.[6]

[6] Ignazi (2003) points out that the third wave of PRPs was different from the first and second waves. The former two were the heirs of the conflicts derived from the development of the industrial society and are by-products of the Industrial Revolution. The third wave was by-products of the conflicts of the post-industrial society, where material interests are no longer so central, and bourgeoisie and working class are not so clearly defined. The post-war

Their persistence at this stage is even described as a 'normal pathology' of Western democracies (Mudde, 2004: 541).[7] However, the rise of PRPs is not a universal phenomenon. In some countries, such as in Austria, Belgium, and France, PRPs have been growing strikingly, which were able to command more than 10% of national vote, and were even invited to join coalition governments. In other countries, such as in the Netherlands, Germany, and Spain, they had not been electorally successful and labelled as 'flash parties' (Goodwin, 2011: 1–3; Rydgren, 2005: 413–4; Van der Brug and Fennema, 2007: 475).

Despite their different fortunes and performances, the third wave of PRPs has been able to command sustainable electoral support in nearly a half of European countries, and this political reality caused what Messina phrases: 'the most disturbing and intractable challenges to democracies' (2007: 2–3).

How to explain the persistence of PRPs in contemporary Europe? There are two families of explanations—one focusing on the demand-side factors and the other on supply-side explanations.

## 2.1 Public Demand-Side Factors

This group explains the electoral support of PRPs from macro-structural factors that have changed voters' interests, emotions, attitudes, and preferences.

### 2.1.1 Relative Deprivation/Modernization Losers Account

The relative deprivation thesis is built on people's frustration arising from declining market situations or from fear of economic decline in the near future. This account argues that such economic frustration and fear, associating with the loss of social status or fear of loss of status, explain why people support PRPs (Rydgren, 2007: 247–8).

economic and cultural transformation, such as the development of services sector, the decline of labour relations, atomization, and secularization process, all have blurred class identification and loosened traditional loyalties to social groups. See Piero Ignazi (2003), *Extreme Right Parties in Western Europe*, Oxford: Oxford University Press, pp. 33–4, for more details.

[7] However, Mudde (2010) does not agree with 'normal pathology thesis'. He argues that the ideology of PRPs should be seen as 'a radicalization of mainstream values', and therefore PRPs should be regarded as a pathological normalcy, not normal pathology. See Cas Mudde (2010), 'The populist radical right: A pathological normalcy', *West European Politics*, Vol. 33, Issue 6, pp. 1167–86, for more details.

The modernization losers account further develops that the rise of PRPs can be understood as 'the radical effort to undo social change associated with modernization' (Minkenberg, 2003: 151). Betz (1994: 26–7) argues that the support for PRPs is largely 'a consequence of a profound transformation of socio-economic and socio-cultural structure of advanced Western European democracies' from an industrial to a post-industrial economy. Those who cannot cope with the 'acceleration of economic, social and cultural modernization' and/or run risks of falling into new underclass, or unemployment, may favour PRPs, as their anxiety, discontent, resentment, and insecurity could only be channelled into support for such kind of parties. Bell, accordingly, describes support for PRPs as 'politics of frustration' because it is based on 'the sour impotence of those who find themselves unable to understand, let alone command, the complex mass society that is the polity today' (cited from Rydgren, 2007: 248). In practical terms, Minkenberg (2000: 187) describes modernization losers being at 'the second-to-last fifth' stratum of society, which is rather secure but still can lose something.

This account echoes with Lipset's well-known argument that interwar fascist parties were disproportionately supported by old middle class. Empirical studies support the class profile of PRPs' supporters, but unemployment rates are found not a good predictor for PRPs' electoral performance. For example, several studies show that PRPs gained very high support from economically insured working and old middle class with lower- and mid-school educational qualifications, while very low support from more secure and higher-paid sections of the middle classes with a university-level education (Goodwin, 2011: 6–9; Ivarsflaten, 2005: 465; Lubbers et al., 2002: 364; Norris, 2005: 139; Arzheimer and Carter, 2006: 422 & 439; Gunduz, 2010: 40; Arzheimer, 2009: 259).[8] Also, unemployed people are more likely than others to vote for PRPs (Lubbers et al., 2002: 134). But unemployment rates are not a good predicator for PRPs' support. For example, a number of cross-national surveys find either insignificant relationship (Kessler and Freeman, 2005: 283; Lubbers et al., 2002: 370–1) or negative relationship (Coffe et al., 2007: 152–3; Arzheimer and Carter, 2006: 437; Knigge, 1998: 249) between

[8] According to Goodwin's survey (2011: 6–9), working class was two times of middle class to be PRPs' supporters in Austria, three times in Belgium and France, and four times in Norway. See Mathew Goodwin (2011), *Right Response: Understanding and Countering Populist Extremism in Europe*, London: Chatham House, pp. 6–9 and 17, for more details.

unemployment rates and electoral support of PRPs. Swank and Betz (2003: 230–3) find no significant relationship between unemployment rates, slower economic growth, or inflation rates and the electoral support of PRPs, but confirm a significant negative relationship between universal welfare state system and PRPs' support. Arzheimer (2009: 274) also supports that unemployment benefits can effectively reduce PRPs' support. On the other hand, Jackman and Volpert (1996: 501), Kestila and Soderlund (2007: 787), Arzheimer (2009: 274), and Rydgren and Ruth (2011: 202, 2013: 723) confirm a positive relationship between unemployment rates and PRPs' support. Boomgaarden and Vliegenthart (2007: 412) and Golder (2003a: 525) further find that unemployment correlates with PRPs only when it interacts with immigration issue. Anderson's case study on Denmark and Norway also suggests that unemployment would correlate with PRPs' support when it became a serious political problem in elections (1996: 506).

### 2.1.2 *Ethnic Competition Thesis*

This account argues that immigration issue is the main, if not the only, reason for voters' support for PRPs, because they want to reduce competition from immigrants over scarce resources such as job market, housing, welfare state benefits, or even the marriage market.[9] Following these arguments, it is assumed that PRPs' support will be more manifest in areas where there is high presence of immigrants, and among voters of lower-educated, unskilled, male voters who are confronted competition from immigrants foremost (Norris, 2005: 11; Fennema, 2005: 1–24; Mudde, 2007: 220; Goodwin, 2011: 16; Lubbers and Scheepers, 2000: 63; Kriesi et al., 2006: 921; De Koster et al., 2012: 15; Rydgren and Ruth, 2013: 723; John et al., 2005: 14–5).

A number of empirical studies support this account. For example, Knigge (1998: 249), Lubbers et al. (2002: 370–1), Swank and Betz (2003: 230), Coffe et al. (2007: 153), Anderson (1996: 507), Van der Brug et al. (2005: 562–3), Rydgren and Ruth (2011: 222–3), and

[9] Voters' perceptions of immigrants vary with the income level of countries. According to O'Connell (2005: 73), immigrants are perceived as an economic threat in lower-income countries, such as in Portugal, Greece, and Spain, while they are seen as a problem of social integration in wealthier countries, such as in Norway, Denmark, Switzerland, and Austria. See Michael O'Connell (2005), 'Economic forces and anti-immigrant attitudes in Western Europe: A paradox in search of an explanation', *Patterns of Prejudice*, Vol. 39, No. 1, pp. 60–74, for more details.

Arzheimer (2009: 274) find there is a positive relationship of the number of immigrants, and asylum seekers, with PRPs' support. But some researchers point out that such co-relationship between the number of immigrants and PRPs is conditional. For example, Golder (2003b: 454) found that it is significant only when unemployment rate exceeded 1.3%. Rydgren (2008: 737), Williams (2006: 5), and Givens (2005: 78) also found that immigration is effective to PRPs' support only when this issue links with other meaningful issues such as criminality, social unrest, unemployment, and economic crisis. Fligstein et al. (2012: 116) suggest that the effects of immigration depend on how the electorate perceive of it, rather than the actual threat of immigrants. On the other hand, Kestila and Soderlund (2007: 789–90) and Norris (2005: 169–172) find no significant relationship between the two, and Rydgren (2007: 250) is also critical of these surveys as 'an ecological fallacy', because 'most competition is more local in character', while most surveys are conducted at country level. His study, using individual-level data, shows that there are country variances between immigration issue and PRPs' support, for example, its correlation is significant in Denmark and the Netherlands, but not in Austria, Belgium, France, and Norway (Ibid.: 250–1).

### 2.1.3 *Political Discontent*

This account claims that the growing political alienation and discontent in Western European democracies have created an audience who are receptive to anti-establishment and anti-system appeals and thus provided opportunities for PRPs to gain support from protest voters. Some empirical studies, indeed, support this account that voters who are dissatisfied with the political establishment or have lower trust and confidence in politicians and democratic institutions are more likely to support PRPs (Kessler and Freeman, 2005: 283; Lubbers et al., 2002: 371; Norris, 2005: 157–9; Oesch, 2008: 368). However, Van der Brug et al. (2005: 77) find no significant relationship between protest voters and PRPs' electoral support. Furthermore, it is argued that protest voters play more important roles in PRPs' breakthrough elections than in subsequent elections, as Rydgren (2007: 251) confirms this tendency in the case of France's Front National. On the other hand, Norris (2005: 164) disagrees with this account as mistrust of politicians and political institutions has been widespread in many Western European democracies, but PRPs are not successful in every country. Also, as Rydgren (2007: 251) points out, this account cannot clarify why protest voters would turn to PRPs, instead of any other opposition party. Therefore, protest vote is 'a concept that in itself contains biased ambiguities' (Van der Brug and Fennema, 2007: 479).

In short, demand-side explanations share one feature in common that, whether they are from socio-economic, socio-cultural, or political perspective, they are in different ways based on a strain or grievance theory, focusing on objective conditions that have caused voters' grievances and discontents (Rydgren, 2005: 415). Demand-side explanations have been criticized for their limitations as 'relationship between belief and action is complex' and voters' attitudes and interests 'changes more frequently and less predictably than issue preferences' (Ivarsflaten, 2005: 467). Other researchers thus turn to the so-called supply-side approach.

## *2.2 Supply-Side Factors*

This group explains the rise of PRPs from political opportunity structures—electoral system, elite responses, media, and so on and party organization and programmes—their ideology and discourse that PRPs offer.

### *2.2.1 Political Opportunity Structures*

This account argues that opportunities from de-alignment and realignment processes, from convergence between established parties in political space, from open electoral system with low entrance thresholds, from mass media coverage, and from presence or absence of elite allies all provide favourable political structures for PRPs to emerge and develop (Rydgren, 2007: 252–7).[10]

For de-alignment and realignment processes, this account suggests that contemporary Western European democracies are characterized with two cleavage dimensions. One is economic, which concerns class issues, interest distribution between workers and capitalists, and the subsequent issue of state intervention in the economy; the other is socio-cultural, which concerns values and issues such as immigration, law and order, abortion,

[10] Rydgren (2005: 418) suggests that some political opportunity structures are stable and enduring so can be qualified as structures, and some are rather situational. Stable and enduring political opportunity structures are useful in explaining long-term cross-country variations, while situational ones are good at explaining variations within one specific country over time. See Jens Rydgren (2005), 'Is extreme right-wing populism contagious? Explaining emergence of a new party family', *European Journal of Political Research*, Vol. 44, p. 418, for more details.

and so on (Rydgren, 2004: 489, 2005: 420–1). In recent decades, it has been witnessing socio-cultural cleavage dimension has increased its salience at the expanse of the economic one. This realignment process provides an opportunity for PRPs' rise as they are able to appeal to working-class voters, who used to be conventional voters of the centre-left parties in socio-economic politics. As Lipset argues, manual workers have been traditionally at odds with the left parties' positions on socio-cultural issues, but this did not affect their voting behaviour as long as they identified with socialist parties' economic positions. With economic cleavage dimension losing its salience and socio-cultural one gaining its salience, socialist parties found them more difficult to hold their traditional voters as working-class voters are receptive to PRPs' appeals on socio-cultural issues. Therefore, it is argued that PRPs are less successful in countries where centre-left parties or institutions, such as trade unions, have retained strong hold on working-class voters (Oesch, 2008: 353; Eatwell, 2000: 407; Rydgren, 2004: 490–1).

For convergence thesis, it has been argued that convergence between established parties expands opportunities for PRPs, as this may produce a feeling of established parties 'being all the same' and fuel voters' distrust and discontent in politicians and parties, so as to create a niche market for PRPs to mobilize protest voters (Rydgren, 2005: 423). Most empirical studies tend to support this account, as Van der Brug et al. (2005: 562–3), Abedi (2002: 551), Arzheimer and Carter (2006: 439) all found correlation between PRPs' electoral success and the convergence of mainstream parties. Only Norris (2005: 192–6) found no support for the convergence thesis.

For electoral system and entrance thresholds, this account argues that the openness or closure of electoral systems is critical to PRPs' development. It is believed that a political system that has an entrance threshold of 2% or 4% would make a difference for the emergence of PRPs (Rydgren, 2007: 254). This account received mixed support from empirical studies. For example, Van der Brug et al. (2005: 568) and Arzheimer and Carter (2006: 439) found PRPs were not particularly successful under proportional electoral systems, while Swank and Betz (2003: 238), Jackman and Volpert (1996: 501), and Golder (2003b: 461) found PRPs did get more votes with proportional electoral systems.

For access to the mass media, many researchers argue that media, including mass media and the internet, play a vital role in the developments of PRPs, as 'action of gatekeepers produce the first and most basic selection mechanism' (Koopmans, 2004: 8). For example, Rydgren (2006: 30–1) points out that Sweden's PRP—New Democracy—has benefited greatly from a variety of commercial TV channels developing in the 1990s, and Cammaerts (2009: 555) found that the internet is instrumental in Belgium's case. Eatwell (2005: 101–20) also argues that French Front National reached its electoral breakthrough shortly after its leader was given access to state television. The different attitudes between Danish and Swedish newspapers on publishing PRPs' articles, the former more generous while the latter more warily, are believed to be a reason for why PRPs have been more successful in the former than in the latter (Rydgren, 2004: 474). Plasser and Ulram (2003: 40) and Boomgaarden and Vliegenthart (2007: 413) also confirm the positive relationship of media coverage on immigration issues with PRPs' support. However, Green-Pedersen and Krogstrup's case study on Denmark and Sweden suggests that mass media only has limited power in setting political agenda. To a large extent, its effects depend on how issues that media reported fit with party competition and electoral strategy (2008: 628–9).

For presence or absence of elite allies, there are two opposing hypothesis on this relationship. One is that cooperation with established parties would lend legitimacy to PRPs and result in more electoral success for them (Dahlstrom and Sundell, 2012: 354). The other, on the contrary, argues that PRPs' cooperation with established parties would result in losing voters as they would find themselves more difficult to use anti-establishment strategy and mobilize protest voters, and eventually facing shrinking niches in the political market (Van der Brug et al., 2005: 548). Empirical studies, so far, have been inconclusive over this relationship (Rydgren, 2007: 255–6).

### 2.2.2 *Party Organization*

This thesis argues that, even if political opportunity structures are favourable, it still depends on how well PRPs can exploit these opportunities (De Lange and Art, 2011; Mudde, 2007: 264; Betz, 1998: 8–9). The ideology/discourse they present,[11] the party organization they operate, and the

[11] Rydgren (2004: 475–8, 2005: 426) argues that France's Front National's innovation of new master frame combining ethno-nationalism, cultural racism, and anti-political establishment populism was the major reason for this party's electoral breakthrough in 1984. This new master frame has been diffused to other Western European countries and becomes a main reason of the electoral sustainability of the third-wave PRPs. However, he reminds that only the new master frame was not sufficient for PRPs' electoral success, it still requires the

internal resources they can employ are all critical to PRPs' capability to rise and to develop (Mudde, 2007: 275–6; Lubbers et al., 2002: 361; Rydgren, 2007: 256–7, 2005: 432). Mudde (2007: 275–6) and Eatwell (2005: 101–20) even argue that the personal charisma of PRPs' leaders is a major factor for PRPs' electoral success. However, Van der Brug et al. (2005: 542 & 567) disagree with this argument, as successful politicians 'are easily called charismatic, and an unsuccessful politician will never be called charismatic', and this reasoning, therefore, becomes circular.

In spite of the fact that significance of party organization factor to PRPs' rise has been recognized, there lacks systematic research on party dynamics being conducted (Rydgren, 2007: 257).

In sum, demand-side approaches of relative deprivation/modernization losers, ethnic competition, and political discontent derive from a macro-perspective. Supply-side accounts of political opportunity structures and party organization explain PRPs' development from a micro-level analysis. As with its use of terminology, there lacks consensus on the explanations of PRPs' rise, despite numerous literature and empirical studies mentioned above.[12]

conditions of favourable political opportunity structures for them to operate. See Jens Rydgren (2004), 'Explaining the emergence of radical right-wing populist parties: The case of Denmark', *West European Politics*, Vol. 27, No. 3, pp. 474–502; (2005), 'Is extreme right-wing populism contagious? Explaining emergence of a new party family', *European Journal of Political Research*, Vol. 44, pp. 413–37, for more details.

[12] Several commentators provide explanations for the inconsistency of these studies. For example, Hooghe and Reeskens (2007: 185 & 195) point out that cross-country, quantitative surveys may not be a good way to conduct empirical studies on PRPs, as there will be technical bias and response bias which both lead to measurement bias and lack cross-cultural external validity in this measurement. Kestila and Soderlund (2007: 780) also suggest that the reason why quantitative studies produce different, and often contradictory, results is because they differ in data magnitude, method precision, and the number and quality of variables included in surveys. Rydgren and Ruth (2013: 712) argue that cross-national studies cannot avoid ideological, programmatic, and institutional variances in different countries. See Marc Hooghe and Tim Reeskens (2007), 'Are cross-national surveys the best way to study the extreme-right vote in Europe?', *Patterns of Prejudice*, Vol. 41, No. 2, pp. 177–96; Elena Kestila and Peter Soderlund (2007), 'Subnational political opportunity structure and the success of radical right: Evidence from the March 2004 regional elections in France', *European Journal of Political Research*, Vol. 46, p. 780; Jens Rydgren and Patrick Ruth (2013), 'Contextual explanations of radical right-wing support in Sweden: Socioeconomic marginalization, group threat and the halo effect', *Ethnic and Racial Studies*, Vol. 36, No. 4, pp. 711–28, for more details.

## 3 Competing Interpretations for the 2014 EP Election: Identifying Causes

How can these theoretical accounts guide us to understand the rise of PRPs in the 2014 EP election? In accordance with these accounts, there are three different kinds of interpretations for explaining the 2014 EP election result.

### *3.1 Economic Interpretation: The Euro Crisis Factor*

Echoed with the relative deprivation/modernization losers account, policy practitioners and media commentators tend to interpret the 2014 EP election result from an economic perspective. For example, *The Economist* explains the election result that 'after years of the euro crisis, the biggest danger to the European project is economic stagnation' that has caused political rejection to European integration (26 May 2014a). Another leading newspaper, *Financial Times*, similarly interprets the election result as the increasing discontent of Europeans for the EU as a consequence of the euro crisis that has led to record unemployment (26 May 2014a). The then president of the European Commission, José Manuel Barroso, also maintains such economic explanations that 'this election follows the biggest financial, economic and ultimately social crisis in decades' (*Financial Times*, 26 May 2014a).

On the surface, the EU's economic context seemed to justify the economic interpretation. The EU's overall unemployment reached 24.4 million, 10% on average, in October 2014. The high level of unemployment is just part of the EU's economic picture. The European Commission points out in its annual report that one in four Europeans is at risk of poverty because of the EU's fragile economic situation, even when 'unemployment is gradually reducing'. This is because increasing numbers of part-time and low-wage jobs mean that finding a job cannot lift workers out of poverty and no longer equate with a decent standard of living (*EU Observer*, 22 January 2014e). The situations in France and the UK were especially alarming. Unemployment in France reached a record high of 3488 million people, 10.5%, in November 2014 (*EU Observer*, 26 December 2014a). On the other hand, according to the OECD report (Andre et al., 2013: 13), labour market reforms in the UK have eased the increase in unemployment, but this has come at the price of large underemployment and low wages. Both income inequality and absolute poverty were increasing, while social transfer was being cut, which all contributed to the fact that the UK is one with the widest gap of income growth among OECD countries. In an EU survey, French people were the most anxious and pessimistic about the economic future. Sixty per cent of the surveyed responded that they would have a darker future. Another major EU country that was also more worried about the economic future was the UK, with 45% of respondents holding a pessimistic outlook (*EU Observer*, 25 July 2014b). Against this backdrop, it is therefore not surprising why PRPs in France and the UK rose to become the largest party in the 2014 EP election.

However, such an economic interpretation cannot explain why Italy, another EU major country which was also pessimistic, 48%, about its economic future, was not witnessed the rise of PRPs. Neither can it explain that it was not PRPs but radical left parties that did well in the euro crisis-hit EU members in the 2014 EP election (*BBC*, 27 May 2014b).[13] An economic interpretation, understandably, is a plausible explanation after the euro crisis. However, such interpretation, which had been popular since Hitler's rise to power in Weimar Germany in the early 1930s (Mudde, 2014), cannot fit in neatly with the whole picture across the EU.

Different from policy-makers and practitioners' economic interpretation, some academics, following the ethnic competition thesis, interpret the 2014 EP election result from a socio-cultural perspective.

### 3.2 *Socio-cultural Interpretation: Immigration Factor*

Mudde (2014) explains the rise of PRPs in the 2014 EP election as a post-materialist phenomenon, which emphasizes socio-cultural issues and is involved in identity politics, while economic issues are secondary. He argues that the role that the euro crisis played in this election is in a socio-cultural way. PRPs framed the EU's bailout policies with their nationalistic and populist rhetoric and most importantly framed the crisis leading to immigrants from crisis-hit countries that caused problems to their economy and culture. Goodwin (2011: 9–11) also agrees that, although PRPs

[13] In Spain, the United Left Coalition and the newly formed Podemos Party, both anti-austerity, came third and fourth, respectively. In Greece, radical left party Syriza came first. In Portugal, the opposition party, Socialist Party, and the Communist Party, which campaigned for a referendum on leaving the euro, were the two biggest winners. See *BBC* (2014), 'European election result: At a glance', 27 May 2014, available at http://www.bbc.com/news/world-europe-27575869, for more details.

voters are mainly from economically insured working and lower middle classes and they have high level of dissatisfaction with and distrust of political elites, economics and political protest are not their major motives to vote for PRPs. According to the European Social Survey, it is the immigration issue to be the 'most important factor' of voters to support PRPs. These voters are not simply protest voters or merely the losers of globalization but are concerned about immigration and rising ethnic and cultural diversity as threats to their culture, national identity, and the way of life.[14]

In terms of policy issue, immigration, indeed, is the most concerned issue singled out by PRPs voters in numerous surveys. In the 2014 EP election campaign, all PRPs revealed explicit hostile languages to immigrants, to ethnic diversity, and to multiculturalism, which all were argued to derive from the EU and European integration. For example, the leader of National Front, France's PRP, Marine Le Pen, who won the largest share of votes in the election, accused the EU's 'posted workers directive', which allows workers from poor EU countries to work in France and put thousands of French people out of work, and thus appealed to recovering 'our identity from the EU' (*The Irish Times*, 2 May 2014; *Financial Times*, 26 May 2014a).

However, socio-cultural interpretation cannot explain why in Italy and Spain, where both countries have been struggling with the surge of African immigrants,[15] PRPs were not successful in the 2014 EP election. This inconsistency between the surge of immigrants and the electoral success of PRPs is more evident in the case of Germany, which has topped the EU list as the choice of immigrants and asylum seekers since 2012 (*EU Observer*, 26 August 2015c), but its PRPs have constantly failed to progress in elections.[16] Neither can this interpretation explain why PRPs gained as

[14] In a survey of 18 European countries, concerns over culture are five times more important than those about the national economy. See Mathew Goodwin (2011), *Right Response: Understanding and Countering Populist Extremism in Europe*, London: Chatham House, p. 17, for more details.

[15] The migrant smuggling has escalated into humanitarian crises in the Mediterranean Sea and led to the EU's launch of a military operation to sink migrant smugglers' boats in May 2015. See *EU Observer*, 'EU countries agree boat-sinking operation', 18 May 2015, available at https://euobserver.com/foreign/128743, for more details.

[16] The surge of refugees from the Middle East to Europe had escalated into a migrant crisis in August, 2015, and Germany took a leading role by announcing that it could receive up to 800,000 refugees that year. See *The Economist*, 'Europe's migrant crisis: Merkel the bold', 5

much as their losses in elections between 2005 and 2013 (*The Economist*, 4 January 2014b) but were able to make a breakthrough in the 2014 EP election. More importantly, if the immigration issue was as vital as PRPs and their voters keep claiming, and has become the most concerned issue by the electorate since the EU's enlargement in 2003 as Goodwin argues (2011: 14), why the same PRPs suffer from instability of electoral support, for example, National Front performed badly in elections in the last decade while UKIP's votes were halved a year later in the UK general election from the 2014 EP election?

The inapplicability of socio-cultural interpretation across countries and across different period of times exposes its limitations. These unanswered questions lead to the third interpretation emerging—the political explanation.

### *3.3 Interpretation of Trust Crisis: Disillusion with Political Establishment from the Euro Crisis Mismanagement*

Several commentators from think-tanks and a few from the academia believe that EU political elites' mismanagement of the euro crisis has caused the collapse of the electorate's confidence in political establishment and the deep disillusion with the EU. For example, Jamie Bartlett, the director of Demos, a UK think-tank, explains that it is neither economics nor culture, but a wider collapse of trust in the political establishment that caused the rise of PRPs in the EU politics (*EU Observer*, 28 January 2014f). Stratfor, a US think-tank, also argues that 'the wide-spread criticisms on the German-imposed solutions to the crisis, from both bailed-out and financing countries, caused the loss of legitimacy for European mainstream parties, which fell in line with the German consensus', and 'this anti-establishment sentiment for protesting European political elites' has facilitated the rise of PRPs and provoked the first serious political debacle in the eurozone (24 March 2011). European Policy Centre, a Brussels-based think-tank, explains that, from the 2014 EP election results, it shows that a financial crisis has turned into a political crisis because of a representation crisis in EU members and disenchantment with European leaders (2014: 2–4).

September 2015, available at http://www.economist.com/news/leaders/21663228-refugees-germanys-chancellor-brave-decisive-and-right-merkel-bold, for more details.

Some academics echo with such interpretation. For example, Collignon (2015), Papadopoulou (2014: 11), and Karakasis (2014: 5–6) all interpret the 2014 EP election result as European voters' disagreement to, rejection to, and distrust with the political establishment through ballots due to their euro crisis mismanagement. As Lifland (2013: 20) points out, the EU's, mainly Germany's, euro crisis management, which has been criticized by both bailed-out and financing countries, has exacerbated Euroscepticism that characterizes PRPs. Karakasis (2014: 5–6) further warns that the image of the EU and the euro have become synonymous to austerity and existing poverty, and if European leaders do not read into the reasons of the 2014 EP election result correctly, they may face bigger surprise in future elections.

Caritas, a pan-European charity, explains further the real picture of the EU's austerity in its 'Crisis Monitoring Report'. It points out that the EU's management to the euro crisis is structural reforms and austerity. When these reforms translated into reality, the real pictures are that pensioners and disabilities had to wait for their allowances and pensions for months because there are no enough public servants to process all the claims because austerity has made public sector cut. This had great impact on the most vulnerable at risk, who had no part in decisions causing the euro crisis, but it was them who paid the highest price (*EU Observer*, 27 March 2014c, 19 February 2015a). An official report from the OECD also reminds the EU that public services benefit every income group, but they have a larger effect in lower-income groups. Austerity could hit the poor the hardest, as they rely on public services much more than other income groups, and thus public services and redistribution policies are crucial in alleviating poverty (Andre et al., 2013: 20–1). In his report, Alejandro Cercas, a Spanish MEP, backed by the EP's employment committee, accuses that austerity being imposed by troika—the EU, ECB, IMF, breached the European Social Charter and had caused a 'social tsunami'.

The euro crisis management, indeed, was criticized fiercely in the 2014 election campaign. For example, one slogan from National Front is to end austerity policies (*Financial Times*, 26 May 2014a). The interpretation of political disillusion and trust crisis seems to be in line with more empirical evidences.

According to the Eurobarometer survey in July 2014, over half, 52%, feels their voice does not count in the EU, down from 66% last year, while the number believing their voice is heard has increased significantly from 13% to 42%. Pollsters believe this change should be attributed to the shocking result of the 2014 EP election. On the other hand, trust at both the EU and national levels remained low, only 31% for the EU. The same figure in 2007, before the euro crisis, was 57%. Interestingly, low trust in the political establishment did not reduce the public's support for the euro in principle. Majority of Europeans, 55%, viewed the euro in a positive light, and the support for the euro has raised even in the euro crisis-hit countries, such as Portugal, Cyprus, and Greece (*EU Observer*, 25 July 2014b).

Furthermore, in Portugal, Spain, and Italy, where unemployment, especially youth unemployment, remained very high, there appeared little risk of the rise of anti-EU, anti-euro, and anti-immigration PRPs, as it has been seen in France, the UK, and Denmark. In a survey on six largest members, which accounted for 70% of the EU's population, Spain (63% of respondents) and Italy (64%) held much more positive attitudes than those in the UK (only 51%) and France (55%) (*EU Observer*, 2 June 2015b). And the electorate's trust in the political establishment remained solid in most euro crisis-hit countries, except for Greece. By the end of 2014, a Eurobarometer survey shows that faith in Portugal's mainstream parties remained strong as it has been in the case of Spain, Italy, and Ireland.[17] Only Greece is different, where people's faith in the political establishment has been discredited in clientelism.[18] Antonio Costa Pinto, a professor of Lisbon University, explains the survey results on Portugal in that 'political parties are ... strong in their ability to frame the attitudes of society' (*Financial Times*, 4 December 2014b).

These surveys show that the electorate were not as anti-euro, neither were they that anti-immigration even in their economic hardships, as PRPs

[17] O'Malley (2008) argues that Irish mainstream parties' populist and nationalistic rhetoric and policy reduce the space for PRPs to develop in Ireland. For example, citizenship referendum in 2004, in which removed citizenship to those who was born in Ireland, reduces the controversy over immigration that many PRPs tend to develop on. See Eoin O'Malley (2008), 'Why is there no radical right party in Ireland?', *West European Politics*, Vol. 31, Issue 5, pp. 960–77, for more details.

[18] For a long time, Greece has not witnessed the rise of PRPs because of its legacy of authoritarianism and the absence of welfare state. Ellinas (2013) argues that the Greek debt crisis provided an electoral breakthrough for Greece's PRP—Golden Dawn in 2012, as the crisis exposed the chronic failure of the Greek political establishment and de-legitimatized its governance. The political de-alignment and realignment of the electorate gave rise to calls for radical political changes and thus can explain the rise of Golden Dawn's rise after 2012. See Antonis A. Ellinas (2013), 'The rise of the Golden Dawn: The new face of the far right in Greece', *South European Society and Politics*, Vol. 18, Issue 4, pp. 543–65, for more details.

claim so. Rather, they lack trust in the political establishment from their performance in the euro crisis management and their subsequent economic governance. In countries, where ruling parties failed the electorate's expectations, the political establishment lost people's trust in politics as a result. For example, one argument that National Front criticized the government most is that President Hollande was elected on the promise to end austerity and create jobs, but his government has been putting its effort to austerity and reform public sector since his election. Not surprisingly, Hollande's popularity lowering to a record low of 12% and National Front progressing to become the largest party in the 2014 EP election have been witnessed (*The Economist*, 26 May 2014a; *EU Observer*, 26 December 2014a). As Niblett (2015) argues, 'the quality of individual political leadership' is a more convincing account than a pure economic perspective when explaining the public disenchantment with the political establishment.

It is in these countries where political leadership was viewed as incapable and disappointing, PRPs became the electorate's protest outlet and rose sharply as a result, as can be seen in France, the UK, and Greece. By contrast, in countries where ruling parties have a strong hold on the electorate and policy debates, the political establishment dominated electoral markets, and PRPs failed to gain large and stable bases of electoral support, as can be seen in Portugal, Spain, Italy, and Ireland.[19] Unfavourable economic conditions, such as the euro crisis, and cultural factors, such as controversy over immigration, indeed, are not sufficient explanations for the rise of PRPs in the 2014 EP election. They only provided a political scene for ruling parties to demonstrate their governing capability and to fulfil their electoral promises. As Kulinska (2010: 58) argues, nationalistic tendencies and PRPs exist in domestic politics for decades, but they were marginalized on the European scene. Thus, PRPs' significant rise in the 2014 EP election was not a constant phenomenon either within the EU or within individual members, even in countries where PRPs grew to the largest parties in the election. Moreover, as Kulinska points out, the rise of PRPs was not due to their changes of ideology or behaviours; they continued to follow the same pattern and strategy of anti-immigration, anti-EU, and strong nationalistic appeals as their predecessors (2010: 60). Therefore,

[19] For the full details of the 2014 EP election results, see *BBC*, 'European election result: At a glance', 27 May 2014, available at http://www.bbc.com/news/world-europe-27575869.

the supply-side explanations are not applicable to the 2014 EP election case. Their sharp rise in the 2014 EP election was provoked by the public demand side—the electorate's disillusion with the political establishment from their performance of the euro crisis management over years, which accumulated into a political trust crisis eventually. Thus, the whole picture of the 2014 EP election result is more related with the interaction between the changes of political trust and PRPs' electoral support. This can explain why PRPs' support varies in different EU counties in the 2014 election and in different periods of time in the same country. However, this is not to say the EU's governance is irrelevant to the 2014 EP election. In the most euro crisis-hit countries, anti-austerity radical left parties gained momentum in a relatively short period of time, such as Spain's Podemos Party and Greece's Syriza.

## 4 Implications for European Integration

After identifying the causes of PRPs' rise in the 2014 EP election, what does it imply for European integration and what does it suggest to national and EU policy-makers?

### *4.1 Implications for the EU and European Integration*

When commenting on what the 2014 EP election results imply for European integration, Fabian Zuleeg, the head of European Policy Centre, a Brussels-based think-tank, points out that they 'mean major difficulties' for European integration, 'particularly because of France', as it is a co-founder and an engine of this project. The senior advisor of the French Institute of International Relations, Dominique Moisi, a well-known French political scientist, comments that 'the legitimacy of Europe is weakened, the legitimacy of France in Europe is weakened further' (*Reuters*, 27 May 2014). Indeed, as the history of European integration in the 1960s demonstrates, any projects cannot be advanced if there lacks the commitment and support of France. Moreover, the rise of Eurosceptical PRPs in the 2014 EP election implies that any move to deepen integration was hard to envisage, as European integration would encounter 'a period of political stagnation' (European Policy Centre, 2014: 4–5) and political mainstream parties were said to try to attract the anti-EU vote (*Financial Times*, 26

May 2014a). The rise of PRPs, as Cakmak and Postaci rightly point out, threatens not only immigrants but also the very roots of European integration—'unity in diversity' (2013: 1). European integration has been linked closely by PRPs with ethnic and cultural diversity and described as a threat to national identity and economic welfare (Cakmak and Postaci, 2013: 1; John et al., 2005: 14–5). Fligstein et al. (2012: 106–7) comment such developments, after European integration has been developing for decades, are counter-evidence to neofunctionalism proposed by Haas, as it has not spilled over to the development of a European identity but spilled back to the emphasis on national identifications, which became popular after the euro crisis. Gunduz (2010: 37) further comments that, with the EU celebrating its 50th anniversary, paradoxically, we have witnessed the rise of PRPs. It is surely not a right direction for European integration, because it manifestly violates the Treaty of the European Union and the Treaty of Lisbon regarding the regulations of fundamental and human rights.[20] How to effectively respond to this development, as he argues, becomes the most important issue faced by European integration (Ibid.: 45).

The clarification of PRPs' rise in the 2014 EP election in the previous section—disillusion with political establishment and political trust crisis—indicates that the political establishment, not economic hardships nor immigration policy, should account for this policy challenge. The (mis) management of the euro crisis by European political elites, which has hit the poor and the most vulnerable seriously, has deepened the divide of winners and losers of European integration and highlighted the issue of economic justice and evenness of European integration. As Fligstein et al. (2012: 118–9) rightly point out, 'the ultimate fate of the EU is how ordinary citizens view the role of Europe in their lives', because after all, democracies follow the preferences of the electorate and PRPs reflect such perceptions. Therefore, this chapter argues that the rise of PRPs in the 2014 EP election is not the real threat to European integration. They were just the reflection of voters' disillusion and sentimental outlets and should not be overestimated. It is the distributional justice and fairness of both economic benefits and costs derived from European integration that caused the collapse of the electorate's trust in the political establishment. As Fligstein et al. (Ibid.) argue, European integration has created far more

[20] Refer to Article 6 of the Treaty of the European Union, Article 6 of the Lisbon Treaty, and Articles 20 and 21 of the Charter of Fundamental Rights of the European Union, which is an integral part of the Lisbon Treaty for details.

economic and political integration than social and cultural projects that unify Europe. Due to the lack of social and cultural integration, it is thus not surprising that supporters and opponents of European integration accord with the fault lines of economic classes. Those who support European integration most, usually with a European identity, come from higher end of socio-economic group, for example, owners of businesses, managers, professionals, and other white-collar workers, the so-called winners. On the contrary, those who support European integration least and have lower degree or even none of European identity come from the lower end of economic classes, for example, blue-collar, low white-collar, services and older workers who economically benefit less from market opening and economic liberalization and may even be the victims of it, the so-called losers (Ibid.: 109–10 & 118). They are consequently the target group that PRPs appeal to. The fact that the support for and objection to European integration correspond to the divide of economic classes implies the imperative of addressing to the distributional justice of European integration by national and EU policy-makers, which was worsened after the mismanagement of the euro crisis. The deterioration of distributional justice has damaged the legitimacy of both national and EU governance and accumulated into a trust crisis for the political establishment.

### 4.2 Policy Responses: Did Policy-Makers Read the Message Right?

After the EP election results were revealed, the French prime minister, Manuel Valls, responded that 'the EU must react' to the breakthrough of PRPs. France's president, François Hollande, perceives the rise of PRPs as seizing on the 'disenchantment' with Europe. He, accordingly, proposed strengthening the leadership for the eurozone governance by six EU founding members so as to provide more support to growth and employment (*EU Observer*, 20 July 2015e; *Financial Times*, 26 May 2014a). His call for redirecting the eurozone governance from the current austerity and structural reforms to growth and employment was echoed with some practitioners. For example, Alejandro Cercas, a Spanish MEP who was in charge of a social survey across the EU for the European Parliament, calls for an EU job recovery plan, and those social benefits which had been cut by structural reforms should be brought back (*EU Observer*, 14 February 2014d). Caritas, a pan-European charity, suggests EU decision-makers to shift away from its focus on austerity because '[it] is not working' and calls for other policy alternatives. From its empirical experiences across the EU, it also reminds EU decision-makers to assess the social impact of any economic measures before implementing them (*EU Observer*, 27 March 2014c, 19 February 2015a).

These initiatives for policy change received supports from a few of academics. For example, Papadopoulou (2014: 12) contends that the EU needs to change its policy direction to aim at boosting growth because the only way that the EU could gain back its credibility is to serve citizens' interests first, not just require them to adjust to the euro crisis. Collignon (2015) also agrees that the right medicine to the euro crisis management is not austerity but to set up an economic government to stimulate growth, stabilize financial markets, and restore social welfare. Liakopoulos (2014: 15) similarly argues that EU leaders and mainstream parties should regain their lost voters by redefining Europe's direction to introducing a big investment plan in quality jobs and to a social Europe, which cares for its citizens.

Indeed, as argued above, the economics is just a half of the answer to the challenge of PRPs' rise; the other, and more important, half is the social dimension of European integration—distributional justice of economic gains and prices. From the outset, European integration is not just an economic project of producing winners and losers, although economic integration is the major means to its aims. It is, in nature, a political project aimed for pursing perpetual peace and prosperity for Europe by its architects. The neglect of a social Europe would counteract the gains from an economic Europe and lead to a political Europe disintegrated, which reflects in the rise of PRPs, and eventually harm the core of European integration—unifying Europe. It is for these reasons that this chapter supports policy suggestions from Barslund et al. (2015: 1–3) and Frank Vandenbroucke (2015). The former suggest the EU to create a European unemployment insurance (EUI) that could direct financial flows to the unemployed whenever they are in Europe and support EU members that suffer from increasing unemployment. This could be a way to stress to social dimension of European integration and be seen as a direct solidarity link between the EU and European citizens. The latter, a former Belgium's social affair minister, suggests the EU to prioritize the agenda of 'Social Investment Package' on education, training, and skills,[21] at the highest

[21] More details of the EU's Social Investment Package are available at http://ec.europa.eu/social/main.jsp?catId=1044.

level of budget, which has been slipping down in EU policy-making recently because on its emphasis on structural reforms and fiscal disciplines.

How are these calls for policy change from France and suggestions from practitioners and academics perceived by the German and EU policy-makers? Right after the elections, the German chancellor, Angela Merkel, did not respond to the French call directly, but noted that high unemployment did damage political trust in the EU in some countries (*Reuters*, 27 May 2014). A year later, however, the French and German economy minister co-published the 'Gabriel-Macron' proposal, without treaty changes, to push further eurozone integration by allowing the eurozone to have an institution with its own budget and own revenues through taxing, in all but name an economic government (*EU Observer*, 4 June 2015d) to coordinate the divergent economic performance of euro members.

Policy change can also be traced from the EU's new initiatives. The newly elected president of the European Commission following the 2014 EP election, Jean-Claude Juncker, claims that his top priority is to create jobs and growth. In January 2015, his Commission proposed to establish the European Fund for Strategic Investments (EFSI) to mobilize at least €315 billion investment in Europe in the following three years. After being approved by the European Council and Parliament, the EFSI was scheduled in operation from September 2015.[22]

Another observable policy change of the Juncker Commission is its address to the idea of a social Europe. Juncker explains in his twitter that his goal is to reduce the divide between the EU and ordinary people and to highlight the social dimension of the EU is crucial to achieve this aim. European Commissioner for Employment, Social Affairs, Skills, and Labour Mobility, Marianne Thyssen, further illustrates in a speech that 'a new start for Social Europe' implies 'fair and balanced growth that leads to the creation of decent, quality jobs' so as to promote 'upward social convergence' (European Commission, Announcements on 19 June 2015). The Commission swiftly revived social dialogue between EU executive, employers, and trade union, explained as necessary in the making of new economic governance of 'social market economy' (*EurActic.Com*, 6 March 2015).

[22] For Juncker's Commission's top priority on jobs, growth, and investment and the EFSI, see http://ec.europa.eu/priorities/jobs-growth-investment/index_en.htm for more details.

Strengthening the eurozone leadership through a coordinating economic institution and setting up the EFSI, viewed by this chapter, are right policy responses to the rise of PRPs and can demonstrate policy-makers capable of having strong hold on directing an economic Europe. However, concrete elements of a social Europe are missing. The effects of reviving social dialogue remain to be seen, and initiatives that address to economic fairness and distributional justice are absent. Without addressing to the social dimension of European integration, a recovering euro economy, underpinned by the EFSI, would not guarantee the fall of PRPs. Neither would policy-makers find it sufficient to restore the legitimacy of European integration and the political trust of the electorate.

## 5 Conclusion: Is the EU Still a Role Model of Regional Integration?

This chapter explores why PRPs rose in the 2014 EP election and identifies the causes of this election result from competing theoretical accounts. To explain the electoral performance of PRPs, indeed, as Arzheimer rightly points outs, 'persistent country effects prevail' (2009: 259). It is then difficult to provide a universal explanation to various election results across different EU countries. After examining competing interpretations, however, this chapter argues that the interpretation of disillusion and trust crisis in the political establishment from the euro crisis mismanagement is more applicable to explain the whole picture across the EU. It agrees with Martin Schulz, the president of the EP, that 'the result conveyed the electorate are disappointed and lost trust and hope' (*The Wall Street Journal*, 27 May 2014). Such deep political disillusion and trust crisis derived from the long neglect of distributional justice arising from European economic and monetary integration, which became acute after the mismanagement of the euro crisis, termed as 'social tsunami'. The shocking results of the 2014 EP election thus could be interpreted as protest vote against the political establishment. Therefore, the audiences that PRPs can appeal to were not just 'losers of modernity' but rather wider social strata, as Van der Brug and Fennema rightly remind (2009: 589).

It is at this point that the trust crisis in the political establishment, reflected in the rise of PRPs in the 2014 EP election, should not be underestimated. It could imply for a stagnation, even a spill back of European integration, and eventually undermine the legitimacy of the whole European project. This chapter, accordingly, suggests that policy redirection from the current austerity to economic recovery and addressing to social dimension of European integration at the same time are required in order to regain the credence of good governance from the electorate for both national and EU policy-makers. Policy responses taken by the EU, so far, conform to the former suggestion, but not to the latter.

Having celebrated its 50th anniversary only few years ago, European integration now has witnessed the rise of anti-EU political forces. This is not just counter-evident to neofunctionalism but also highlights the insufficiency of intergovernmentalism. For an advanced model of regional integration such as the EU, one-sided emphasis on economic integration, an economic Europe, without addressing to social dimension, a social Europe, was doomed to result in anti-forces, as economic integration only produces winners and losers, while distributional fairness and justice that are felt by a wider part of the electorate are left untouched. European integration, as history shows, has been experiencing numerous ups and downs, and this is not the first time for this movement to encounter a crisis. However, it is the first time that European integration encountered such a serious political trust crisis of Euroscepticism that allows anti-EU PRPs to make an electoral breakthrough in the 2014 EP election. Such developments are ironic to the achievements that European integration has fulfilled. For a long time, the EU has been a role model of regional integration for the rest of the world to emulate. This is because it is not only the most advanced model but also the most successful one. One key to its advancement and success is the common sharing of the core values of European integration between the political elites and the public, and its self-learning capability from trial and error. However, such a common value-sharing, which political trust is built on, has been jeopardized by the deteriorating distributional justice. Whether or not key policy-makers can rightly read the massage from the 2014 election result and rectify its mismanagement through self-learning once again will determine how far European integration can go and demonstrate to the rest of the world that whether or not it is still qualified as a role model of regional integration.

## References

Abedi, Arim (2002), 'Challenges to established parties: The effects of party system features on the electoral fortunes of antipolitical-establishment parties', *European Journal of Political Research*, Vol. 41, No. 4, pp. 551–83.

Anderson, Christopher (1996), 'Economics, politics, and foreigners: Populist party support in Denmark and Norway', *Electoral Studies*, Vol. 15, No. 4, pp. 497–511.

Andre, Christophe, Clara Garcia, Giulia Giupponi, Jon K. Pareliussen (2013), 'Labour Market, Welfare Reform and Inequality in the United Kingdom', *OECD Economics Department Working Papers*, No. 1034, Paris: OECD.

Arzheimer, Kai (2009), 'Contextual factors and the extreme right vote in Western Europe, 1980–2002', *American Journal of Political Science*, Vol. 53, pp. 259–75.

Arzheimer, Kai, and Elisabeth Carter (2006), 'Political opportunity structures and right-wing extremist party success', *European Journal of Political Research*, Vol. 45, pp. 419–43.

Bale, T., C. Green-Pedersen, A. Krouwel, K.R. Luther and N. Sitter (2010), 'If you can't beat them, join them? Explaining social democratic responses to the challenge from the populist radical right in Western Europe', *Political Studies*, Vol. 58, pp. 410–26.

Barslund, Mikkel, Claeys Gregory, and Anne Macey (2015), 'A single labour market: moving it closer', *Discussion Paper for Brussels Think Tank Dialogue*, held on 28 January 2015 in Brussels.

Betz, Hans-George. (1994), *Radical Right-Wing Populism in Western Europe*, Basingstoke: Macmillan.

———. (1998), 'Introduction', in Hans-George Betz (ed.), *The New Politics of the Right: Neo-Populist Parties and Movements in Established Democracies*, New York: St. Martin's Press, pp. 1–9.

Boomgaarden, Hajo G. and Rens Vliegenthart (2007), 'Explaining the rise of anti-immigrant parties: The role of news media content', *Electoral Studies*, Vol. 26, pp. 404–417.

Cakmak, Gizem and Asli Postaci (2013), 'The rise of extreme right in Europe: The case of Greece', paper presented at *LSE 6th biennial Hellenic Observatory PhD Symposium on Contemporary Greece and Cyprus*, held on European Institute of London School of Economics and Political Science, 6–7 June 2013, London.

Cammaerts, Bart (2009), 'Radical pluralism and free speech in online public spaces: The case of North-Belgian extreme right discourses', *International Journal of Cultural Studies*, Vol. 12, No. 6, pp. 555–75.

Coffe, Hilde, Bruno Heyndels, and Jan Vermeir (2007), 'Fertile grounds for extreme right-wing parties: Explaining the Vlaams Blok's election success', *Electoral Studies*, Vol. 26, pp. 142–55.

Collignon, Stefan (2015), 'Why the "bitter medicine" of austerity isn't working', *Europe's World*, Issue 29, available at http://europesworld.org/2015/02/25/bitter-medicine-austerity-isnt-working/#.VUDQDssf6B0, last viewed 29 April 2015.

Dahlstrom, Carl and Anders Sundell (2012), 'A losing gamble. How mainstream parties facilitate anti-immigrant party success', *Electoral Studies*, Vol. 31, pp. 353–63.

De Lange, Sarah and David Art (2011), 'Fortuyn versus Wilders: An agency-based approach to radical right party building', *West European Politics*, Vol. 34, No. 6, pp. 1229–49.

De Koster, Willem, Peter Achterberg and Jeroen van der Waal (2012), 'The new right and welfare state: The electoral relevance of welfare chauvinism and welfare populism', *International Political Science Review*, Vol. 34, No. 1, pp. 3–20.

Eatwell, Roger (2000), 'The rebirth of extreme right in Western Europe?', *Parliamentary Affairs*, Vol. 53, No. 3, pp. 407–25.

——— (2005), 'Charisma and the revival of the European extreme right', in Jens Rydgren ed., *Movements of Exclusion: Radical Right-Wing Populism in the Western World*, New York: Nova Science, pp. 101–20.

Ellinas, Antonis A. (2013), 'The rise of the Golden Dawn: The new face of the far right in Greece', *South European Society and Politics*, Vol. 18, Issue 4, pp. 543–65.

European Commission (2015), 'Announcements on 19 June 2015-Speech at Seminar on "A new start for social Europe", Luxemburg', available at https://ec.europa.eu/commission/2014-2019/thyssen/announcements/speech-seminar-new-start-social-europe-luxembourg_en, last viewed 16 September 2015.

European Policy Centre (2014), *Post-European Parliament Elections Analysis*, Brussels: EPC.

Fennema, Meindert (2005), 'Populist parties of the right', in Jens Rydgren ed., *Movements of Exclusion: Radical Right-Wing Populism in the Western World*, New York: Nova Science, pp. 1–24.

Fligstein, Neil, Alina Polyakova and Wayne Sandholtz (2012), 'European integration, nationalism and European identity', *Journal of Common Market Studies*, Vol. 50, No. S1, pp. 106–22.

Givens, Terri (2005), *Voting Radical Right in Western Europe*, Cambridge: Cambridge University Press.

Golder, M. (2003a), 'Electoral institutions, unemployment and extreme right parities: A correlation', *British Journal of Political Science*, Vol. 33, No. 3, pp. 525–34.

———. (2003b), 'Explaining variation in the success of extreme right parties in Western Europe', *Comparative Political Studies*, Vol. 36, No. 4, pp. 432–66.

Goodwin, Matthew (2011), *Right Responses: Understanding and Countering Populist Extremism in Europe*, London: Chatham House.

——— (2014), 'How Europe's far-right will-and won't flourish in 2014', *New Statesman*, 2 January 2014, available at http://www.newstatesman.com/politics/2014/01/how-europes-far-right-will-and-wont-flourish-2014, last viewed 22 April 2015.

Green-Pedersen, Christopher and Jesper Krogstrup (2008), 'Immigration as a political issue in Denmark and Sweden', *European Journal of Political Research*, Vol. 47, pp. 610–34.

Gunduz, Zuhal Y. (2010), 'The European Union at 50—Xenophobia, Islamophobia and the rise of the radical right', *Journal of Muslim Minority Affairs*, Vol. 30, No. 1, pp. 35–48.

Hix, Simon (2013), 'Why the 2014 European elections matter: The key votes in the 2009–2013 European Parliament', *European Policy Analysis*, Issue 15, pp. 1–15.

Hooghe, Marc and Tim Reeskens (2007), 'Are cross-national surveys the best way to study the extreme-right vote in Europe?', *Patterns of Prejudice*, Vol. 41, No. 2, pp. 177–96.

Howard, Marc M. (2010), 'The impact of the far right on citizenship policy in Europe: Explaining continuity and change', *Journal of Ethnic and Migration Studies*, Vol. 36, No. 5, pp. 735–51.

Ignazi, Piero (2003), *Extreme Right Parties in Western Europe*, Oxford: Oxford University Press.

Ivarsflaten, Elisabeth (2005), 'The vulnerable populist right parties: No economic realignment fuelling their electoral success', *European Journal of Political Research*, Vol. 44, No. 3, pp. 465–492.

——— (2010), 'What unites right-wing populists in Western Europe? Re-examining grievance mobilization models in seven successful cases', *Comparative Political Studies*, Vol. 41, pp. 3–23.

Jackman, Robert W. and Karin Volpert (1996), 'Conditions favouring parties on the extreme right in Western Europe', *British Journal of Political Science*, Vol. 26, Issue 4, pp. 501–21.

John, Peter, Helen Margetts, Stuart Weir (2005), '1 in 5 Britons could vote far right', *New Statesman*, Vol. 134, Issue 4723, pp. 14–5.

Karakasis, Vasileios (2014), 'Reflections on the outcome of the European elections', Bridging Europe Pamphlet on European Parliament Elections 2014: Assessment *Report*, Athens: Bridging Europe.

Kessler, Alan E. and Gary P. Freeman (2005), 'Support for extreme right-wing parties in Western Europe: Individual attributes, political attitudes, and national context', *Comparative European Politics*, Vol. 3, pp. 261–88.

Kestila, Elena and Peter Soderlund (2007), 'Subnational political opportunity structure and the success of radical right: Evidence from the March 2004 regional elections in France', *European Journal of Political Research*, Vol. 46, No. 6, pp. 773–96.

Knigge, Pia (1998), 'The ecological correlates of right-wing extremism in Western Europe', *European Journal of Political Research*, Vol. 34, No. 6, pp. 249–79.

Koopmans, Ruud (2004), 'Movement and the media: Selection processes and evolutionary dynamics in the public sphere', *Theory and Society*, Vol. 33, pp. 367–91.

Kriesi, H., E. Grande, R. Lachat, M. Dolezal, S. Bornschier and T. Frey (2006), 'Globalization and transformation of national political space: Six European countries compared', *European Journal of Political Research*, Vol. 45, pp. 921–56.

Kulinska, Elena (2010), 'The European extreme right in 2010': A new phenomenon or the same pattern?', *Western Balkans Security Observer*, Vol. 5, No. 17, pp. 50–62.

Liakopoulos, Dimitris (2014), 'This time is different. Was it?', *Bridging Europe Pamphlet on European Parliament Elections 2014: Assessment Report*, Athens: Bridging Europe.

Lifland, Amy (2013), 'Right wing rising: Eurozone crisis and nationalism', *Harvard International Review*, Vol. 34, No. 3, pp. 9–10.

Lubbers, Marcel, Merove Gijsberts and Peter Scheepers (2002), 'Extreme right-wing voting in Western Europe', *European Journal of Political Research*, Vol. 41, pp. 345–78.

Lubbers, Marcel and Peter Scheepers (2000), 'Individual and contextual characteristics of the German Republikaner vote: A test of complementary theories', *European Journal of Political Research*, Vol. 38, pp. 63–94.

Messina, Anthony M. (2007), *The Logic and Politics of Post-WWII Migration to Western Europe*, Cambridge: Cambridge University Press.

Minkenberg, Michael (2000), 'The renewal of the radical right: Between modernity and antimodernity', *Government and Opposition*, Vol. 35, No. 2, pp. 170–88.

——— (2003), 'The West European radical right as a collective actor: Modelling the impact of cultural and structural variables on party formation and movement mobilization', *Comparative European Politics*, Vol. 1, No. 2, pp. 149–170.

Mudde, Cas (1996), 'The war of words': Defining the extreme right party family', *West European Politics*, Vol. 19, No. 2, pp. 225–48.

——— (2004), 'The populist zeitgeist', *Government and Opposition*, Vol. 39, No. 4, pp. 541–63.

——— (2007), *Populist Radical Right Parties in Europe*, Cambridge: Cambridge University Press.

——— (2010), 'The populist radical right: A pathological normalcy', *West European Politics*, Vol. 33, Issue 6, pp. 1167–86.

——— (2013), 'Three decades of populist radical right parties in Western Europe: So what?', *European Journal of Political Research*, Vol. 52, No. 1, pp. 1–19.

——— (2015), 'The far right in the 2014 European elections: Of earthquakes, cartels and designer fascists', *Washington Post*, 30 May 2014, available at http://www.washingtonpost.com/blogs/monkey-cage/wp/2014/05/30/

the-far-right-in-the-2014-european-elections-of-earthquakes-cartels-and-designer-fascists/, last viewed 22 April 2015.

Niblett, Robin (2015), 'What next for the EU?', *Expert Comments of Royal Institute of International Affairs*, published on 5 August 2015, London: Royal Institute of International Affairs, available at https://www.chathamhouse.org/expert/dr-robin-niblett-cmg, last viewed 1 October 2015.

Norris, Pippa (2005), *Radical Right: Voters and Parties in the Electoral Market*, Cambridge: Cambridge University Press.

O'Connell, Michael (2005), 'Economic forces and anti-immigrant attitudes in Western Europe: A paradox in search of an explanation', *Patterns of Prejudice*, Vol. 39, No. 1, pp. 60–74.

Oesch, Daniel (2008), 'Explaining workers' support for right-wing populist parties in Western Europe: Evidence from Austria, Belgium, France, Norway and Switzerland', *International Political Science Review*, Vol. 29, No. 3, pp. 349–73.

O'Malley, Eoin (2008), 'Why is there no radical right party in Ireland?', *West European Politics*, Vol. 31, Issue 5, pp. 960–77.

Papadopoulou, Maria (2014), 'Abstention rates and rejection of traditional elites', Bridging Europe Pamphlet on European Parliament Elections 2014: Assessment *Report*, Athens: Bridging Europe.

Plasser, F. and P.A. Ulram (2003), 'Striking a responsive chord: Mass media and right-wing populism in Austria', in G. Mazzoleni., J. Stewart and B. Horsfield (eds.), *The Media and Neo-Populism: A Contemporary Comparative Analysis*, Westport: Praeger, pp. 21–43.

Rydgren, Jens (2004), 'Explaining the emergence of radical right-wing populist parties: The case of Denmark', *West European Politics*, Vol. 27, No. 3, pp. 474–502.

——— (2005), 'Is extreme right-wing populism contagious? Explaining the emergence of a new party family', *European Journal of Political Research*, Vol. 44, pp. 413–37.

——— (2006), *From Tax Populism to Ethnic Nationalism: Radical Right-Wing Populism in Sweden*, New York: Berghahn Books.

——— (2007), 'The sociology of the radical right', *Annual Review of Sociology*, Vol. 33, pp. 241–62.

——— (2008), 'Immigration sceptics, xenophobes or racists? Radical right-wing voting in six West European countries', *European Journal of Political Research*, Vol. 47, pp. 737–65.

Rydgren, Jens, and Patrick Ruth (2011), 'Voting for the radical right in Swedish municipalities: Social marginality and ethnic competition?', *Scandinavian Political Studies*, Vol. 34, No. 3, pp. 202–25.

——— (2013), 'Contextual explanations of radical right-wing support in Sweden: Socioeconomic marginalization, group threat and the halo effect', *Ethnic and Racial Studies*, Vol. 36, No. 4, pp. 711–28.

*Stratfor Analysis* (2011), 'Eurozone finances inspiring anti-establishment sentiment', 24 March 2011, p. 122.

Swank, Duane and Hans-George Betz (2003), 'Globalization, the welfare state and right-wing populism in Western Europe', *Socio-Economic Review*, Vol. 1, pp. 215–45.

Van der Brug and Meindert Fennema (2007), 'What causes people to vote for a radical-right party? A review of recent work', *International Journal of Public Opinion Research*, Vol. 19, No. 4, pp. 474–87.

——— (2009), 'The support base of radical right parties in the enlarged European Union', *Journal of European Integration*, Vol. 31, Issue 5, pp. 589–608.

Van der Brug, Meindert Fennema, and Jean Tillie (2005), 'Why some anti-immigrant parties fail and others succeed: A two-step model of aggregate electoral support', *Comparative Political Studies*, Vol. 38, No. 5, pp. 537–73.

Vandenbroucke, Frank (2015), 'Unequal Europe: A more caring agenda for the new Commission', *Europe's World*, issue 29, available at http://europesworld.org/2015/02/23/unequal-europe-caring-agenda-new-commission/#.VUHM18sf6B0, last viewed 30 April 2015.

William, M. Hale (2006), *The Impact of Radical Right-Wing Parties in West European Democracies*, New York: Palgrave Macmillan.

## Media Consulted

*BBC* (2014a), 'Eurosceptic "earthquake" rocks EU elections', 26 May 2014, available at http://www.bbc.com/news/world-europe-27559714, last viewed 22 April 2015.

——— (2014b), 'European election result: At a glance', 27 May 2014, available at http://www.bbc.com/news/world-europe-27575869, last viewed 24 April 2015.

*EU Observer* (2014a), 'French unemployment reaches new high', 26 December 2014, available at https://euobserver.com/social/127045, last viewed 27 April 2015.

——— (2014b), 'Poll: French most pessimistic about economic future', 25 July 2014, available at https://euobserver.com/economic/125112, last viewed 27 April 2015.

——— (2014c), 'Charity documents "human cost" of EU austerity', 27 March 2014, available at https://euobserver.com/social/123643, last viewed 30 April 2015.

——— (2014d), 'MEPs accuse troika of causing "social tsunami"', 14 February 2014, available at https://euobserver.com/news/123135, last viewed 30 April 2015.

——— (2014e), 'Jobs not lifting Europeans out of poverty, commission warns', 22 January 2014, available at https://euobserver.com/news/122825, last viewed 30 April 2015.

———(2014f), 'EU-wide protest movements set for gains in European elections', available at https://euobserver.com/political/122897, 28 January 2014, last viewed 24 April 2015.

———(2015a), 'Bailout austerity hurts most vulnerable, charity says', 19 February 2015, available at https://euobserver.com/economic/127707, last viewed 30 April 2015.

——— (2015b), 'Spanish and Italians more positive about EU', 2 June 2015, available at https://euobserver.com/news/128938, last viewed 17 June 2015.

——— (2015c), 'Xenophobic violence "shames" Germany', 26 August 2015, available at https://euobserver.com/migration/129998, last viewed 10 September 2015.

——— (2015d), 'Berlin and Paris propose radical eurozone integration', 4 June 2015, available at https://euobserver.com/economic/128964, last viewed 17 September 2015.

———(2015e), 'Hollande calls for vanguard of states to lead strengthened eurozone', 20 July 2015, available at https://euobserver.com/economic/129695, last viewed 17 September 2015.

*EurActic.Com* (2015), 'Commission seeks to revive battered social dialogue', 6 March 2015, available at http://www.euractiv.com/sections/eu-priorities-2020/commission-seeks-revive-battered-social-dialogue-312678, last viewed 16 September 2015.

*Financial Times* (2014a), 'Eurosceptics storm Brussels', 26 May 2014, available at http://www.ft.com/intl/cms/s/0/fd3975ce-e424-11e3-8565-00144feabdc0.html#axzz3YCc7v0Pb, last viewed 24 April 2015.

———(2014b), 'Euro crisis fails to undermine faith in Portugal's two-party political system', 4 December 2014, available at http://www.ft.com/intl/cms/s/0/112beb50-6023-11e4-88d1-00144feabdc0.html, last viewed 26 April 2015.

*Irish Times* (2014), 'National Front campaign is vehemently anti-EU', 2 May 2014, available at http://www.irishtimes.com/news/ireland/irish-news/national-front-campaign-is-vehemently-anti-eu-1.1780713, last viewed 18 May 2015.

*Reuters* (2014), 'Eurosceptic election surge gives EU a headache', 27 May 2014, available at http://uk.reuters.com/article/2014/05/27/uk-eu-election-idUKKBN0E40Q620140527, last viewed 17 September 2015.

*The Economist* (2013), 'Europe: The anti-European question', 18 November 2013, available at http://www.economist.com/news/21589051-once-european-elections-may-will-matter-both-eu-and-its-members-anti-european, last viewed 21 April 2015.

——— (2014a), 'European elections: The Eurosceptic Union', 26 May 2014, available at http://www.economist.com/blogs/charlemagne/2014/05/european-elections-0, last viewed 22 April 2015.

——— (2014b), 'Europe's populist insurgents: Turning right', 4 January 2014, available at http://www.economist.com/news/briefing/21592666-parties-nationalist-right-are-changing-terms-european-political-debate-does, last viewed 24 April 2015.

——— (2014c), 'The National Front's victory: France in shock', 26 May 2014, available at http://www.economist.com/blogs/charlemagne/2014/05/national-fronts-victory, last viewed 27 April 2015.

*The Wall Street Journal* (2014), 'Anti-EU, far right parties post strong gains in European elections', 27 May 2014, available at http://www.wsj.com/articles/SB10001424052702304811904579583503825611192, last viewed 18 May 2015.

CHAPTER 5

# Brexit and Its Implications for the EU and Beyond

## 1 Introduction

On 23 January 2013, the then UK prime minister, David Cameron, announced in a speech that he would hold a referendum on EU membership if he got re-elected in the next general election. He indicated that, after 40 years, the European Union (EU) has been evolving from a common market that the UK voted to join in a direction that people did not sign up for. As a result, 'domestic consent for the EU is wafer thin,…, and public disillusionment with the EU is at all time high'. It is then required to regain the public mandate for the UK's EU membership (Cameron, 2013). In May 2015, the Conservative Party led by Cameron unexpectedly won the parliamentary majority, and the EU referendum became a reality. After successfully striking a deal through renegotiations with the EU on the new terms of the UK's EU membership in February 2016, Cameron announced to hold an in/out referendum on 23 June 2016, in which'[the British people will make] the biggest economic and political decision… in our lifetimes' (Cameron, 2016; Cameron and Osborne, 2016).

The referendum has drawn the world's attention since then, and the unusual, high-profile interventions from international leaders and

Part of this chapter was first published by *European Review*, 25(4): 519–531.



C.-M. Luo, *The EU's Crisis Decade*,
https://doi.org/10.1007/978-981-13-6565-2_5

organizations during the campaign[1] highlight the significance of the referendum not just to the UK but to the wider world. The unexpected outcome was confirmed to be the British exit from the EU (Brexit) with 51.9% of votes in favour of leaving the EU and 48.1% in favour of remaining in the EU (Bremain) (The UK Electoral Commission, 2016). The Brexit outcome has caused immediate political and economic repercussions across the UK and the world. For the UK itself, as Glencross (2014: 2) comments, this result was the UK's 'most momentous political decision in the peacetime period since the Irish Home Rule'. Whitman (2016a) believes such an outcome presented 'the most formidable challenge to the UK' since World War II, while the commentator of *Financial Times*, Martin Wolf (2016), describes it as 'the single worst event in the British post-war history'. For Europe, as Barysch and Bildt (2016), the director of Allianz SE and former prime minister of Sweden, point out, 'Brexit is the most consequential event in Europe since the fall of the Berlin Wall', and Niblett (2016a) indicates that the EU faced 'the most difficult period in its history'.

This historic event has caused profound impact on European integration and the post-war consensus on promoting free trade. The German chancellor, Angela Merkel, comments Brexit as 'a turning point in the history of European integration' (*Politico*, 26 August 2016a), while there is widespread concern about its spillover to other Western advanced economies, as the *New York Times* expresses in its editorial (28 June 2016). The Chinese president, Xi Jin-Ping, also warns the rise of protectionism and anti-globalization after the UK referendum. Whether or how Brexit will have impact on European integration and wider regional integration requires thorough examinations into how this issue emerged and developed first, and to explore under what circumstances, the Brexit outcome has been produced. This research is an attempt to answer such questions. It will discuss how the issue of Brexit emerged and developed first, followed by the analyses on how it has led to the result of Brexit in the referendum in the second section. The third and fourth sections will explore its implications for European integration and beyond.

[1] The then US president Barack Obama, the Chinese president Xi Jin-Ping, leaders of G7, finance ministers of G20, the OECD, and the IMF all issued pleas to the UK public to vote for Bremain. See Sect. 3.1 for more details.

## 2 The Brexit Issue

Since the UK joined the EU, EU membership, as Oliver points out (2015: 77), is one of the most divisive issues in the UK politics. What are the characteristics of the UK's relation with the EU? How can these characteristics explain why EU membership is so divisive in the UK politics? And more importantly, how did these divisions on this issue finally lead to an in/out referendum on the EU after its 43-year membership? These are the issues this section will look into.

### *2.1 The UK and the EU*

The UK joined the EU in 1973. Although the UK was invited to join the EU from its conception in 1957, it wasn't until the 1960s that it applied for membership. After two failed applications, the UK was granted membership status in the EU's first expansion. The reason for this two-decade delay was simply because European integration was not conceived by the UK as essential either to its national interests, as it was to France, or to its national identity and reorientation, as it was to Germany. European integration was considered only as a means to achieving economic aims. How to halt the economic decline and modernize the UK economy had dominated post-war UK domestic politics. With the economic benefits of European integration increasingly evident in contrast to the UK's declining economy in the 1960s, EC membership was sought as a solution to economic revitalization (George, 1999: 1–19; Hix, 2002: 47–68; Warner, 2002: 871; Menon and Salter, 2016: 1298).

In other words, the UK sought for EU membership not because of its commitment to the ultimate objectives of European integration, nor for its big picture of an ideal Europe, but rather, it was simply out of economic imperative. European integration, as Wall (2012: 516) describes, was only a 'business arrangement' and a means to growth and prosperity rather than a desirable end itself as it was for other EU members (Raines, 2013, 2016a; Goodwin, 2015; *The Economist*, 12 March 2016). The EU was expected to raise national economic well-being; otherwise, it lost appeal to the UK. The public support for the EU in the UK therefore has been volatile. When economic benefits of this movement were obvious, the UK was supportive; when they were not so evident nor debatable, the UK either vetoed or opted out. For example, the UK did not join the euro, nor was it a member of Schengen project. This economic-benefits-only tendency has led the UK's participation in European integration to focusing only on economic and trading issues and opposed to any directions towards political integration. These characteristics thus presented the UK as the least integrationist within the EU and most Eurosceptical member, often labelled as an 'awkward partner' and revealed in its largely negative, even hostile domestic media coverage (Menon and Salter, 2016: 1298–9).

### 2.2 *Euroscepticism in the UK Society*

With such a pragmatic and utilitarian approach to European integration, the UK examined and debated the benefits and costs of EU membership constantly since it joined in the movement. As the UK industry did not magically revive as expected and there lacked a consensus on economic benefits of EU membership among economists, EU membership has been a never-ending debate and divisive issue in the UK politics, accompanied by an increasing continuity in Euroscepticism in the UK society (Glencross, 2014: 1–2).

The regular Eurobarometer surveys of public opinions, carried out by the European Commission, show that the UK has been one of the most Eurosceptical member in the EU. Thirty-one per cent of UK respondents thought the EU as a positive thing, compared to the EU average of 34%, while 36% of UK respondents held a negative view on the EU, compared to the EU average of 27%. The UK was also one of the few EU countries who viewed the future of the EU more pessimistic than optimistic (European Commission, 2016a: 16 & 20).

Commentators attribute the UK's Euroscepticism to a number of factors. First, the geographical factor, an island on the edge of the continent, and the effect it has had on the UK history, once a maritime power, have orientated the country more to other parts of the world, such as North America, Africa, and Asia, than just the continental Europe. This character was captured by Churchill who told de Gaulle that when facing with a choice between the continent and *le grand large*, the UK would always choose the wide open seas (Grant, 2008: 2). Second, unlike other EU members, the UK was the victory country in World War II, to which the war was the country's 'finest hour'. Memories of war endow the UK people a sense of pride and moral superiority, as the former UK prime minister, Margaret Thatcher, often said that the continental Europe has been a source of the UK's problems (Grant, 2008: 2–3; *The Economist*, 3 March 2014). Third, distinct from EU members, there existed a uniquely

Eurosceptical media community in the UK. Three quarters of UK newspapers were viewed as Eurosceptical. Balanced accounts that covered EU issues were very rarely seen. For example, *The Times* and *The Daily Telegraph*, two popular broadsheet newspapers, hardly published opinions that were supportive of the EU, while tabloid newspapers, such as the best-selling *Sun*, can often be found publishing bogus stories about the EU (Grant, 2008: 3–5). Fourth, research by the Institute for Public Policy Research found there is a link between English national identity and Euroscepticism in some areas of England. The stronger the sense of English national identity, the more Euroscepticism there was (Oliver, 2015: 84–5).

However, Euroscepticism does not mean the support for the UK's exit from the EU. As Oliver points out (2015: 78), in spite of the UK's distant and aloof relations with the EU, all the mainstream political parties were committed to EU membership in order to secure UK interests. Also, according to the regular surveys of the British Social Attitudes (Curtice, 2016: 2–5), only a minority of UK people, 30%, could be identified as 'Brexiteers', whereas there was a vast majority, 60%, supportive of EU membership by 2015 (see Table 5.1). Indeed, although Euroscepticism was pervasive in the UK as more than two-thirds of the surveyed, 65%, would like the UK to maintain a looser relationship with the EU (Curtice, 2016: 6), there were more than a half, 53%, of UK respondents who felt themselves as a citizen of the EU in the latest survey of Eurobarometer (European Commission, 2016a: 38).

Curtice (2016: 14–16), who has conducted annual surveys of the British Social Attitudes, further points out that the high level of Euroscepticism in the UK was, indeed, a reflection of widespread concerns about cultural consequences of EU membership on the UK national identity. But such a concern did not translate into a request for withdrawal from the EU. Among people who felt the EU undermined the UK's identity, only 42% would like to withdraw from the EU, while a larger proportion, 46%, would like to stay (see Table 5.2). That is to say, Euroscepticism on its own was not sufficient to explain why the UK had to hold a Brexit referendum. It can explain the UK's inclination of checking on the EU's power and their distant relationship, but it does not mean a dramatic step of leaving. Also, as Jensen and Snaith's survey indicate (2016: 1304–8), there cannot be found any demands from domestic interest groups to pressure for such an issue. The reason why the UK had to hold such a

**Table 5.1** Attitudes towards Britain's membership of the EU, 1983–2015

| | *1983* (%) | *1984* (%) | *1985* (%) | *1986* (%) | *1987* (%) | *1989* (%) | *1990* (%) | *1991* (%) | *1992* (%) | *1997* (%) | *2014* (%) | *2015* (%) |
|---|---|---|---|---|---|---|---|---|---|---|---|---|
| Continue | 53 | 48 | 56 | 61 | 63 | 68 | 76 | 77 | 72 | 54 | 57 | 60 |
| Withdraw | 42 | 45 | 38 | 33 | 32 | 26 | 19 | 17 | 22 | 28 | 35 | 30 |
| Unweighted sample size | 1761 | 1675 | 1804 | 3100 | 2847 | 3029 | 2797 | 1445 | 2855 | 1355 | 971 | 1105 |

Source: Curtice, 2016: 5, Table 1

**Table 5.2** Attitudes towards the EU by level of cultural concern: Withdraw versus continue

| *EU is undermining Britain's distinctive identity* | | | | | |
|---|---|---|---|---|---|
| | *Strongly agree (%)* | *Agree (%)* | *Neither (%)* | *Disagree (%)* | *Strongly disagree (%)* |
| Withdraw | 80 | 42 | 9 | 4 | 3 |
| Continue | 17 | 46 | 75 | 92 | 95 |
| Unweighted sample size | 198 | 350 | 216 | 242 | 65 |

Source: Curtice, 2016: 14, Table 8

historic referendum, as Ignacio-Torreblanca (2016), a Spanish EU official, indicates, was political: 'using Europe as a battlefield for domestic politics'.

### 2.3 *How Has Euroscepticism Led to the Brexit Referendum?*

Euroscepticism was not uncommon in the EU politics. What made the UK distinct from other EU members, as Glencross points out (2014: 2), was that it was found in mainstream parties rather than just in radical right populist parties as in other EU countries, and thus it posed serious challenges to the parties when they were in power. Euroscepticism was first found in the Labour Party in the 1970s, and the internal divisions within the then Labour Wilson government over EU membership finally led to the 1975 referendum. The turning point occurred when the president of the European Commission, Jacques Delors, addressed to the Trade Union Congress (TUC) about the social dimension of the future EU with tougher labour and social protection in 1988. This became the watershed in the UK politics where the Conservative Party replaced Labour 'as the party of Euroscepticism' (*The Economist*, 12 March 2016). The then Conservative prime minister Margaret Thatcher, who firmly believed in economic liberalism, attacked the EU for excessive interferences and refused to sign up to further EU integration of the single currency. Since then, the party has been preoccupied with this 'totemic issue'. Numerous rebellions, defections, and the downfall of Thatcher have been caused over the EU controversy, and these internal divisions partly accounted for the party's landslide defeat in 1997 (Whitman, 2016c: 518; Menon and Salter, 2016: 1301–2; Moore, 2015).

When Cameron led the Conservative Party back to power in the form of the coalition government with the Liberal Democrat Party in 2010, he faced with a deep and strong Eurosceptic force within the party after successive Eurosceptic party leaders,[2] where more than 100 Conservative parliamentary members (MPs) demanded for holding an EU referendum. On the other hand, the anti-EU party, UK Independence Party (UKIP), was found in some surveys to have 15% of the electoral support by 2012. Some marginal seats of Conservative MPs looked precarious as they might lose to Labour if the UKIP took enough votes. In order to 'end 40 years of political squabbles' (in the words of former prime minister, John Major) within the party and 'shoot the UKIP fox' in the next general election at the same time, Cameron, reportedly a Eurosceptic himself, agreed to hold a referendum on EU membership in his 2013 Bloomberg speech (Bale, 2013: 12–13; Oliver, 2015: 77; Jensen and Snaith, 2016: 1304; Menon and Salter, 2016: 1303–4; *The Independent*, 3 May 2016d).

It was reported that, in Cameron's calculations, such a promised referendum would never have to be delivered, as, by that time, all polls suggested that neither Conservative nor Labour could win an overall majority in the 2015 general election and another coalition government looked more likely. In that case, the promised EU referendum would have to be dropped at any coalition governments as both Labour and Lib Dem were against it. It was to Cameron's surprise when Conservative won a clear majority in the 2015 election, and holding the EU referendum therefore became inevitable (*The Independent*, 3 May 2016d).

As Whitman (2016b: 518) and Oliver (2015: 81–3) both point out, Cameron's motive to promise an in/out referendum was driven mainly, if not totally, by endogenous rather than exogenous factors. It was resorted to de-politicize the EU controversy within the Conservative Party so as to minimize the damages of internal divisions to the precarious coalition government and to the electability in the next election by externalizing the issue. The referendum was not a desire to renew the 'wafer thin' consent of the UK electorate on the EU, as Cameron claimed. But rather, it was an instrument to manage long-term power struggles and rifts on the EU within the ruling party where Cameron did not enjoy the advantage of a

[2] According to Moore's quantitative survey (2015), two factors explain Euroscepticism in the Parliamentary Conservative Party (PCP). One is its nationalist ideology and the other is the demography of constituencies where the level of employment and numbers of retired people were associated with Euroscepticism in the PCP.

clear parliamentary majority and could not afford any defections, or repeat any past failures on managing Europe issue. The UK's historic referendum, rooted in Conservative Party's Euroscepticism and developed in such a political structural context, accidentally became a reality out of Cameron's miscalculations on the changing domestic politics.

## 3 Interpreting the Referendum Result: Brexit

Since the referendum was bound to be delivered, challenges ahead of Cameron were to win the case. Resorted to the same strategy with Wilson in 1975, Cameron started renegotiations with the EU over the issues that concerned the UK public most about EU membership before calling into the referendum so as to increase the odds of winning the referendum. After marathon talks with leaders of other 27 EU members, a 'special status' agreement, including 'emergency brake' on in-work benefits of immigrants and the UK exempt from the EU's political integration of 'an ever closer union',[3] was struck in February 2016. Right after securing what he called 'the best of both worlds' in the UK's renegotiated EU membership, Cameron immediately announced the referendum to be held on 23 June 2016 (*EU Observer*, 9 February 2016a; *BBC*, 20 February 2016a, 2016b; Hammond, 2016b).

### *3.1 The Bremain Versus Brexit Campaign*

In terms of resources, financial capability, and heavyweight campaigners, the Bremain camp enjoyed overwhelming advantages over the Brexit camp, as political and business elites, both national and international, were at its side.

Since the campaign was initiated, international interventions appeared from time to time. International leaders, from those of the world's largest three economies—the US president, Barack Obama; the German

[3] Thomas Raines (2016b) and Daniela Annette Kroll and Dirk Leuffen (2016: 1315–17) all argue that the demands that the Cameron government proposed to the EU were rather modest than grandstanded and the results were rather symbolic and rhetorical than substantial and exceptional as the government claimed so. However, Francisco Gomezmartos, an EU official speaking on his personal capacity, disagrees that the UK was, indeed, granted 'special status'. He criticizes the EU has crossed the red lines and gambled on its principles. Accordingly, he views this new deal as 'a very bad agreement' (interviewed with the author on 9 May 2016).

chancellor, Angela Merkel; and the Chinese president, Xi Jin-Ping—to those of Commonwealth countries such as the Canadian and Australian prime ministers all issued public pleas for the UK public to support Bremain (*The New York Times*, 21 June 2016; *CBC*, 22 June 2016; *BBC*, 1 May 2016). So did prominent international organizations, such as the G7, G20, IMF, OECD, and NATO (G7 Ise-Shima Leaders' Declaration, 2016, *The Independent*, 28 February 2016; *The Wall Street Journal*, 17 June 2016; OECD, 2016: 6–7; *The Telegraph*, 20 June 2016).

Within the UK, the Bremain camp also received tremendous support across business, trade unions, academic and political communities. A total of 1280 UK business leaders from 51 FTSE 100 companies issued an open letter to back the UK remaining in the EU. So did the vice chancellors of 103 UK universities, who seldom publicly involved in political affairs. The TUC also issued public support for Bremain for better protection of workers' right (University Vice Chancellors, 21 June 2016; *The Independent*, 23 June 2016c & 3 May 2016d). The major three parliamentary parties—Conservative, Labour, and Lib Dem—were all behind the Bremain camp, except from a fraction of Conservative MPs (Hague, 2016; Benn, 2016).[4] By contrast, the Brexit campaign was backed only by a few big names such as the former London mayor, Boris Johnson; the minister of justice, Michael Gove; and the leader of UKIP, Nigel Farage.

The discourses that the Bremain and Brexit camps presented to the public also marked a clear contrast. The Bremain camp resorted to economic rationale of maintaining the access of the European single market and potential costs of losing such a market access. For example, the prime minister, David Cameron, reminded that the European single market put '500 million customers on our doorstep' and sources of jobs, trade, opportunities, and wealth, and Brexit would lead 'in the short term [to] recession, in the medium term [to] a decade of uncertainty and in the long term [to] living with fewer jobs, lower wages and higher prices'. Therefore, Brexit would be 'an act of economic self-harm'. Together with his chancellor of exchequer, George Osborne, they described Brexit as 'a DIY recession' (*EU Observer*, 21 & 3 June 2016; Cameron and Osborne, 2016).

In contrast, the Brexit camp appeal was much simpler and straightforward—'take back control' on the policy areas such as immigration, public finance and taxation, national health system (NHS), social welfare, and so

[4] There were 6 of 21 cabinet ministers who were publicly supportive of Brexit.

on.[5] They projected 'hope' in the post-Brexit scenario of freeing from the bureaucracy of Brussels and accused the Bremain camp of 'scaremongering' over its warning that Brexit was economic self-harm (*EU Observer*, 22 June 2016).

During the campaign, the Brexit camp drew criticisms over its poster that was reminiscent of the 1930s fascist propaganda. The shocking killing of the Labour MP, Jo Cox, who was a Bremain supporter, also seemed to lean the tight competition favourable to the Bremain camp (*EU Observer*, 17 & 20 June 2016). However, the support for Brexit did not decrease because of the negative effects of these events, but increased with the campaign being progressing. Gareth Harding (2016a), an expert of polls, points out that, in February 2016, the month that Cameron announced the date of referendum, only 6 out of 20 national surveys showed a majority in favour of Brexit. Two months later, the number increased to 7 out of 12 surveys that showed a majority in favour of Brexit. Benjamin Fox (2016a) also observes an interesting phenomenon that every time an influential leader, may it be a foreign leader, the Bank of England governor, a well-known economist or academic, made a rational, economic case to justify the benefits of Bremain, the support for Brexit went up. He explains that the Brexit's appeal to 'take back control' was a concept that was hard to disagree and this powerful slogan made the possible economic costs of Brexit seem like a small price to pay. On the contrary, the Bremain arguments were hard to touch people, as Jacques Delors, the former president of the Commission, once said that 'no one falls in love with a market'. The competition accordingly became a tug of war between hearts and heads.

A report of the House of Lords also suggests that 'a campaign based upon narrow national economic-interest, alongside fear of the alternatives to membership, would be insufficient'. Jeroen Dijsselbloem, the president of the Eurogroup and the Dutch finance minister, also reminded the Bremain campaign to engage more on voters' feelings, and not just on the rational part of the debate (*EU Observer*, 31 March & 2 June 2016). However, Harding (2016a) disagrees that the dichotomy between hearts and heads may be too simplistic, as Brexit supporters were more pragmatic

[5] Robin Niblett (2016b: 6 & 25) refutes the anti-EU campaign's powerful argument on 'take back control' as 'a worthless proposition', as, apart from immigration from the EU, the vast majority of policy issues of greatest concerns to UK voters were determined by the UK government and devolved administrations. In the 2014–15 financial year, the UK parliament still decided more than 98% of public spending.

than they were thought to be. He predicts that people would be persuaded to vote for Brexit if they did not see any personal gains from EU membership and believed that more migrants depressed wages and took jobs from them. It would be a vote cast with both their hearts and heads.

It was in capturing people's feelings that the Brexit campaign seemed more effective than the Bremain one. Waldman (2016) and Menon and Salter (2016: 1297) all point out that Brexit campaigners' skills and capability to empathize with voters' feelings and perceptions were key to their success. The Bremain camp, as Fox (2016a) points out, was pictured by Brexit campaigners as the advocates of global banks, such as Goldman Sachs and JP Morgan, and the EU served only multinational companies, not workers. On the other hand, Brexit campaigners pictured themselves as striking for the 'little guy' and ordinary people. This can explain why political and business leaders' and elites' economic pleas for Bremain were counter-productive, as they were described as siding with the 'undeserving rich'.

### 3.2 *The Referendum Outcome of Brexit: Who Voted for It?*

In spite of the growing and resilient support for Brexit during the campaign, few, including Brexit campaigners themselves, were expecting the referendum outcome to be a Brexit one. It is not only because past referendums suggest that support for the 'change' option often declined and the 'status quo' would be gaining ground as the polling day approached (Lord Ashcroft Polls, 2016; Goodwin and Heath 2016; Kellner, 2015), but also because among 168 surveys, most predict Bremain would win the referendum (*The Guardian*, 24 June 2016d). Therefore, when the outcome of the referendum was confirmed to be Brexit by a majority of nearly 52%, there has been a phenomenon of 'sinking feeling', as Stella Creasy, a Labour MP (2016: 20), describes. Such a feeling derives not just from deep divisions, revealed in the referendum result, along social, geographical, generational, and income lines, but also from widespread uncertainty about the future.

Indeed, the Brexit result exposed clear divisions between regions, generations, and social classes. In terms of regions, Scotland and North Ireland voted for Bremain; England and Wales voted for Brexit (see Fig. 5.1). To be more precise, among 12 UK areas, only 3 areas—London, Scotland, and North Ireland—were for Bremain; the other 9 areas were for Brexit. The highest shares of support for Brexit were found in the

**Fig. 5.1** The result of the Brexit referendum. Source: *BBC* (24 June 2014)

North England, East England, West and East Midlands, while the highest shares for Bremain were found in Scotland and London (see Chart 5.1) (*BBC*, 24 June 2016d). That is to say, the result reveals divisions not just between four nations of the UK—England, Wales, Scotland, and North Ireland—but also between London and non-London areas within England.

The second contrast revealed in this vote was in different generations. According to the poll of Lord Ashcroft after the vote (2016), the older the voters, the higher they were to vote for Brexit, while the younger the voters, the higher they were to vote for Bremain. Sixty per cent of those aged 65 or older voted for Brexit. The second highest group of Brexit voters was those aged 55–64. By contrast, 73% of aged 18–24 voted for Bremain,

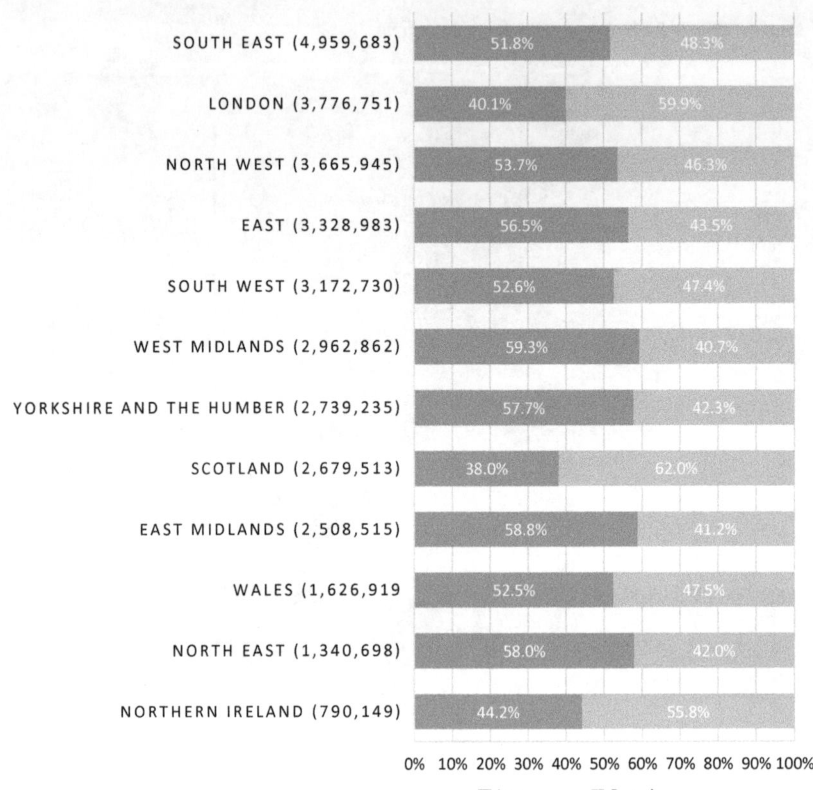


**Chart 5.1** Results in different areas. Source: *BBC* (24 June 2014)

and the second highest group of Bremain voters was those aged 25–34. Aged 45 was a watershed between Bremain and Brexit votes, at which Brexit votes outweighed Bremain ones. Brexit votes increased proportionally over aged 45 and decreased proportionally under aged 45 (see Chart 5.2).

The third sharp contrast that can be observed in this vote was in the differences of educational background. The poll of Lord Ashcroft (2016) indicates that the higher the educational attainment, the more likely they were to vote for Bremain. A majority, 57%, of those with a university degree voted for Bremain, so did 64% of those with a higher degree. There was an overwhelming majority, 81%, of those still in full-time education

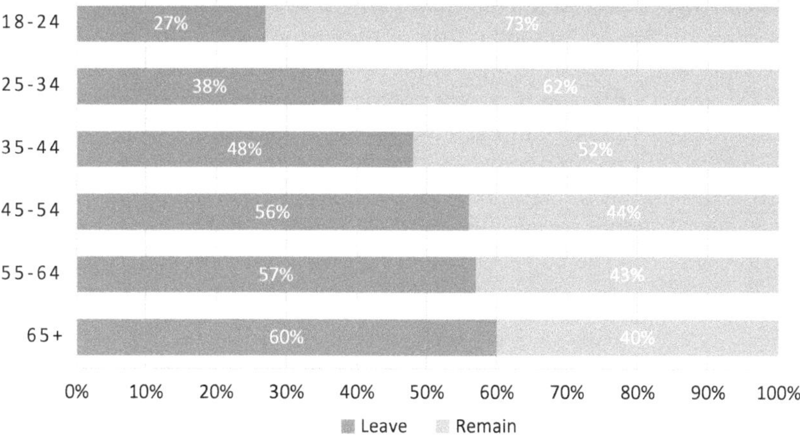


**Chart 5.2** Results in different age groups. Source: *BBC* (24 June 2014)

that voted for Bremain. By contrast, a large majority of those with a secondary school degree or lower voted for Brexit. Barr (2016) exemplifies that, in Wandsworth, Richmond upon Thames and Cambridge where population has higher education qualification, over two-thirds of their votes were for Bremain. In Great Yarmouth, one of the top five areas that supported Brexit, only 14.2% have higher education qualification and 71.5% of its population voted for Brexit.

The fourth contrast was found in different economic and social groups. Professionals and managers (AB group) were the only social group among whom a majority, 57%, voted for Bremain. Lower middle class (C1 group) was slightly leaning over to Brexit, while two-thirds of the three lower social and economic groups—skilled workers (C2 group) and working class (DE group)—voted for Brexit (Lord Ashcroft Polls, 2016).

In short, the surveys show that there were a strong correlation of voting behaviours with age, education, and income levels. Only Scotland was an exception. People voted for Bremain regardless of their education and income background. For example, in North Lanarkshire, just 17% of its population has higher education qualification, but 61.7% of its votes went to Bremain (Barr; *BBC*, 24 June 2016d). Burn-Murdoch (2016) therefore concludes the following characteristics of the vote. First, areas with higher numbers of degree-educated voters tended to vote Bremain. Second, areas with large numbers of voters whose jobs required university degrees also tended to vote Bremain. Third, areas where large numbers of people did not hold a passport—an indication of they being abroad or not—tended to vote Brexit. Fourth, the highest Brexit voters tended to come from low-income areas. Fifth, young people voted overwhelmingly for Bremain but were fewer in number. Surprisingly, the extent of economic link with the EU had no effects on people's voting behaviour. The regions where the most economically intertwined with the EU were also the ones with highest share of Brexit votes. For example, East Yorkshire and Northern Lincolnshire had the highest share of exporting their economic output to the EU than any other regions. Yet, 65% of their electorate voted for Brexit.

### 3.3 *Identifying the Causes to the Outcome: Why Did They Vote for Brexit?*

Some commentators attribute the outcome of Brexit to provisional factors. The most-debated factor was the turnout. For example, Speed (2016) and Chowdhury (2016) suggest that if the turnout of young voters, who were most likely to vote for Bremain, would be higher, the result might not be the triumph of the Brexit campaign. Fox (2016b) also suggests before the polling day that a turnout of 80%, which implies a higher turnout of young people, would be more likely to result in a Bremain vote. The actual turnout was 72%. However, their perspectives were not seen as plausible by others. First, as Singh (2016) points out, the turnout of 72% was already high by modern standards. Goodwin and Heath (2016: 325) further confirm that this turnout was the highest in a nationwide vote since the 1992 general election. Furthermore, according to the post-referendum survey of Bruter and Harrison of LSE for Opinium Research, the turnout was 64% in the group of aged 18–24; 65% in the group of aged 25–39; and 66% in the group of aged 40–54. By contrast, the turnout increased to 74% in the group of aged 55–64 and 90% in the group of aged 65 and over. The turnout of younger voters, indeed, was significantly lower than older ones. However, they do not think that a higher turnout of younger voters would be enough to overturn the result, but only to narrow down the victory margins of Brexit votes (*The Guardian*, 10 July 2016).

Another debate on the turnout was the unexpected lower turnout in Scotland, North Ireland, and London, the only 3 regions among the overall 12 UK regions that voted for Bremain. All three regions were among the areas with the lowest turnout. The unexpected lower turnout in

Scotland was explained by its electoral exhaustion as they just had a national election in May and the independence referendum last year. The case of London was explained by the flash floods as several polling stations were forced to move (Dunford and Kirk, 2016). However, Roger Scully (2016), the professor of Cardiff University, points out that even if Scotland and North Ireland had the same turnout as high as England, the result would not be changed (Scully, 2016).

Others blame the passive campaign of the Labour Party's leadership. Goodwin (2015) points out that this is the first time that the leadership of the Labour Party held a less positive view on EU membership and some trade unions clearly indicated that they would vote for Brexit. The former Labour prime minister, Tony Blair (2016), criticizes publicly in his article of the *New York Times* that the Labour leader, Jeremy Corbyn, was lukewarm in campaigning for Bremain and failed to send a clear message to Labour supporters. This led to Labour supporters being drawn by the Brexit campaign and used this vote 'as an opportunity to register an anti-government protest'. Most Labour MPs shared with his view and asked for Corbyn to resign over his incapable performance in the campaign right after the Brexit result was confirmed (*The Independent*, 24 June 2016a, e).

However, such criticisms do not stand up to empirical examinations. According to the survey of Lord Ashcroft Polls (2016), 63% of Labour supporters voted for Bremain. This share was almost as much as those of the Scottish National Party (SNP), 64%, whose party leader, Nicola Sturgeon, campaigned enthusiastically for Bremain. Moreover, if there was any party leader to be blamed for the result of Brexit, it would be the Conservative leader, David Cameron, who campaigned strongly for Bremain but failed to persuade the majority of Conservative supporters to vote for Bremain, as 58% of its supporters voted for Brexit.

Kellner (2015), on the other hand, suggests that contemporary events happening in the EU affected people's voting behaviours. He observes that, according to the regular surveys of YouGov, until the first half of 2015, there was a constant lead of Bremain over Brexit by 6–12%. But following the Greek bailout events in June and the refugee crisis escalating from that time, the two sides have been neck and neck since August 2015. The crisis-ridden EU thus made the status quo, Bremain, less appealing and the scenario of Brexit less frightening.

Vasilopoulou (2016: 222–3), Thielemann and Schade (2016: 139), Menon and Salter (2016: 1309–10), and Goodwin and Heath (2016: 328) all recognize that the issue of immigration from the EU and border controls seemed to dominate the debates in both the government's renegotiations with the EU and throughout the whole campaign. However, the connection between immigration and voting behaviour was rather mild and was not as determining as it was expected. Goodwin and Heath (2016: 329) find that among 20 areas in the UK with the lowest level of EU migration, 15 voted for Brexit; among 20 areas with the highest level of EU migration, 18 voted for Bremain.

In her pre-referendum survey, Vasilopoulou (2016: 224–5) predicts that utilitarian concerns of voters regarding the cost and benefits of EU membership would be more influential in their voting decisions. Her findings coincide with those of Curtice. Curtice (2016: 15–17) points out in his pre-referendum survey that people would need to be persuaded about the economic disadvantages of EU membership to vote for Brexit. Immigration and identity were, indeed, the foundation of many doubts and grievance about the UK's EU membership, but they were unlikely to be sufficient to persuade people to vote for Brexit. Only when people were convinced of the economic disadvantages of EU membership, 68% of them would vote for Brexit. Similarly, if they were convinced of the economic advantages of EU membership, 88% would vote for Bremain and only 8% would vote for Brexit (see Table 5.3).

A number of commentators tend to agree that the referendum result was a vote on the economic case, but they point to more structural rather than contemporary European issues. Wright (2016: 20), Farvis (2016: 17), Goodwin (2016), Eagle (2016: 6), Fox (2016c: 8), Menon and Salter (2016: 1315), Goodwin and Heath (2016: 331), Jack (2016), and Bailey (2016: 3) all point out that the characteristics of voting behaviours revealed

**Table 5.3** Attitudes towards the EU by evaluations of the economic consequences of leaving

| *If Britain left the EU economy would be …* | | | | | |
|---|---|---|---|---|---|
| | *Much better (%)* | *Better (%)* | *Neither (%)* | *Worse (%)* | *Much worse (%)* |
| Withdraw | 80 | 68 | 31 | 8 | 2 |
| Continue | 14 | 26 | 55 | 88 | 98 |
| Unweighted sample size | 87 | 184 | 355 | 313 | 103 |

Source: Curtice, 2016: 15, Table 9

in the referendum meaning people voted on their personal economic experiences over the past years. A large majority of working-class voters who feel left behind by the rapid economic transformation and cut adrift from mainstream parties have led to the outcome of Brexit. It is, indeed, a rational and economic vote, and less to do with the personal charisma of individual politicians. It was a vote from those 'left behinds' to express their frustration with the established parties and rejection to 'an economic status quo that had failed them', as the Labour leader, Jeremy Corbyn, puts it (*The Guardian*, 15 September 2016).

Indeed, it was in northern and eastern England where economic backbones—traditional industries—had been hit most by globalization and de-industrialization, and the support for Brexit was the highest. Wright (2016: 20), a Labour MP, exemplifies with his constituency that jobs have been lost not to immigrants but to automation and Asian emerging economies. Wage stagnation and the rise of 'gig economy', in which people accepted short or intermittent period of works without employment protection, were the facts of life. For them, globalization did provide cheaper imports, but that could be at the cost of their jobs. Reeves (2016: 17–18), a Labour MP whose constituents also voted for Brexit overwhelmingly, further explains that many workers blamed the EU for keeping their wage lower and living costs higher because of more EU workers coming into the UK. They also resented the increasing inequality between the rich and poor, mostly between London and the rest of the country. A stereotypical thinking was that: 'who cares if leaving Europe meant fewer jobs? The jobs all go to foreigners anyway'. Reynolds (2016: 24–5) also confirms that the main reason of why a large number of her constituents voted for Brexit was immigration.[6] But underlining their concerns about immigration, she observes, was a sense of insecurity that globalization and economy were not favourable to them as pay restraint became a new normal.

These actual pictures from people's real life explain why economic appeals made by the Bremain campaign failed to persuade people, as people felt and experienced EU membership in their personal way, not to mention such economic appeals were pictured by the Brexit campaign as serving for multinationals and global banks, those 'undeserving rich'. The same logic also explains why younger generation who benefited from the

[6] *The Economist* (2016b) and Goodwin and Heath (2016: 329) all point out that it was the change in numbers of migrants in a short period of time, rather than the total number of them, that have effects on voting.

EU's Erasmus exchanging project across the EU, Londoners who benefited from the City of London being the EU's financial centre, and people with higher education and income levels who benefited from more opportunities offered by the EU for professionals tended to vote for Bremain. This is all because EU membership was personally favourable to them. The referendum outcome thus has become a showdown between the beneficiaries/winners and victims/losers of European integration and globalization.

While economic rationales provide justifications for the general picture of the Brexit vote in England, they alone cannot explain the whole picture of voting outcomes across the UK. The majority in affluent southern England who also voted for Brexit just as the result in deprived northern England was clearly an exception. Neither can they explain the case of Wales. The region has benefited greatly from the EU's financial supports, but the majority of Welsh voters also delivered an outcome of Brexit.

For the case of southern England, Williams (2016a) points out that those who were council house tenants voted for Brexit. But so did those who owned their houses outright. The only groups that voted for Bremain in this region were private renters and people with mortgages. She explains such a paradoxical outcome as 'plot voting against housing', which has to be understood in a local context and cannot be explained merely by the dichotomy of economic and social classes.

Perhaps the most surprising result was delivered by Welsh voters. Unlike widespread Euroscepticism in England, Wales has been very supportive of the EU. One of four flags that fly outside the Welsh Assembly was that of the EU, which cannot be seen outside the UK parliament (Williamson, 2016). The fact that Wales has been one of UK regions benefiting most from EU membership explains the positive views held by Welsh people on the EU just as in the case of Scotland. At a very conservative estimate, the EU offered an annual net benefit of 245 million pounds for Wales (Wales Governance Centre, 2016: 4). Most polls before the referendum also suggested Wales to be a region of voting for Bremain. Yet, the majority, 52.5%, of the Welsh electorate voted for Brexit in the referendum, and this outcome 'appears to be bizarrely self-defeating' (Jones, 2016). Richard Wyn Jones (2016), a professor of Welsh politics at Cardiff University, attributes such a surprising outcome to a number of factors: firstly, the lack of legitimacy of the referendum viewed by Welsh people—it was for Cameron's tactical rather than principled reasons; secondly, the undersourced and disorganized Bremain campaign in Wales; and, thirdly, the higher numbers of Wales than the UK average of voters with low education attainment, the so-called left behinds. Daniel Evans of Welsh Institute of Social and Economic Research, on the other hand, singles out the factor of the absence of a Welsh national media. He explains that, unlike Scotland which has its own media, Welsh people were preoccupied by mostly Eurosceptic England-based media which focused primarily on English issues such as immigration, instead of the implications of Brexit for Wales itself (O'Hagan, 2016). However, as Ellie Mae O'Hagan (2016), the editor of openDemocracy, reminds, Wales was the UK's poorest region and has been excluded from mainstream politics for a long time. It should also be reminded that Welsh people were well-known for their strong opposition to the austerity policies posed by the Conservative government (Jones, 2016). Carole Cadwalladr (2016), a famous Welsh writer, observes that the sense of inequality, both economic and political ones, explains the Brexit vote than the sums of other facts. Thus, Jones (2016), O'Hagan (2016), and Daran Hill (*BBC*, 24 June 2016d) all view the surprising outcome of Wales' vote for Brexit as an anti-government, anti-establishment vote. Their argument of protest vote was verified by a post-referendum survey in which the majority, 53%, of Welsh voters would change to vote for Bremain if there was a second referendum. It was a 6% swing in the direction and the so-called 'Bregret' votes for being cast to protest the government (*The Independent*, 5 July 2016f).

To sum up, as the former UK representative to Taiwan, Michael Reilly, concludes, both economic rationales and political dissatisfaction explain the overall outcome of Brexit (interviewed with the author on 30 August 2016). Together with local factors in southern England, frustration and dissatisfaction of disadvantaged voters with the economic status quo in northern and eastern England and protest votes to the then Conservative government in Wales finally led to the unexpected outcome of Brexit.

## 4 The Implications of Brexit for European Integration

The immediate impact of Brexit to the rest of the world was economic. The outcome has caused immediate downfalls in the worldwide financial markets. The IMF also cut its forecasts for global growth for 2016 and 2017 both by 0.1% to 3.1% and 3.4%, respectively, as a Brexit result, despite claiming that economic consequences of Brexit were still unfolding (IMF, 2016: 1–3). The chaos of financial markets could be settled and cleared after some times, but the implications of Brexit for worldwide regional integration were more enduring and challenging. What messages were delivered from Brexit and how these messages imply for European integration need to be identified. They are the focuses this section addresses to.

### *4.1 Lessons from the Brexit Referendum*

There are several phenomena that emerged from the Brexit referendum.

First, it is an exception to the conventional wisdom that political and economic elites are capable and influential of shaping public opinions. According to Goodwin and Milazzo's survey (2015: 9) before the referendum, they suggest that endorsements by political leaders act as cues to voting behaviours and the 'signalling power' of elites can play an important role in winning the referendum. They estimate that the effects of such cues from political elites could increase support for Bremain by between 20 and 30 percentage points. Parakilas and Wickett (2016) also point out, under normal circumstances, the support across party lines for Bremain should have ensured a comfortable victory. To the contrary, it lost by a not-insignificant 52–48% margin. The conventional wisdom did not apply to the Brexit referendum this time. The unexpected, counterintuitive Brexit result, accordingly described by the UK's post-Brexit prime minister, Theresa May, was a 'quiet revolution' (*Reuters*, 7 October 2016).

A number of commentators interpret such 'a revolution' as a wake-up call for political elites. It was seen as a shock from voters who were angry and distrustful of political elites. The unexpected Brexit result reveals that elites no longer necessarily hold the preponderance in the politics (Erlanger, 2016; Parakilas and Wickett, 2016). In fact, not just political elites found themselves powerless in the wake of the Brexit outcome, so did international leaders as well as business and social elites. International interventions were proved not just invalid but only counter-productive. The most frustrated group may come from business leaders. There were as many as 1280 UK businesses publicly calling for Bremain, but they did not change even the minds of their own employees. For example, Paul Willcox, the chairman of Nissan Europe, which employs 6000 people in Sunderland, issued an internal note to all employees asking them to vote for Bremain. A significant majority, 61.3%, of voters in Sunderland, however, voted for Brexit (*International Business Times*, 20 June 2016; *BBC*, 24 June 2016d). The unusual call from 108 university chancellors only serves another living example of elites' declining influences and their enlarging gap with common people.

Why and since when the electorate lost their confidence and trust with political, economic, and social elites was hard to trace. Some politicians from mainstream parties attribute specifically to austerity policies adopted by the Cameron government in the last six years. For example, Nick Clegg, the former deputy prime minister of the then government and former leader of the Liberal Democratic Party, indicates that people still feel the scars of the 2008 financial crisis in the government's austerity policies (*The Guardian*, 27 July 2016). The Conservative succeeding prime minister after the referendum, Theresa May, echoes such a view by indicating that 'it was ordinary working-class families' had made the biggest sacrifices after the global financial crisis (*Reuters*, 7 October 2016). Farvis (2016: 17), a Labour MP, points out directly that austerity policies led to the loss of people's trust with the government and 'Britain cannot afford austerity' any longer. Another Labour MP, Rachel Reeves (2016: 17), whose constituents voted for Brexit overwhelmingly, also points out that governing elites lost their appeal to the electorate because the former were seen by the latter as incapable during the euro crisis. In her attempt to persuade her constituents to vote for Bremain, she was confronted by a reply that 'there was a massive recession when we were in the EU, so you can't say leaving the EU will cause a recession'.

It may not be fair to blame the outbreak of the global financial crisis or euro crisis solely on the governing elites, but the mismanagement of these crises surely can. According to the UN's Committee on Economic, Social and Cultural Rights' report (2016), the UK government's austerity policies caused 'disproportionate adverse impact…on disadvantaged and marginalized individuals and groups'. Measures such as 'various changes in the entitlements to, and cuts in, social benefits' have adversely affected 'women, children, persons with disabilities, low-income families and families with two or more children'. As a result of these austerity policies, the UN report accuses the UK government to breach its obligations to international human rights. The World Economic Forum's 2017 report (2017: 7) also contends that the breaking-up of social protection system was the cause of the rising political and economic disaffection with status quo. The survey of McKinsey Global Institute (2016: 16) further specifies that four-fifths fiscal measures associated with austerity policies were spending cuts, for example, cuts to benefits. They had disproportionately effects on working-class people, especially on the bottom quintile, with disposable income growth decreasing by 6%.

It is then explainable why Brexit voters came from all parts of political spectrum beyond the traditional right/left divide. As Parakilas and Wickett (2016) suggest, the Brexit result is not an ideological split. Brexit voters, may they be older generation or working-class families, were all from economically less advantaged people trying to find their own way to fight back to the negative impacts of globalization. The governing elites supposedly should provide protection for them, but instead, they put the most economically vulnerable people at the front of cost-bearing in the form of austerity policies. Their votes for Brexit therefore, as May said, were not just a demand for bigger control on their lives but also the voices for a fairer society, which was ignored by the 'privileged and powerful' governing elites, for too long and too often (*BBC*, 5 October 2016).

Second, the Brexit outcome shows that the emphases of assessing policies were not about how large positive effects they had produced, but about how widely and evenly these effects spread out among population and how people experienced them personally. Distributive justice of policy effects, accordingly, is far more important than benefits that policies produced at the aggregate level. In spite of many authoritative national and international assessments on the positive effects of EU membership, they were just figures indifferent to the common public. The fact that Bremain and Brexit voters were divided along with the lines of beneficiaries/winners and victims/losers of EU membership highlights the importance and imperative of addressing to distributive justice by political leadership. As commentators point out (Erlanger, 2016; Parakilas and Wickett, 2016), political leadership has to consider how to stop large numbers of voters feeling left out of economic change and success and find solutions to social and economic inequality brought by EU membership.

It is noteworthy that the Brexit outcome was delivered at a time when the UK economy was in recovery. It is obvious that a rising economy cannot lift all boats; neither can it automatically alleviate economic inequality and distributive justice, as policy-makers who upheld economic liberalism assume so. A recovering UK economy cannot prevent Brexit only shows that markets alone are not sufficient to the functioning of regional integration; instead, they alone could sow the seeds of disintegrating the whole project as distributive injustice aggravates. As Williams (2016b) suggests, the reasons of voting for Brexit, such as to halt the flow of EU labours, cannot be said extreme themselves, but isolation and protectionism can be seen as the symptoms of political extremism. Without political redress, there is only one step far between economic inequality and political extremism. Distributive injustice that EU membership produced should not and cannot be left to markets to solve.

For too long, political leadership in Western advanced economies, under the guise of economic liberalism, has been shirking their duties on distributive justice and left the issue to markets to take care. The Brexit outcome is a backfire to their irresponsibility and a price to pay for their ignorance of the deterioration of distributive justice. Being authoritative arbitrators and allocators of resources, political leadership should not sit and watch but ensure the benefits of policies to reach broader population and its costs to be better mitigated. The Brexit referendum proves that the continuing ignorance of distributive injustice is not just a quicker way to lose power but a confirmed answer to reverse the UK's EU membership around.

Third, as a response to 'a quiet revolution' of Brexit, there seems to lead to reflections on the contemporary economic governance in the UK politics. Economic liberalism has been the doctrine held by UK mainstream parties since the 1990s after Labour forwent its dogma on state control over the economy and embraced the so-called third-way politics (also known as 'New Labour') out of the challenges of globalization externally and electability domestically (Hay, 1999: 3–11; Heffernan, 2001: 170). Internally, economic liberalism upholds the role of market mechanism and minimizes state intervention, and austerity policies are the product of such an ideology. Externally, it promotes international free trade and market integration, and the EU's projects of common market and currency are its realization in its regional form.

The superiority of economic liberalism[7] in governance, however, has been questioned and reflected after the Brexit referendum. In its survey, Joseph Rowntree Foundation (2016: 4), a UK NGO focusing on poverty and inequality, asks policy-makers to address uneven economic growth and opportunities immediately, as the referendum result proves that these issues were 'not just a moral imperative, but also a political and economic

[7]Economic liberalism, explained by Ostry et al. (2016: 38), was established on two principles: first, the increase of competition, mainly through deregulation, liberalization, and market opening; second, the limits on ability of government to run public deficits and debt, mainly through fiscal consolidation and austerity.

necessity'. A surprising criticism on economic liberalism was from the governor of the Bank of England, Mark Carney. Carney (2016: 7–8) admits that economists' belief in economic liberalism was 'totemic'. But uneven gains from trade and technology already prove that it was not 'Pareto optimal'. The succeeding prime minister after the referendum, Theresa May, recognizes the outcome of the Brexit referendum as not just a vote to leave the EU but a vote for more profound change as 'liberalism and globalization have left too many people behind'. In contrast to her Conservative predecessors, she introduces an idea of 'responsible capitalism' in which the government should 'repair' free market and take action to injustice so as to build 'a society based on fairness'.[8] Her ideas contradict with the decades-long consensus on economic liberalism held by successive UK governments since Margret Thatcher, who once declared that there is 'no such thing [fairness] as society' (*BBC*, 5 October 2016; *Reuters*, 7 October 2016; May, 2016).

Reflections on capitalism also emerged from international elites. In its annual meeting, the World Economic Forum (2017: 6–11 & 23), which was composed of international business, political, and academic leaders, called for reforming market capitalism towards an 'inclusive growth' model. Otherwise, 'rising income and wealth disparity' would be the biggest risk for the global economy in the next ten years. By the time of writing, it is not clear whether and how such reflections on capitalism in the UK and beyond would result in any paradigm shift of economic governance, but it is for sure that the Brexit result shows that regional integration, as a conduit of global capitalism, was no longer seen as a means to enhancing economic welfare at least for the UK electorate. Whether and how these reviews and reflections on economic liberalism will result in the paradigm shift of the contemporary economic governance in the UK remain to be seen. It is noticeable that the political correctness of economic liberalism since the 1990s was being under reviewed.

Fourth, the Brexit event shows the unpredictability of referendum even in an age of unprecedented information and data. Among 168 polls being conducted from the wording of the referendum was decided in September 2015 to the voting day in June 2016, more than two-thirds of them pre-

[8] In his first statement on the May government's annual budget, the chancellor of exchequer (2016), Philip Hammond, confirms that the government would increase the benefits of working people by raising national living wage, lowering taxes, and providing more affordable homes.

dicted a victory for Bremain (*The Guardian*, 24 June 2016d). While the flaws of polling designs and techniques are beyond the discussions of this chapter, the inaccuracy of polling on Brexit reveals the unpredictability and dangers of having referendums. As the former UK representative to Taiwan, Michael Reilly, points out (interviewed with the author on 30 August 2016), the Brexit vote was not just a vote on the issue itself. It was also 'a channel for people to express their dissatisfaction with current politics in a way they don't think there will be a cost'. The unexpected Brexit outcome in Wales is a living example. The region supposedly should deliver the same result of Bremain as in Scotland for both have been major beneficiaries of EU funding. Instead, Brexit was the outcome of political discontent from Welsh voters. As the decision-maker's motives of holding such a referendum were not focusing on the issue itself but on Cameron's party management, so were the motives of voters. Referendums have never been as simple and clear-cut as they should be. They are always the synergy of perceivable and non-perceivable factors altogether and therefore increase the difficulties of predictabilities. The Brexit referendum should serve as a caveat to politicians who manipulate referendums for their personal purposes.

## 4.2 The Implications for European Integration: How to Interpret and Respond to Brexit?

Alongside the UK, the other party in the Brexit event was the EU. Being one of the EU's top three economies, Brexit undoubtedly will cause both political and economic impact to the EU. Tangibly, the UK accounts for 15% of the EU economy and one-eighth of its population. Intangibly, it is the first time that the EU encountered an exit from its member state after it has been initiated more than 60 years ago. As Munich Security Conference indicates (2017: 16), Brexit reverses the EU's developments towards an 'ever closer union' by creating an exit precedent.

On the eve of the voting, the first vice president of the European Commission, Frans Timmermans, comments that the outcome of Brexit would be 'a failure of all European politics' (2016). His view echoes among most EU citizens. In a survey of the Pew Research Center, 70% of people surveyed in nine EU members considered Brexit as 'bad for the EU' (*EU Observer*, 7 June 2016). Another survey of Lord Ashcroft shows that the majority, 60%, of public opinions of other 27 EU members supported the UK staying in the EU and the UK was viewed by citizens in other EU members as Europe's 'Big Three' (Raines, 2016c: 14). Along with the public's support and positive perception of the UK's EU membership, what worried EU leadership most, however, was the political contagion of the Brexit referendum to other EU members. Calls for holding similar referendums on EU membership emerged in some EU members such as France, Italy, the Netherlands, and Denmark (*EU Observer*, 23 February & 9 May & 8 June 2016). In his personal reply to the author, an anonymous senior EU official confirms that the Commission worked hard to prevent Brexit from taking place, especially that [Brexit] 'would have no domino effect on other member states' (reply received on 26 July 2016). Deep worries of political contagion by EU leadership and the EU public's sympathy to the UK Cameron government's request for limiting the EU's power explain why the UK was granted 'the special status' in the EU-UK renegotiations on the terms of the UK's EU membership (*EU Observer*, 7 June 2016).

Yet, the outcome of Brexit materialized. In his response to the Brexit outcome, the president of the European Council, Donald Tusk, tried to downplay the significance of the event from his pre-referendum remarks such as Brexit 'will change Europe forever' to the post-referendum comment as it is 'just one incident and not a start of a process' (*EU Observer*, 25 February & 8 July 2016). The president of the European Commission, Jean-Claude Juncker, on the other hand, admits in his State of the Union Address that the EU was 'at least in part, in an existential crisis', but insists that it was not at risk of 'disintegration' (Juncker, 2016). Indeed, the EU will not dissolve just because of one single event of Brexit. But its credential of being the centre of uniting divisive countries in Europe, which is its very original purpose, was questioned. As Oliver (2016: 1323) observes from 59 analyses that most commentators view Brexit to cost the UK economy much more than to the EU's and its impact to the EU, therefore, was rather political than economic. As Germany's economic minister, Sigmar Gabriel, indicates, Brexit was not an economic challenge to the EU but more a psychological and political one (*The Guardian*, 30 August 2016). Raines (2016b) argues that, after Brexit, the EU has to prove it is still a model for the future international cooperation. As Luxembourg's foreign minister, Jean Asselborn, rightly points out, the EU has to explain 'why we needed the European Union after World War II and why we need the European Union for this century' (*EU Observer*, 25 July 2016). Barysch and Bildt (2016) predict that the Brexit incident, in the short term, will lead to anti-EU populist parties growing stronger and louder in their demands. It will also put a pause to European integration as only one in four Germans and one in five Italians prefer to see more EU integration, while 40% of people surveyed would rather see some powers to be returned from the EU to national governments. What is more significant, they argue, is Brexit's long-term effects on the EU. They point out that, for over 50 years, the EU has been the driving force of European politics. It has helped overcome national divisions and stabilize democracy for its member states. Brexit has made the EU's magnetism substantially diminished and thus exposed the continent to the risk of reverting to historical old patterns of national divisions and divergences. In the light of its political and psychological significance to the EU, Sigmar Gabriel reminds EU leaders to deal with Brexit rightly; otherwise, the EU will be in deep trouble (*The Guardian*, 30 August 2016).

To deal with Brexit rightly, the EU has to recognize the implications of the event rightly first. This is the issue that caused many debates and contentions in the EU politics. Why the UK, being a very privileged member in the EU for more than four decades, decided to exit from the EU seems a puzzle for some of its continental counterparts. Jo Leinen (2016: 27), a German MEP, points out that the UK has enjoyed so 'many opt-outs, opt-ins and derogations while maintaining full involvement in the EU's decision-making' during its 43 years of EU membership. It is thus hard to understand why a member state as privileged as the UK would give up such an advantageous position. Interpretations emerged alongside three different lines as follow.

### *4.2.1 Brexit as an Issue of Misinformation and Miscommunication*

Some view the Brexit vote as a misinformation and miscommunication problem. For example, a senior EU official indicates in her reply to the author that the misinformation and disconnection between the EU and its citizens, to a very substantial extent, was due, on the one hand, to the EU's bad public diplomacy and communication and, on the other hand, to the 'tendency of EU governments to turn Brussels into their favorite scapegoat when things don't go well' (reply received on 28 July 2016). Civis Europaeus, a pan-Europe NGO, also argues that the absence of a genuine EU perspective in national and local media to communicate to the public and national political elites' constant bashing on the EU as their scapegoat altogether contributed to the derogation of its image. It cited the remarks of the previous president of the Commission, José Manuel Barroso, to exemplify that 'if you spend all week blaming Europe, you can't ask people to vote for Europe on Sunday' (Civis Europaeus, 2016). Matti Maasikas (2017), the deputy foreign minister of Estonia which took over the presidency of the European Council after Brexit, therefore asks national politicians to demonstrate their courage and conviction to explain the positive effects of EU membership.

Sharing with such views, the president of European Council, Donald Tusk, asked EU leaders to stop the blame game in the post-Brexit summit in Bratislava, and EU leaders agreed to improve communications not just with each other, with EU institutions but, most importantly, with their citizens in their Bratislava Declaration (*Reuters*, 18 September 2016; European Council, 2016a).

#### *4.2.2 Brexit as an Issue of the Failure of Leadership*

However, many EU leaders on the Bratislava summit considered the implications of Brexit for the EU beyond further than just communication problems, but rather representing 'a symptom of broader issues' and it would take more than PR or media strategy to win back the public's support for the EU (*The Guardian*, 16 September 2016; *EU Observer*, 25 July 2016). Some leaders of smaller EU members point out to the problem of the EU's failed leadership. Czech Republic's prime minister, Bohuslav Sobotka, contends that in the past few years, the EU has been plagued by a number of 2 crises, from the euro crisis to the refugee crisis, and now the Brexit crisis. A common feature that can be seen in these crises was the EU's slow and wavering reactions. The lack of rational, systematic approach to these crises, but only reactive crisis management taken by EU leadership under the pressure of these events resulted in the loss of people's confidence in and trust with the competence of the EU (Sobotka, 2016). When taking over the presidency of the EU Council, Slovakia's prime minister, Robert Fico, also suggests that the EU cannot only focus on crisis management and have to come up with substantial answers; otherwise, it will lose the public's confidence in the EU and lead to the rise of populism (*EU Observer*, 6 July 2016). Finland's president, Sauli Niinistö, indicates more bluntly in his public speech that the EU has reached an impasse in many aspects, but this result was self-induced rather than externally imposed. 'Too often, decisions are made to postpone genuine decisions until later. And even when decisions are made, their implementation often adds up to no more than good intentions'. By acting this way, the EU has undermined its own future by losing the confidence of its citizens and nourishing political discontent. He reminds EU leaders that 'discontent is part of democracy', but 'what is essential is where and how it is channeled, and by what kinds of leaders'. Brexit is a case in point.

### *4.2.3 Brexit as an Issue of Wrong Economic Governance*

Other politicians and practitioners contend that it is not the inactive leadership that caused the collapse of the EU's appeal to the public. Rather, it is the wrong governance of EU leadership that caused the EU's impasse. Tomáš Prouza (2016: 28), the Czech State Secretary for European Affairs, points out that all formerly industrialized regions in the UK voted for Brexit. The EU was seen as a catalyst for globalization and industrial restructuring, which brought higher economic output but also exacerbated inequality. Indeed, the president of Germany's central bank, Bundesbank, Jens Weidmann; the former prime minister of Italy, Enrico Letta; and the former EU Council official, Luuk van Middelaar, all agree that, for many Europeans, the EU lost its shine and became the 'Trojan horse of globalization' (Zalan, 2016). Antonio Costa, Portugal's prime minister, further indicates that failing to regulate globalization 'is one of the greatest failures of the European Union' (*Euronews*, 17 November 2016). Therefore, the EU was experiencing a rupture between the winners and losers of globalization and divided the EU society into two houses between elites and common people that have two kinds of world views. Brexit was the most dramatic, backward step taken by those who feel left behind. Letta (2016: 24), therefore, argues that economic inequality within the EU cannot be ignored any longer and the EU cannot be only for globalization's winners.

Indeed, the chief economist of the World Economic Forum, Jennifer Blanke (2016), points out that, since its eastern enlargement in 2004, the EU has encountered a series of setbacks such as the rejection of the European Constitution, the lower and lower turnouts of European Parliament elections, the euro crisis, and the recent refugee crisis. However, among all these issues, the most serious one was inequality. Recent decades have seen a significant increase in income and wealth inequality across Europe. Unemployment, particularly the young, remained high in many EU countries. Median income was kept stagnant, which means growth has simply not been inclusive. These facts naturally led average citizens to a belief that their lives and those of their children would be worse off than previous generations and the EU was held to blame.

Evidences from the International Labour Organization (ILO) especially point out to the economic inequality that young Europeans were experiencing. In its report, the ILO warns that, under the policy of 'jobs at any cost' in many EU members, Europeans between 18 and 24 years old faced 'relative poverty' because of low-paid jobs, mostly in the form of temporary or part-time jobs. Young people have replaced the elderly as the group at the greatest risk of living in poverty. A large majority of young people, 60% in Spain and Greece and 70% in Italy and Romania, took temporary jobs because of the lack of permanent employment since the 2008 financial crisis. Such involuntary part-time employment, accordingly, was closely associated with the youth poverty (*EU Observer*, 2016q).

But since when the EU changed from its proudly claimed social market model to the one that only aggravated economic inequality? A number of commentators point to the management of the euro crisis during 2008–2015. In his reply to the author, Francisco Gomezmartos, the senior official of the European Parliament, explains that the EU used to be seen by its citizens as a solution to peace (after the war in ex-Yugoslavia), prosperity, and jobs linked to its achievements of the world's largest internal market and introduction of a new currency, the euro. However, such perceptions were changed after the breakout of the euro crisis because of the decisions and policies adopted at EU level. Austerity policies, as responses to the crisis, required EU members to reform social security and pension systems, and they had direct impacts on 'the core of economic and living conditions'. His comments echoed among several EU politicians.

The vice president of the European Parliament, Dimitris Papadimoulis (2017), asserts that austerity politics worsen social inequalities and weaken the welfare state. Letta (2016: 24), being Italy's prime minister during 2013–2014, also agrees that the euro crisis and, most importantly, the way that the EU dealt with the crisis overturn the equity of the EU, in which the majority of its population was turned from the winners of globalization to the losers. In their joint statement, the prime ministers of Portugal and Greece criticize austerity policies failing on its own terms as it had caused the economy depressed and the society divided by reducing the social safety net that enables equitable growth (Tsipras and Costa, 2016). Middelaar points out that this is why the old narratives of the EU being a provider of peace and prosperity were no longer sufficient to convince dissatisfactory and disillusioned voters (Zalan, 2016), and the EU's legitimacy, based on providing common benefits, was 'in question' (Maurice, 2016: 20). Therefore, Taylor (2016) calls for breaking the link between 'Europe and austerity', while Papadimoulis (2017) and Dean Baker (*Politico*, 25 June 2016b), the co-director of the Washington-based Center for Economic and Policy Research, both contend that the EU must 'take a new political and economic model' in order to save the EU from dissolution.

Other commentators, on the other hand, prescribe to more long-term and structural roots rather than just austerity policies. In his talk to the author, Jan Zielonka (2016), a professor of politics at Oxford University, contends that the EU was supposed to reconcile the strong and the weak, the large and the small. As a matter of fact, the EU has been undergoing a long economic revolution of neo-liberal ideology, referred by some as globalization or Americanization. Such a process manifests itself in deregulation, marketization, and privatization, and cuts in social welfare benefits and environmental protection so as to pursue better competitiveness and leave redistribution to the markets. The EU's 'Stockholm consensus', a global brand of functional and generous welfare state, has been prevailed by the 'Washington consensus' of its free and unregulated market ideas. The harsh austerity policies after the euro crisis were only the products of such an ideology. This is then understandable why many people, especially those unemployed, see the EU as an agent of multinational banks or German industrialists (the talk was held on 8 August 2016). Luuk van Middelaar, who served on the cabinet of the EU Council under the presidency of Herman Van Rompuy, also verifies that, for a long time, EU policy-makers believed in the so-called Brussels Doctrine, in which economic interdependence through free-market integrations among EU countries were believed to lead to 'grateful societies' (Zalan, 2016). Lang (2016) exemplifies such liberal economic governance with the recent example of Apple's legal tax evasion in Ireland. She argues that this case vividly shows, instead of taxing multinational corporations and investing in social welfare, European leaders yielded to and served their interests. Such economic mismanagement was much more harmful than the refugee crisis to public trust with EU leadership.

A survey of the Pew Research Center (2016: 6) confirms the negative perceptions of EU citizens on the EU's management of the economy. Among ten EU members being surveyed, the overwhelming majority of public opinions across Europe disapprove the EU's economic governance, only in two countries, Germany and Poland, the share of approval outweighs that of disapproval. In Italy, France, and Spain, there were as many as around two-thirds of people expressing their disapprovals, while the highest proportion was found in Greece (92%). On the issue of the refugee crisis, public opinions in ten countries surveyed all disapprove the

EU's governance. In other words, on two issues that citizens feel most personally and directly in their daily life, the EU was seen as incompetent, and Euroscepticism therefore became 'the new normal' as Harding describes (2016b). As Fligstein et al. (2012: 118–19) remind, 'the ultimate fate of the EU is how ordinary citizens view the role of Europe in their lives', because, after all, democracies follow the preferences of the electorate.

Reading the messages of growing economic inequality and deteriorating distributive justice implied from Brexit in the EU, most commentators suggest EU leadership to return to the European social model. Prouza (2016: 28) argues that the EU has to find a common approach to moderating the costs of globalization by restoring the European social model; otherwise, the increase in economic inequality and decrease in social cohesion will result in popular discontent growing and extremist populism rising. Blanke (2016) similarly suggests the EU to introduce a new type of social contract to attack on the inequalities both within and across the Union. Middelaar (Zalan, 2016) asks the EU to stop undermining the European welfare state and should provide not just freedoms and opportunities but also protection for its citizens both in external border and in economic life. As Weidmann (*The Guardian*, 19 September 2016) points out, '[market] integration cannot be an end in itself, it has to make sense'.

### *4.3 Perspectives Held by This Research*

These three factors outlined above, to a larger or lesser extent, all contributed to the public's anti-EU sentiment. However, the EU's problem of misinformation and miscommunication is not a new phenomenon. Since the rectification crisis of the Maastricht Treaty in 1992, the EU has been suffering from this disadvantage. The veto on the EU Constitution Treaty in 2005 is another example. However, such a disadvantage has not substantially affected the public's commitment to European integration. According to Eurobarometer, from 1994 to 2013, a clear majority (47–54%) of people surveyed were supportive of the EU. Even during the period of 2009–2013, the height of the euro crisis, there was as much as 47% of people surveyed supported the EU, while only a minority, 17%, thought EU membership was 'a bad thing', despite the fact that only 29% of respondents thought they were 'well-informed' regarding EU information (European Commission, 2014). On the other hand, a post-Brexit referendum survey showed that, compared to other political institutions, the EU received higher support than national governments and parliaments of member states (European Commission, 2016c: 14).

In other words, the majority of European citizens, indeed, have been 'badly informed' about EU-related information. However, such a permanent weakness did not cause a challenge to the EU or diminish the public's trust in it. Compared to the EU, member states enjoyed much more resources and channels in propaganda, but the latter did not gain higher public support as a result. Therefore, to interpret Brexit as an issue of misinformation and miscommunication was hardly convincing.

As to the explanation of leadership failure, indeed, leading countries, especially Germany, were heavily criticized for their inadequate behaviours in recent crises that the EU encountered, and their bad performance, to some extent, aggravated the seriousness of the crises. Germany's inaction and slow responses to the euro crisis helped the crisis expand from the periphery of the eurozone to core economies. However, when active leadership finally demonstrated after Germany forcefully put the fiscal compact passing through among 22 EU members in just two months, the crisis was far from over. Similarly, Germany's strong leadership in the refugee crisis was not appreciated by a number of EU members, but rather increased more internal disputes and conflicts over the relocation system and the public's dissatisfaction with the EU. In other words, the failure of leadership in crisis management, indeed, has escalated the situations; nevertheless, strong leadership has not solved, if not complicated, the crises either, let alone restore the public's confidence in the European project.

Viewing from this perspective, the collapse of the public's faith in the EU, as Brexit revealed, was not due to the lack of strong leadership but due to wrong policy answers they provided. Empirical evidences revealed in the Brexit referendum—clear divisions between regions, generations, educational background, income levels, and social classes—highlight the distributive (in)justice as the deciding factor behind voting behaviours. The increase in economic inequality and deterioration of distributive injustice were largely the products of the EU's wrong governance and the symptoms of the EU's two structural flaws in its governance. First, EU leadership, with their firm belief in economic liberalism, has been shirking their duties on distributive justice and left the issue to markets to take care for a long time. The fact that Brexit outcome was delivered at a time when the UK economy was in recovery explains that a rising economy cannot lift all boats. Neither can market mechanism automatically alleviate economic inequality. The Brexit outcome, therefore, is the price for EU leadership's ignorance of the deterioration of distributive justice. Second, following the same economic ideology, European integration has been reduced to a large economic project with its major achievements of creating the single market and currency that focus on enhancing market efficiency only. No policy attention to social cohesion and integration has been ever properly addressed. In other words, 60 years on, European integration has realized only in economic and monetary aspects without social integration and protection in parallel. The EU, as a result, has been simplified as an 'economic/capitalist Europe', but not a 'social Europe'. Furthermore, in order to pursue 'economic Europe' better functioning, social protection at the member-state level has to be dismantled without replacements substituted at the EU level. The receding social safety net within the EU, accordingly, aggravated the distributive injustice, especially at a time of economic crisis. The EU, therefore, was experiencing a rupture between the winners and losers of 'economic Europe', and divided the EU society into two houses between the elite and the common people who had two kinds of world view. Brexit was the most dramatic, backward step taken by those who feel left behind from this 'economic Europe'.

Such wrong governance exercised by EU leadership not only distorts the very aims of European integration—achieving a 'political Europe', aimed at perpetual peace and unity—but also would backfire on their own economic project. The Brexit outcome, thus, should be seen as the most serious warning to the EU's long wrong and distorted governance.

### 4.4 Responses to Brexit from EU Leaders: Competing Arguments Between 'More Europe' and 'Less Europe'

In their common statement to the result of the Brexit referendum, EU leaders of 27 member states, the Council, and Commission indicate that they will start a political reflection on the EU's future (European Council, 2016b). However, such a reflection failed to produce any consensus on reforms or policy changes in the post-Brexit EU. Instead, EU leaders, reportedly, were divided on how the EU should react to Brexit and the rising Euroscepticism. One view, supported by France, Italy, Spain, Portugal, and Greece, was inclined to further integration to encounter the common problems of growth and security, the so-called more Europe (*The Guardian*, 23 August 2016; *EU Observer*, 26 August & 9 September 2016). In its Italian Economic and Finance Ministry's report (2016: 2–8), the Italian government recognizes the inappropriateness of the EU's management of the euro crisis as it exacerbated divergences and segmentation between core and periphery. It therefore calls for EU leaders to change economic governance from the current austerity policies to more growth-friendly fiscal ones and to introduce pan-EU unemployment benefit and insurance schemes as the first steps to build necessary trust for more further integration (Italian Ministry of Economy and Finance, 2016).

By contrast, the other view, supported by Germany, Czech Republic, Hungary, Poland, and Slovakia, was inclined to less interfering but more efficient EU powers, the so-called better Europe. Two sub-groups, EU-Med and Visegrad group of four eastern European countries, emerged to compete within the EU as a result (*The Guardian*, 23 August 2016; *EU Observer*, 26 August & 9 September 2016). Germany's refusal to yield on the governance of the economy and immigration led to Italy's prime minister, Matteo Renzi, refused to co-host the press conference with the German and French leaders after the post-Brexit summit in Bratislava. As Lithuania's president, Dalia Grybauskaitė, comments, the fragmentation among EU leadership casts a more serious challenge than Brexit (*EU Observer*, 16 September 2016). The open discords between leading EU countries embody what John Holmes (2016), the director of Ditchley Foundation, describes a core and fundamental dilemma that the EU faced: it cannot solve recurrent crises without further integration, but such an approach was less acceptable than ever after Brexit.

Indeed, in his post-Brexit speech to the European Parliament, the European Commission president, Jean-Claude Juncker, warns EU leaders that he has witnessed EU integration for several decades but never seen so much fragmentation and so little commonality in the EU at a moment when it had 'a very important choice to make'. Although aligning with the positions of Italy, Juncker did not make any significant policy change from the current EU governance. He recognizes the harms of unemployment and social inequality to citizens' trust with the EU and emphasizes the EU as 'a social market economy', not the Wild West, but without having the mandate from EU members, little concrete measures were added to his 'social Europe' idea, and there were seen only moderate changes to the current economic governance by promising to apply austerity rules flexibly (Juncker, 2016).

The competing views on the EU's responses to Brexit, in essence, reflect the long battle between intergovernmentalism and neofunctionalism in the history of European integration. Only this time was different in that Germany, in contrast to its traditional integrationist characteristic, behaved more nationalistic. Due to the lack of consensus on policy responses among EU leaders, the EU, again, was expected to muddle the impact of Brexit through, and this only re-confirms people's negative perceptions of the EU's inapt leadership and economic mismanagement. The unsolved trust crisis with the EU would only guarantee the continuing growth of Euroscepticism and promise another crisis to develop in the near future.

## 5 The Implications Beyond Europe: For Worldwide Regional Integration

As a response to the Brexit outcome, global stock markets immediately fell by 10%, and the IMF (2016: 1–3) cut down the global growth forecasts by 0.1% to 3.1% for 2016 and 3.4% for 2017, respectively, as the event materialized 'an important downside risk for the world economy'. While as the IMF (2016: 1) rightly warns, the economic effects of Brexit were still unfolding, the greater damages of this event to the world economy and worldwide regional integration were those non-quantifiable. Brexit, no doubt, was a backlash to the mainstream governance of economic liberalism and its major policy achievement—globalization.

Given that the EU has been a role model of regional integration, Blanke (2016) argues that Brexit made the logic of regional integration no longer inevitable. Not just regional integration, this event challenges the heart of post-war economic establishment—globalization in the form of global free trade. As Niblett (2017) contends, since 1945, Western policy-makers have believed in open markets, and the EU has been the advance guard of this liberal international order. Brexit represents the demise of such a liberal dream. In its 2017 report, the World Economic Forum (2017: 11) interprets such an event as 'a tipping point' of globalization. Indeed, as the former UK prime minister, Gordon Brown (2016), indicates, 'the elephant in the room [of Brexit] is globalization'. Voters from 'the hollowing out of industrial towns as a result of the collapse of manufacturing in the face of Asian competition' voted for Brexit. They, who felt on 'the wrong side of globalization' and did not see globalization tamed in their interests, decided to 'take back control' to protect themselves against global change. Mark Carney (2016: 3), the governor of the Bank of England, explains further that, to these people, globalization was associated with 'low wages, insecure employment, stateless corporations and striking inequalities'. Voters' negative perceptions on globalization were justifiable. According to the World Economic Forum report (2017: 23), the incomes of the top 1% grew by 31%, while the incomes of the remaining 99% barely improved (less than 0.5%) in the US between 2009 and 2012. The Munich Security Conference (2017: 9) also indicates that 65–70% of households in advanced economies faced stagnant and declining incomes during 2005–2014. The same figure during 1993–2005 is just 0–2%. Jeremy Corbyn, the leader of the UK's Labour Party, therefore argues that, for the majority of people, it can no longer be argued that free trade and free markets alone would deliver prosperity (*The Guardian*, 15 September 2016).

Most commentators, such as Parakilas and Wickett (2016), Creasy (2016: 21), Kettle (2016), Baker (2016: 3), and Ip (2016: 1 & 6), share similar views. Baker (2016: 3), Ip (2016: 1 & 6), and the *New York Times* (24 June 2016) agree that there were, indeed, some specific contexts to the UK in this referendum, but there were commonalities across Europe and the US. Brexit represents a watershed in two related trends: anti-establishment politics and anti-globalization. It was the first time in the post-war era that voters in an advanced economy decided to withdraw from a regional free trade area. *The Economist* (24 June 2016) also argues that the UK, being a champion of free trade for a long time, can vote to revoke a regional trade deal; how much faith can businesses put in other international trade agreements? As Kettle (2016) points out, since the end of the twentieth century, capitalism and democracy have triumphed in a way that economic liberalism has been the only orthodox. Brexit was a revolt against such a modern economic liberalism.

What were the factors that led to such a revolt? Brown (2016) argues that it was the massive inequalities brought by globalization and the former became the latter's Achilles' heel. Creasy (2016: 21) also agrees that globalization creates gaps that swallow communities and individuals and the UK's vote for Brexit was partly driven by the issue of economic inequality being ignored for too long. Ip (2016: 6) especially specifies the effects of the 2008 global financial crisis and the following economic slump that fuelled the public's disillusion with the established politics. Approval ratings of governments in 20 major democracies have been in steady decline since 2010. The continuity of economic hardship has led to a majority of the electorate ignoring the warnings of political elites over economics, as the benefits of globalization did not show on them. Parakilas and Wickett (2016) also argue that the Brexit vote has changed the world fundamentally as it was the first time when political elites could call the shot has gone because of the growing social and economic inequalities. Danielle Pletka (*Politico*, 25 June 2016b), the senior vice president of American Enterprise Institute, also contends that although there was a mob quality of Brexit supporters, their resentments and complaints on economic inequality, tides of refugees, and anger at government were real. Nelson (2016: 8–9) interprets the Brexit referendum as 'socio-economic battles' between the losers of globalization against its winners and as an attempt to manage globalization by their, not Brussels', hands. Brown (2016), Ip (2016: 6), and Pletka (*Politico*, 25 June 2016b) thus predict a retreat from the post-war political and economic consensus on promoting worldwide free trade, if the benefits of globalization cannot be shared more fairly. Parakilas and Wickett (2016), Hawking (2016), and Pletka (*Politico*, 25 June 2016b) further warn of the risk of returning to 1933, a time when the world was fragmented by isolationism and protectionism.

However, as the chief of the World Trade Organization (WTO), Roberto Azevêdo, and the World Economic Forum both remind, isolationism and protectionism were wrong answers to the challenges of globalization as they create more problems than they solve (*Associated Press*, 7 November 2016; the World Economic Forum, 2017: 25). Farvis (2016: 17) also indicates that developing countries looked into the wealth of the West and aspired to make their lives better. If such expectations were hindered by the rising inequality and protectionism, they would turn to alternative ideologies such as race, nationality, and identity, and the moral foundations of global system would be called into question. Parakilas and Wickett (2016) therefore call for political leadership to find ways to solutions to social and economic inequalities and to ensure the benefits of globalization can reach broader population. Brown (2016) therefore proposes global political leaders to set up a world commission to examine all controversial issues arising from globalization so as to make it fair and inclusive for everyone.

As a matter of fact, even before Brexit, protectionism around the world has been creeping in. The WTO indicates that protectionist measures in the G20 were multiplying at their fastest rate since 2008. But the Brexit outcome only ensures nationalist populism and protectionism to be stronger (*The Economist*, 24 June 2016). Kori Schake from Hoover Institute (*Politico*, 25 June 2016b) also contends that the Brexit vote was a turning point that marks the peak of the global trend of regional integration. She foresees governments to be less confident in actions and more cautious about any signs of public disapproval in signing regional and international free trade agreements. Evidences can be found in the recent examples of the nearly collapsed EU-Canada free trade agreement—Comprehensive Economic and Trade Agreement (CETA)—and the factually dead EU-US trade deal, Transatlantic Trade and Investment Partnership (TTIP).

The CETA was concluded between the EU and Canada in 2014 and scheduled to be put into effect in 2017. As a response to the growing scepticism from the public about the EU's external trade policy, the Commission changed its initial position on fast-track legal procedure only with EU institutions but without the approvals of national parliaments of member states to acceptance that CETA would be sent to national parliaments for rectification at Germany and France's insistence (*DW*, 5 July 2016). The CETA, unexpectedly, was vetoed by the regional parliament of Wallonia in Belgium for the reasons that it put corporate interests before citizens on the eve of signing the treaty in October 2016. Reacting to the failure of signing the CETA, Canada's international trade minister, Chrystia Freeland, said that this episode shows that 'the EU is not capable to have an international agreement even with a country that has values that are so European', while EU leaders responded in that they had to 'take into account the concerns of [European] citizens' (*EU Observer*, 21 & 27 & 28 October 2016). The deadlock was finally unblocked after 36 documents that address to Wallonia's concerns were attached to the CETA and the treaty was finally signed on 30 October 2016 (European Commission, 2016b). Although the CETA was saved at the last minute, the event shows, as a senior EU diplomat puts it, 'the growing contestation of the negative consequences of globalization, of which trade deals are considered a vector' (*EU Observer*, 21 October 2016).

After the Wallonia event, there can be observed some changes emerging in the policy-making of the EU's trade strategy both externally and internally. Externally, there was a shift in the EU's emphasis from free trade to fair trade. EU leaders, reportedly, discussed the so-called trade defence instruments to protect EU economy from trade dumping, especially on Chinese products, a measure which has been blocked in the council of EU trade ministers since 2013. The UK and Nordic countries used to oppose such measures, but now a UK official from the May government said: 'effective trade defense instruments should be proportionate, not protectionist'. Such discussions mark a 'change of atmosphere', and an agreement on trade defence was expected to reach by the end of 2016 (*EU Observer*, 21 October 2016). The president of the Commission confirms such a policy change. In his annual speech to the European

Parliament, Juncker (2016) indicates clearly that his Commission would employ trade defence instruments against China's steel industry by imposing anti-dumping tariff on China's steel industry, as the EU 'should not be naïve free traders' and should 'protect European workers and industries in an increasingly globalized world'. His remarks implicitly responded to the call from Wallonia's leader, Paul Magnette, that the EU's trade agreements need to think about 'which globalization we want' (*EU Observer*, 21 October 2016).

Internally, Wallonia's veto on the CETA also led to a call to review the way that EU negotiates trade deals. In the past, international trade deals were the exclusive power of the Commission. That caused criticisms for the lack of transparency and often resulted in backlashes when national parliaments or NGOs started looking into details, as in the case of CETA (Ibid.). The fact that the CETA, which had been under negotiations for seven years, was nearly strangled by a small Belgian region only shows the end to the EU's top-down trade policy-making. As Olivet of Transnational Institute, a Netherland-based NGO (2016), argues, the Wallonia episode shows the public demand a real debate on the contents of the EU's trade policy. The European Ombudsman (2017a, b) formally issued letters to the European Council and Commission, respectively, requiring them to adopt transparency policy in the following negotiations on Brexit and trade deals, 'because there has been a culture-shift,...,and civic society activism is also forcing EU executive' to do so (*EU Observer*, 2017). More bottom-up inputs to the EU's future trade policy-making, on the one hand, would increase policy legitimacy and decrease public opposition to signing trade agreements, but on the other hand, it also complicate and prolong negotiation processes, which imply more difficult to conclude a full-blown trade agreement in the future.

Other evidences were from the case of the TTIP. Negotiations on the TTIP started from 2013 and aimed for completion before the end of the US Obama administration. After 14 rounds and hundreds of meetings in the past 3 years, nothing was agreed by both sides and no single chapter was able to conclude. A senior official of the EU Council and Germany's TTIP rapporteur both admitted that the TTIP was 'actually dead' (interviewed with the author on 20 July 2016; *EU Observer*, 23 September 2016u & 18 July 2016v). The lack of progress in the TTIP, criticized by France's trade minister, Matthias Fekl, was the result of the US' uncompromised position. However, the pressures of uncompromising derived from both sides of the Atlantic. Unprecedented social protests were invoked in

Germany, France, Spain, and Poland for the fears that the TTIP would threaten the EU's environmental standards and workers' rights and therefore a 'direct path to poverty'. Fekl admits that there was no political support for the TTIP from France (*Financial Times*, 30 August 2016; *Reuters*, 15 October 2016). Neither was in the US. Schneider-Petsinger (2016) points out that of all the pressing problems facing the US was income inequality. More than half, 52%, thought the gap between the rich and the poor was the biggest problem. No other issue, including terrorism, race relations, immigration, or crime, caused so much concerns, and income inequality became the central issue in the 2016 presidential election. Rodgers (2016) further suggests that the rise of Donald Trump in the 2016 election symbolizes the US isolationism of 'America first' for the first time since the 1930s. As he reminds, Trump did not invent economic and cultural conservatism. He just rode on these tides. Protectionism and isolationism run deep in the US economic history, but, as he points out, what was different this time was that such protectionist sentiments coincided with those in other advanced economies such as France, the UK, and Germany in the form of the rise of their populist right-wing parties.

With Trump's victory in the 2016 US presidential election, more uncertainties would be expected in the negotiations on the TTIP and Trans-Pacific Partnership (TPP), the US' two major regional integration projects. James Moore (2016), the deputy business editor of *The Independent*, argues that Trump's election means that the golden age of free trade agreements would be over. It sounded the death knell not only to the TPP, the world's biggest regional free trade agreement, but also to the TTIP. Another under threat was the North American Free Trade Area (NAFTA). At Trump's insistence, NAFTA was renegotiated and replaced by United States-Mexico-Canada Agreement (USMCA). Regional trade agreements, pursued by the Obama administration, were likely to be 'fired' under the Trump administration to materialize his 'America first' promise.

## 6 Conclusion

At the eve of the 60th anniversary of the Rome Treaty, European integration witnessed the UK withdrawing from the EU. It was the first time since the movement was launched 60 years ago. The historic Brexit referendum, indeed, was triggered by a political miscalculation. The unexpected Brexit result, on the surface, was an accident, too, which can be attributed to the storming weather on the voting day which led to a lower turnout, failures of the Bremain campaign, inactive leadership of Labour, and the Bregret votes from Wales. However, the clear divisions between regions, generations, educational background, and social classes revealed in this vote highlight a much more structural and deeper issue—economic inequality and distributive injustice—which have been ignored since the triumph of economic liberalism in the 1990s and aggravated after global financial crisis in 2008. Those who did not benefit from but felt deprived from European integration voted for Brexit. They were just as economically rational as those voted for Bremain. The realities of Brexit and the victory of Trump for the 2016 US presidency mean that if political leaders in the UK, the EU, and the US did not address to economic inequality with timely and concrete policy responses, then Trump's famous remarks that 'globalization…wipe out our middle class and our jobs' would reappear in every referendums and elections in coming years. European Council president, Donald Tusk, indicates after Wallonia's veto on the CETA that it could be the last free trade agreement for the EU 'if we are not able to convince people that we negotiate to protect their interests' (*EU Observer*, 21 October 2016). Indeed, European integration and globalization, both in the form of free trade agreements, were not an end in themselves; they were the means to enhancing people's economic well-being. Without the 'responsible capitalism' and 'fair and inclusive globalization', economic rationales that supported regional and global integration, be it European integration, CETA, TTIP, TPP, or NAFTA, could not be justified.

While EU leaders were stuck in the disputes over 'more or less Europe' as a response to Brexit, messages sent from this historic event to European integration were crystal clear. Whatever the scenario that the EU would evolve into, a 'social Europe' that reconciles an 'economic Europe' more inclusive and fairer is required to move European integration forward and to keep a 'political Europe' sustainable. Whether and how the shocks of Brexit would result in any changes to the EU's distorted governance—its long-held 'Brussels Doctrine'—remains to be seen. What is for sure is that failure to address economic inequality and distributive injustice with timely and correct policy answers would cause justifications underpinning European integration collapse and promise the EU with another crisis emerging in the near future.

# References

## I. Interviews and Replies to Questions

### Interviews with

An anonymous senior EU official at Unit of Economic Affairs and Competitiveness of the Council of the European Union on 20 July 2016 in Taipei.

Gomezmartos, Francisco, Head of the Unit of Relations with National Parliament of European Parliament on 9 May 2016 in Taipei.

Reilly, Michael, the former Representative of the British Office Taipei (2006–2009) on 30 August 2016 in Taipei.

Zielonka, Jan, Professor of European Politics at Oxford University, on 8 August 2016 in Taipei.

### Replies via Emailing from

An anonymous senior EU official at Unit of European Civil Service and Social Dialogue of the European Commission received on 26 July 2016.

An anonymous senior EU official at Unit of Directorate-general Communication and Document Management of the Council of the European Union received on 28 July 2016.

Gomezmartos, Francisco, Head of the Unit of Relations with National Parliament of European Parliament received on 14 May 2016.

## II. Official Publications

Cameron, David (2013), 'Prime Minister David Cameron discussed the future of the European Union at the Bloomberg', Prime Minister's Office, 23 January 2013, available at https://www.gov.uk/government/speeches/eu-speech-at-bloomberg.

——— (2016), 'PM statement following cabinet meeting on EU settlement', Prime Minister's Office, 20 February 2016, https://www.gov.uk/government/speeches/pms-statement-following-cabinet-meeting-on-eu-settlement-20-february-2016.

Carney, Mark (2016), 'The spectre of Monetarism', Speech by Mark Carney, the Governor of the Bank of England, 5 December 2016, http://www.bankofengland.co.uk/publications/Pages/speeches/2016/946.aspx (accessed 21 January 2017).

European Commission (2014), *Eurobarometer 40 Years: Effects of the Economic and Financial Crisis on European Public Opinion*, Brussels: European Commission.

——— (2016a), *Standard Eurobarometer 85: Public Opinion in the European Union*, Brussels: European Commission.

——— (2016b), 'EU-Canada summit: An historic juncture in our political and economic partnership', Press Release on 30 October 2016.

——— (2016c), *Standard Eurobarometer 86: Public Opinion in the European Union*, Brussels: European Commission.

European Council (2016a), 'The Bratislava Declaration', Informal Meeting of the 27 Heads of State or Government, 16/09/2016, available at http://www.consilium.europa.eu/en/meetings/european-council/2016/09/16-informal-meeting/.

——— (2016b), 'Informal meeting at 27 Brussels Statement', 29 June 2016, available at http://www.consilium.europa.eu/en/press/press-releases/2016/06/29-27ms-informal-meeting-statement/.

European Ombudsman (2017a), Letter from the Ombudsman to the President Juncker Concerning information for the Public on the Upcoming Negotiations aimed at reaching agreement on the UK's Withdrawal from the EU, 28 February 2017, https://www.ombudsman.europa.eu/en/cases/correspondence.faces/en/76528/html.bookmark (accessed 5 April 2017).

——— (2017b), Letter from the Ombudsman to the Secretary-General of the Council of the EU concerning Public Information on the UK's Withdrawal from the EU, 28 February 2017, https://www.ombudsman.europa.eu/cases/correspondence.faces/en/77306/html.bookmark (accessed 5 April 2017).

G7 Ise-Shima Leaders' Declaration, issued on G7 Ise-Shima Summit, 26–27 May 2016, available at http://www.mofa.go.jp/files/000160266.pdf.

Hammond, Phillip (2016a), 'Autumn Statement 2016: Phillip Hammond's Speech', House of Commons, 23 November 2016, available at https://www.gov.uk/government/speeches/autumn-statement-2016-philip-hammonds-speech.

IMF (2016), *World Economic Outlook Update*, Issued on 19 July 2016, Washington DC: IMF.

Italian Ministry of Economy and Finance (2016), *A Shared European Policy Strategy for Growth, Jobs and Stability*, Rome: Ministry of Economy and Finance.

Juncker, Jean-Claude (2016), 'Sate of the Union Address 2016: Towards a better Europe – a Europe that protects, empowers and defends', The Speech of the President of European Commission, 14 September 2016, available at http://europa.eu/rapid/press-release_SPEECH-16-3043_en.htm.

May, Theresa (2016), 'PM speech to the Lord Mayor's Banquet: 14 November 2016', UK Prime Minister's Office, 10 Downing Street, https://www.gov.uk/government/speeches/pm-speech-to-the-lord-mayors-banquet-14-november-2016 (accessed 18 January 2017).

OECD (2016), 'The Economic Consequences of Brexit: A Taxing Decision', *OECD Economic Policy Paper No. 16*, Paris: OECD.

The UK Electoral Commission (2016), 'Official result of the EU referendum is declared by the Electoral Commission in Manchester', available at http://www.electoralcommission.org.uk/i-am-a/journalist/electoral-commission-media-centre/news-releases-referendums/official-result-of-the-eu-referendum-is-declared-by-electoral-commission-in-manchester.

Tsipras, Alexis and Antonio Costa (2016), Prime Minister Office of Portuguese Republic, *Joint Statement of the Prime Ministers of Greece and Portugal*, issued on 11 April 2016.

United Nations (2016), 'Committee on Economic, Social and Cultural Rights hear from human rights institutions and civil society from the United Kingdom, the former Yugoslav Republic of Macedonia and Angola', 13 June 2016, available at http://www.ohchr.org/en/NewsEvents/Pages/DisplayNews.aspx?NewsID=20087&LangID=E.

## III. Books and Articles

Baalen, Hans Van (2016), 'Reform the EU, with or without Britain', *EU Observer*, 20 June 2016, available at https://euobserver.com/opinion/133883.

Baker, Gerard (2016), 'Britain fires a loud shot that is heard round the world', *The Wall Street Journal*, 27 June 2016, p. 3.

Bale, Tim (2013), 'Tory Euroscepticism: How did it come to this and where does it go from here', *Euroscope*, 53: 12–13.

Bailey, Olivia (2016), 'Introduction', in O. Bailey ed., *Fabian Policy Report: Facing the Unknown*, London: Fabian Society, pp. 2–3.

Barr, Caelainn (2016), 'The areas and demographics where the Brexit vote was won', *The Guardian*, 24 June 2016, available at https://www.theguardian.com/news/datablog/2016/jun/24/the-areas-and-demographics-where-the-brexit-vote-was-won.

Barysch, Katinka, and Carl Bildt (2016), 'The big questions after the Brexit vote', *World Economic Forum Article*, 24 June 2016, available at https://www.weforum.org/agenda/2016/06/the-big-questions-after-the-brexit-vote/.

Benn, Hilary (2016), 'Making the case for Britain in Europe', 11 February 2016, *Speech of UK Shadow Foreign Secretary at Chatham House*, London: The Royal Institute of International Affairs.

Blair, Tony, 'Tony Blair: Brexit's stunning coup', *The New York Times*, 24 June 2016, available at http://www.nytimes.com/2016/06/26/opinion/tony-blair-brexits-stunning-coup.html?_r=0.

Blanke, Jennifer (2016), '3 factors that could hold Europe together', *Research Paper of World Economic Forum*, 27 June 2016, available at https://www.weforum.org/agenda/2016/06/after-brexit-why-europe-matters-and-what-it-must-do-to-survive/.

Bohuslav Sobotka (2016), 'Our common path: EU cohesion, not trenches', *EU Observer*, 16 September 2016, available at https://euobserver.com/opinion/135121.

Brown, Gordon (2016), 'The key lesson of Brexit is that globalization must work for all of Britain', *The Guardian*, 29 June 2016, available at https://www.theguardian.com/commentisfree/2016/jun/29/key-lesson-of-brexit-globalisation-must-work-for-all-of-britain.

Burn-Murdoch, John (2016), 'The demographics that drove Brexit', *Financial Times*, 24 June 2016, available at http://blogs.ft.com/ftdata/2016/06/24/brexit-demographic-divide-eu-referendum-results/#.

Cadwalladr, Carole (2016), 'View from Wales: town showered with EU cash vote to leave EU', *The Guardian*, 25 June 2016, available at https://www.theguardian.com/uk-news/2016/jun/25/view-wales-town-showered-eu-cash-votes-leave-ebbw-vale.

Cameron, David and George Osborne (2016), 'David Cameron and George Osborne: Brexit would put our economy in serious danger', *The Telegraph*, 22 May 2016, available at http://www.telegraph.co.uk/news/2016/05/22/david-cameron-and-george-osborne-brexit-would-put-our-economy-in/.

Civis Europaeus (2016), 'How to save the EU', *EU Observer*, 13 September 2016, available at https://euobserver.com/opinion/134935.

Chowdhury, Hasan (2016), 'How much impact has voter turnout had on the EU referendum result?', *New Statesman*, 24 June 2016, available at http://www.newstatesman.com/print/node/302983.

Creasy, Stella (2016), 'Easing that sinking feeling', *The World Today*, August and September 2016, pp. 20–1.

Curtice, John (2016), *How Deeply Does Britain's Euroscepticism Run?*, London: NatCen Social Research.

Dunford, Daniel and Ashley Kirk (2016), 'How did turnout affect EU referendum result?', *The Telegraph*, 1 July 2016, available at http://www.telegraph.co.uk/news/2016/06/24/how-did-turnout-affect-the-eu-referendum-result/.

Eagle, Angela (2016), 'We must see Brexit as the end of an era and commit to radically reshaping social democracy', in O. Bailey ed., *Fabian Policy Report: Facing the Unknown*, London: Fabian Society, pp. 6–7.

Erlanger, Steven (2016), '"Brexit" opens uncertain chapter in Britain's storied history', *The New York Times*, 24 June 2016, available at http://www.nytimes.com/2016/06/25/world/europe/brexit-european-union-uncertain-chapter-in-britains-storied-history.html?_r=0.

Farvis, Dan (2016), 'Britain can't afford austerity', *The World Today*, August & September 2016, p. 17.

Fligstein, Neil, Alina Polyakova and Wayne Sandholtz (2012), 'European integration, nationalism and European identity', *Journal of Common Market Studies*, Vol. 50, No. S1, pp. 106–22.

Fox, Ben (2016a), 'Leach the poison from the political well', *EU Observer*, 21 June 2016, https://euobserver.com/opinion/133912.

——— (2016b), 'Young voters could keep UK in EU', *EU Observer*, 10 June 2016, available at https://euobserver.com/uk-referendum/133787.

——— (2016c), 'Brexit by accident', *Europe in Review 2016*, December 2016, pp. 8–9.

George, Stephen (1999), 'Britain: Anatomy of a Eurosceptic state', *Journal of European Integration*, Vol. 21, No. 1, pp. 1–19.

Glencross, Andrew (2014), 'British euroscepticism as British exceptionalism: The Forty-Year "Neverendum" on the relationship with Europe', *Diplomatica*, LXVII (4): 1–12.

Goodwin, Matthew (2015), 'Why a "Brexit" looms large', *Chatham House Research Paper*, 22 September 2015, London: The Royal Institute of International Affairs.

Goodwin, Matthew (2016), 'Inequality not personalities drove Britain to Brexit', *Politico*, 28 June 2016, available at http://www.politico.eu/article/inequality-not-personalities-drove-britain-to-brexit/.

Goodwin, Matthew and Oliver Heath (2016), 'The 2016 referendum, Brexit and the left behind: An aggregate-level analysis of the result', *The Political Quarterly*, 87(3): 323–32.

Goodwin, Matthew and Caitlin Milazzo (2015), 'Britain, the European Union and the referendum: What drives Euroscepticism?', *Chatham House Research Paper*, 9 December 2015, London: The Royal Institute of International Affairs.

Grant, C. (2008), 'Why Is Britain Eurosceptic?', Centre for European Reform Essays, available at https://www.cer.eu/publications/archive/essay/2008/why-britain-eurosceptic (accessed 11 May 2018).

Hague, William (2016), *Why a Eurosceptic should vote to Remain?*, 6 June 2016, Speech of Lord Hague of Richmond at Chatham House, London: The Royal Institute of International Affairs.

Hammond, Philip (2016b), *What Do the Alternatives to EU Membership Look Like?*, Speech of Secretary of State for Foreign and Commonwealth Affairs of UK to Chatham House, 2 March 2016.

Harding, Gareth (2016a), 'Stumbling towards Brexit', *EU Observer*, 17 May 2016, available at https://euobserver.com/opinion/133434 (accessed 7 March 2017).

——— (2016b), 'Euroscepticism: The EU's new normal', 9 June 2016, available at https://euobserver.com/opinion/133747.

Hawking, Stephen (2016), 'Our attitude towards wealth played a crucial role in Brexit. We need a rethink', *The Guardian*, 29 July 2016, available at https://www.theguardian.com/commentisfree/2016/jul/29/stephen-hawking-brexit-wealth-resources.

Hay, Colin (1999), *The Political Economy of New Labour: Labour under False Pretences*, Manchester and New York: Manchester Press.

Heffernan, Richard (2001), *New Labour and Thatcherism: Political Change in Britain*, Basingstoke: Palgrave Macmillan.

Hix, S. (2002), 'Britain, the EU and the Euro', in P. Dunleavy; A. Gamble, R.; R. Heffernan; I. Holliday, and G. Peele (eds.), *Developments in British Politics*, Basingstoke: Palgrave.

Holmes, John (2016), 'After the vote: Britain's future in Europe', Lord Garden Memorial Lecture to Chatham House Members, 4 July 2016 London.

Ignacio-Torreblanca, Jose (2016), 'Spain: What has Britain to moan about?', April & May, *The World Today*, available at https://www.chathamhouse.org/publications/twt/spain-what-has-britain-moan-about.

Ip, Greg (2016), 'Impact on global economy depends on leaders', *The Wall Street Journal*, 27 June 2016, p. 1 & 6.

Jack, Ian (2016), 'In this Brexit vote, the poor turned on an elite who ignored them', *The Guardian*, 25 June 2016, available at https://www.theguardian.com/commentisfree/2016/jun/25/brexit-vote-poor-elite.

Jensen, M. Dagnis and Holly Snaith (2016), 'When politics prevails: The political economy of a Brexit, *Journal of European Public Policy*, 23(9): 1302–1310.

Jones, Richard Wyn (2016), 'Why did Wales shoot itself in the foot in this referendum?', *The Guardian*, 27 June 2016, available at https://www.theguardian.com/commentisfree/2016/jun/27/wales-referendum-remain-leave-vote-uk-eu-membership.

Joseph Rowntree Foundation (2016), *We Can Solve Poverty in the UK: A Strategy for Governments, Businesses, Communities and Citizens*, York: Joseph Rowntree Foundation.

Kellner, Peter (2015), 'Analysis: Why the UK might end up voting for Brexit', *Commentary of YouGov*, 16 November 2015, available at https://yougov.co.uk/news/2015/11/16/why-uk-might-end-voting-brexit/.

Kettle, Martin (2016), 'Brexit was a revolt against liberalism. We've entered a new political era', *The Guardian*, 15 September 2016, available at https://www.theguardian.com/commentisfree/2016/sep/15/brexit-liberalism-post-liberal-age.

Kroll, Daniela Annette and Dirk Leuffen (2016), 'Ties that bind, can also strangle: The Brexit threat and the hardships of reforming the EU', *Journal of European Public Policy*, 23(9): 1311–20.

Lang, Florian (2016), 'Stop the hysteria over Germany's little election', *EU Observer*, 7 September 2016, available at https://euobserver.com/opinion/134952.

Letta, Enrico (2016), 'The EU must relaunch or die', *The Word Today*, August and September 2016, p. 24.

*Lord Ashcroft Polls* (2016), 'How the United Kingdom voted on Thursday…and why', 24 June 2016, available at http://lordashcroftpolls.com/2016/06/how-the-united-kingdom-voted-and-why/.

Leinen, Jo (2016), 'Red lines for Brexit negotiations with the UK', in O. Bailey ed., *Fabian Policy Report: Facing the Unknown*, London: Fabian Society, p. 27.

Maasikas, Matti (2017), 'How the EU can thrive in the time of Trump', EU Observer, 9 January 2017, available at https://euobserver.com/opinion/136475 (accessed 19 January 2017).

Maurice, Eric (2016), 'EU legitimacy in question', *Europe in Review 2016*, December 2016, pp. 20–1.

McKinsey Global Institute (2016), *Poorer than Their Parents? Flat or Falling Incomes in Advanced Economies*, New York: McKinsey Global Institute.

Menon, Anand and John-Paul Salter (2016), 'Brexit: initial reflections', *International Affairs*, 92(6): 1297–1318.

Moore, James, (2016), 'What President Trump's victory means for the most important trade deal in the world', *The Independent*, 9 November 2016, available at http://www.independent.co.uk/news/world/americas/us-elections/donald-trump-president-wins-live-results-us-election-ttip-trade-deal-hillary-clinton-loses-a7394611.html.

Moore, Luke (2015), 'What explains euroscepticism in the Conservative Party', *OXPOL*, November 2015, available at http://blog.politics.ox.ac.uk/what-explains-euroscepticism-in-the-conservative-party/.

Munich Security Conference (2017), *Munich Security Report 2017: Post-Truth, Post-West, Post-Order?*, Munich: Munich Security Conference.

Nelson, Fraser (2016), 'A very British revolution', *The Wall Street Journal*, 27 June 2016, pp. 8–9.

Niblett, Robin (2016a), 'Brexit: The reality', *Chatham House Research Paper*, 24 June 2016, London: The Royal Institute of International Affairs.

——— (2016b), 'Britain, the EU and the sovereignty myth', *Chatham House Research Paper*, May 2016, London: The Royal Institute of International Affairs.

——— (2017), 'Liberalism in retreat: The demise of a dream', *Foreign Affairs*, January/February Issue, https://www.foreignaffairs.com/articles/2016-12-12/liberalism-retreat (accessed 19 January 2017).

O'Hagan, Ellie Mae (2016), 'Wales voted for Brexit because it has been ignored by Westminster for too long', *The Independent*, 25 June 2016, available at http://www.independent.co.uk/voices/brexit-wales-eu-referendum-vote-leave-uk-ignored-by-westminster-a7102551.html.

Oliver, Tim (2015), 'To be or not to be in Europe: Is that the question? Britain's European question and an in/out referendum', *International Affairs*, 91 (1): 77–91.

——— (2016), 'European and international views of Brexit', *Journal of European Public Policy*, 23(9): 1321–8.

Olivet, Cecilia (2016), 'Wallonia's historic stand against Ceta is a stand for democracy', *EU Observer*, 28 October 2016, available at https://euobserver.com/opinion/135706.

Ostry, J. D., P. Loungani and D. Furceri (2016), 'Neoliberalism: Oversold?', *Finance and Development*, 53(2): 38–41.

Papadimoulis, Dimitris (2017), 'New model needed to save EU', 30 March 2017, https://euobserver.com/opinion/137431 (accessed 5 April 2017).

Parakilas, Jacob and Xenia Wickett (2016), 'Does Brexit mean the future is President Trump?', *Chatham House Expert Comment*, available at http://www.chathamhouse.org/expert/comment/does-brexit-mean-future-president-trump (accessed 17 May 2018).

Pew Research Center (2016), *Euroskepticism Beyond Brexit: Significant Opposition in Key European Countries to An Ever Closer EU*, Washington, DC: Pew Research Center.

Prouza, Tomas (2016), 'Lessons for central Europe: We need more unity and less inequality', in O. Bailey ed., *Fabian Policy Report: Facing the Unknown*, London: Fabian Society, p. 28.

Raines, Thomas (2013), 'Britain's EU future: Cameron's gambit', *Chatham House Research Paper*, 25 January 2013, London: The Royal Institute of International Affairs.

——— (2016a), 'Britain's vote will test the limits of the EU experiment', *Chatham House Research Paper*, 21 June 2016, London: The Royal Institute of International Affairs.

——— (2016b), 'Tusk's artful compromise could save Cameron in EU referendum', *Chatham House Research Paper*, 4 February 2016, London: The Royal Institute of International Affairs.

——— (2016c), 'What do our neighbours think?', *The World Today*, April & May 2016, p. 14.

Reeves, Rachel (2016), 'We must see the result as a rejection to the economic status quo, and use the opportunity to build a fairer and more inclusive economy', in O. Bailey ed., *Fabian Policy Report: Facing the Unknown*, London: Fabian Society, pp. 17–8.

Reynolds, Emma (2016), 'We must accept the referendum's outcome and secure the best possible deal', O. Bailey ed., *Fabian Policy Report: Facing the Unknown*, London: Fabian Society, pp. 23–4.

Rodgers, Daniel T. (2016), 'Will angry politics and bitter voters floor the US?', *Chatham House Research Paper*, London: The Royal Institute of International Affairs.

Schneider-Petsinger, Marianne (2016), 'Inequality defines the American election', *Chatham House Research Paper*, 20 October 2016, London: The Royal Institute of International Affairs.

Scully, Roger (2016), 'EU referendum: Crunching the numbers on Brexit vote', *BBC*, 25 June 2016, available at http://www.bbc.com/news/uk-politics-eu-referendum-36625433.

Singh, Matt (2016), 'The 2.8 million non-voters who delivered Brexit', *Bloomberg View*, 4 July 2016, available at https://www.bloomberg.com/view/articles/2016-07-04/the-2-8-million-non-voters-who-delivered-brexit.

Speed, Barbara (2016), 'How did different demographic group vote in the EU referendum?', *New Statesman*, 24 June 2016, available at http://www.newstatesman.com/politics/staggers/2016/06/how-did-different-demographic-groups-vote-eu-referendum.

Taylor, Adrian (2016), 'How to reinvent the EU in the age of populism', *EU Observer*, 14 December 2016, available at https://euobserver.com/opinion/136256.

Thielemann, Eiko and Daniel Schade (2016), 'Buying into myths: free movement of people', *The Political Quarterly*, 87(2): 139–47.

University Vice Chancellors, 'EU referendum: An open letter to UK voters from leaders of 103 British universities', *The Independent*, 21 June 2016, http://www.independent.co.uk/news/uk/politics/eu-referendum-an-open-letter-to-uk-voters-from-leaders-of-96-british-universities-a7092511.html (accessed 26 July 2016).

Vasilopoulou, Sofia (2016), 'UK euroscepticism and the Brexit referendum', *The Political Quarterly*, 87(2): 219–227.

Wall, Stephen (2012), *The Official History of Britain and the European Community, Volume II: From Rejection to Referendum, 1963–1975*, Routledge: Abingdon.

Waldman, Matt (2016), 'Trump and Brexit: The cost of failure to empathize', Chatham House Research Paper, 24 November 2016, https://www.chathamhouse.org/expert/comment/trump-and-brexit-cost-failure-empathize (accessed 18 January 2017).

Wales Governance Centre (2016), *Wales and the EU Referendum: Estimating Wales' Net Contribution to the European Union*, Cardiff: Wales Governance Centre at Cardiff University.

Warner, G. (2002), "Why the general said no', *International Affairs*, Vol. 78, No. 4, pp. 869–82.

Whitman, Richard G. (2016a), 'The EEA: A safe harbour in the Brexit storm', *Chatham House Research Paper*, 27 June 2016, London: The Royal Institute of International Affairs.

——— (2016b), 'Brexit or Bremain: What future for the UK's European diplomatic strategy?', *International Affairs*, 92(3): 509–529.

——— (2016c), 'After the "Leave" vote: The UK's European Year Zero', *Chatham House Research Paper*, 10 March 2016, London: The Royal Institute of International Affairs.

Williams, Zoe (2016a), 'Think the north and the poor caused Brexit? Think again', *The Guardian*, 7 August 2016, available at https://www.theguardian.com/commentisfree/2016/aug/07/north-poor-brexit-myths.

——— (2016b), 'These aren't hard Brexiters. They're political extremists', *The Guardian*, 16 October 2016, available at https://www.theguardian.com/commentisfree/2016/oct/16/hard-brexiters-political-extremists-boris-johnson-cabinet.

Williamson, David (2016), 'Is Wales now a Eurosceptic national that's heading for the EU exit door?' *The WalesOnline*, 15 February 2016, available at http://www.walesonline.co.uk/news/politics/wales-now-eurosceptic-nation-thats-10894382.

Wolf, Martin (2016), 'Brexit will reconfigure the UK economy', *Financial Times*, 24 June 2016, available at http://www.ft.com/cms/s/29a7964c-3953-11e6-9a05-82a9b15a8ee7,Authorised=false.html?siteedition=intl&_i_location=http%3A%2F%2Fwww.ft.com%2Fcms%2Fs%2F0%2F29a7964c-3953-11e6-9a05-82a9b15a8ee7.html%3Fsiteedition%3Dintl&_i_referer=&classification=conditional_standard&iab=barrier-app#axzz4LhJfkMy3.

World Economic Forum (2017), *The Global Risks Report 2017*, Switzerland: The World Economic Forum.

Wright, Iain (2016), 'We must reaffirm and reset employment protection to make clear our position as the workers' party', in O. Bailey ed., *Fabian Policy Report: Facing the Unknown*, London: Fabian Society, pp. 19–20.

Zalan, Eszter (2016), 'EU must protect its citizens', *EU Observer*, 2 August 2016, available at https://euobserver.com/institutional/134546.

## IV. Media Consulted

*Asia Times*, 'Xi warns BRICS summit of globalization backlash', 16 October 2016, available at http://www.atimes.com/article/xi-warns-brics-summit-globalization-backlash/.

*Associated Press* (2016), 'Trade chief: protectionism is not the answer to job losses', 7 November 2016, available at http://bigstory.ap.org/article/3c288a658ab84c989d1a644335a936d1/trade-chief-protectionism-not-answer-job-losses.

*BBC* (2016a), 'EU deal: A hard-headed calculation to avoid Brexit', 20 February 2016, available at http://www.bbc.com/news/uk-politics-eu-referendum-35620434.

——— (2016b), 'EU deal gives UK special status, says David Cameron', 20 February 2016, available at http://www.bbc.com/news/uk-politics-35616768.

——— (2016c), 'EU referendum: Australian would welcome In vote, says PM Turnbull', 1 May 2016, available at http://www.bbc.com/news/uk-politics-eu-referendum-36183444.

——— (2016d), 'EU referendum: The result in maps and charts', 24 June 2016, available at http://www.bbc.com/news/uk-politics-36616028.

——— (2016e), 'EU referendum: Welsh voters back Brexit', 24 June 2016, available at http://www.bbc.com/news/uk-politics-eu-referendum-36612308.

——— (2016f), 'Theresa May: I'll use power of state to build fairer Britain', 5 October 2016, available at http://www.bbc.com/news/uk-politics-37556019.

*CBC* (2016), 'Trudeau makes 'no bones' about his wish for Britain to remain in EU in eve of referendum', 22 June 2016, available at http://www.cbc.ca/news/politics/brexit-trudeau-remain-vote-1.3647807.

*DW* (2016), 'EU Commission: CETA should be approved by national parliaments', 5 July 2016, available at http://www.dw.com/en/eu-commission-ceta-should-be-approved-by-national-parliaments/a-19379263.

*Euronews* (2016), 'Portugal's PM: Failing to regulate globalization a "great failure" of the EU', 17 November 2016, http://www.euronews.com/2016/11/17/failing-to-regulate-globalisation-is-a-great-failure-of-the-european-union (accessed 18 January 2017).

*EU Observer* (2016a), 'EU-UK deal reached in marathon talks', 9 February 2016, available at https://euobserver.com/political/132367.

——— (2016b), 'Lords: Cameron should convey positive Yes message', 31 March 2016, available at https://euobserver.com/political/132851.

——— (2016c), 'Cox murder leaves UK in shock, ugly EU campaign blamed', 17 June 2016, available at https://euobserver.com/political/133868.

——— (2016d), 'Cameron pleads with voters to stay in EU', 21 June 2016, available at https://euobserver.com/uk-referendum/133929.

——— (2016e), 'Cameron in final push, as polls show pro-EU swing', 20 June 2016, available at https://euobserver.com/uk-referendum/133892.

——— (2016f), 'In and Out camps present Brexit scenarios', 15 June 2016, available at https://euobserver.com/uk-referendum/133835.

——— (2016g), 'No EU plan for Brexit, Eurogroup chief says', 2 June 2016, available at https://euobserver.com/institutional/133682.

——— (2016h), 'Cameron warns of Brexit "madness"', 3 June 2016, available at https://euobserver.com/political/133689.

——— (2016i), 'Wider Europe shares Cameron's EU vision', 7 June 2016, available at https://euobserver.com/news/133723.

——— (2016j), 'Tusk: Brexit would "change Europe" for the worse', 25 February 2016, available at https://euobserver.com/tickers/132441.

——— (2016k), 'Obama: Brexit does not mean end of the EU', 8 July 2016, available at https://euobserver.com/foreign/134263.

——— (2016l), 'Poll: Majority of Dutch want EU membership referendum', 23 February 2016, available at https://euobserver.com/tickers/132401.

——— (2016m), 'More Danes want referendum on EU membership', 8 June 2016, available at https://euobserver.com/institutional/133738.

——— (2016n), 'French and Italians want UK-type votes on EU', 9 May 2016, available at https://euobserver.com/political/133367.
——— (2016o), 'EU wonders how to win back people's trust', 25 July 2016, available at https://euobserver.com/eu-presidency/134483.
——— (2016p), 'Fico: EU leaders need to overcome fear', 6 July 2016, available at https://euobserver.com/news/134226.
——— (2016q), 'EU states must act on youth poverty', 29 August 2016, available at https://euobserver.com/education/134788.
——— (2016r), 'Eastern bloc wants fewer EU powers, more security', 26 August 2016, available at https://euobserver.com/news/134775.
——— (2016s), 'Tspiras hopes "Club Med" to soften EU austerity', 9 September 2016, available at https://euobserver.com/economic/134995.
——— (2016t), 'EU 27 meet for "moment of truth"', 16 September 2016, available at https://euobserver.com/political/135123.
——— (2016u), 'EU admits "unrealistic" to close TTIP deal this year', 23 September 2016, available at https://euobserver.com/economic/135217.
——— (2016v), 'Uncertainty stalks EU trade deals with US and Canada', 18 July 2016, available at https://euobserver.com/economic/134385.
——— (2016w), 'Kerry to promote free-trade deal on EU tour', 18 July 2016, available at https://euobserver.com/economic/134395.
——— (2016x), 'Ceta failure deepens EU trade crisis', 21 October 2016, available at https://euobserver.com/economic/135609.
——— (2016y), 'Belgium breaks Ceta deadlock', 27 October 2016, available at https://euobserver.com/economic/135694.
——— (2016z), 'Belgium green lights unchanged Ceta', 28 October 2016, available at https://euobserver.com/economic/135717.
——— (2017), 'Transparency is key EU tactic in Brexit talks', 30 March 2017, available at https://euobserver.com/uk-referendum/137444.
*Financial Times* (2016), 'France urges Brussels to halt TTIP talks', 30 August 2016, available at https://www.ft.com/content/154ecba2-6e82-11e6-a0c9-1365ce54b926.
*International Business Times*, 'EU referendum: Nissan to initiate legal proceedings against Vote Leave campaign', 20 June 2016, available at http://www.ibtimes.co.uk/eu-referendum-nissan-initiate-legal-proceedings-against-vote-leave-campaign-1566521#.
*Politico* (2016a), 'Angela Merkel: Brexit could be "turning point" for EU', 26 August 2016, available at http://www.politico.eu/article/angela-merkel-brexit-breaking-point-warsaw-visegrad-referendum-uk-consequences/.
——— (2016b), 'How Brexit will change the world', 25 June 2016, available at http://www.politico.com/magazine/story/2016/06/brexit-change-europe-britain-us-politics-213990.

*Reuters* (2016a), 'Theresa May pitches Brexit 'quiet revolution' to turn Britain's course', 7 October 2016, available at http://uk.reuters.com/article/uk-britain-politics-idUKKCN1261ZG.

——— (2016b), 'EU needs migration policy, must stop blame game: EU leaders' chairman', 18 September 2016, available at http://www.reuters.com/article/us-europe-migrants-tusk-idUSKCN0RI27J20150918.

——— (2016c), 'Thousands protest TTIP, CETA deals in France, Poland, & Spain as EU vote looms closer', 15 October 2016, available at https://www.rt.com/news/362907-poland-france-protest-ceta/.

*The Economist* (2014), 'Why Britain is so Eurosceptic', 3 March 2014, available at http://www.economist.com/blogs/economist-explains/2014/03/economist-explains-1.

*The Economist* (2016a), 'The roots of Euroscepticism', 12 March 2016, available at http://www.economist.com/news/britain/21694557-why-britons-are-warier-other-europeans-eu-roots-euroscepticism.

——— (2016b), 'Explaining the Brexit vote', 16 July 2016, available at http://www.economist.com/news/britain/21702228-areas-lots-migrants-voted-mainly-remain-or-did-they-explaining-brexit-vote.

——— (2016c), 'Why Brexit is grim news for the world economy', 24 June 2016, available at http://www.economist.com/news/finance-and-economics/21701292-uncertainty-abounds-expect-global-chilling-effect-investment-why-brexit.

*The Guardian* (2016a), 'EU referendum: Youth turnout almost twice as high as first thought', 10 July 2016, available at https://www.theguardian.com/politics/2016/jul/09/young-people-referendum-turnout-brexit-twice-as-high.

——— (2016b), 'Brexit vote was rejection of economic status quo, says Jeremy Corbyn', 15 September 2016, available at https://www.theguardian.com/politics/2016/sep/15/brexit-vote-was-rejection-of-economic-status-quo-says-jeremy-corbyn.

——— (2016c), 'Nick Clegg: Parliament must vote on terms of deal to leave EU', 27 July 2016, available at https://www.theguardian.com/politics/2016/jul/27/nick-clegg-parliament-vote-terms-deal-leave-eu-brexit.

——— (2016d), 'How the pollsters got it wrong on the EU referendum', 24 June 2016, available at https://www.theguardian.com/politics/2016/jun/24/how-eu-referendum-pollsters-wrong-opinion-predict-close.

——— (2016e), 'How the pollsters got it wrong on the EU referendum', 24 June 2016, available at https://www.theguardian.com/politics/2016/jun/24/how-eu-referendum-pollsters-wrong-opinion-predict-close.

——— (2016f), 'Brexit weekly briefing: Splits over timing of talks and single market membership', 30 August 2016, available at https://www.theguardian.com/politics/2016/aug/30/brexit-weekly-briefing-splits-over-timing-of-talks-and-single-market-membership.

——— (2016g), 'Bratislava summit: EU is at critical point, says Angela Merkel', 16 September 2016, available at https://www.theguardian.com/world/2016/sep/16/bratislava-summit-donald-tusk-urges-eu-leaders-not-to-waste-brexit-crisis.

——— (2016h), 'Hard Brexit will cost City of London its hub status, warns Bundesbank boss', 19 September 2016, available at https://www.theguardian.com/world/2016/sep/18/hard-brexit-will-cost-city-of-london-its-hub-status-warns-bundesbank-boss.

——— (2016i), 'Brexit weekly briefing: Is Canada's EU trade deal a blueprint for the UK?', 23 August 2016, available at https://www.theguardian.com/politics/2016/aug/23/brexit-weekly-briefing-is-canadas-eu-trade-deal-a-blueprint-for-the-uk.

*The Independent* (2016a), 'What is Brexit and why are we having an EU referendum?', 24 June 2016, available at http://www.independent.co.uk/news/uk/politics/what-is-brexit-why-is-there-an-eu-referendum-a7042791.html.

——— (2016b), 'Brexit would cause "shock to the world economy", G20 leaders tell George Osborne', 28 February 2016, available at http://www.independent.co.uk/news/uk/politics/brexit-would-cause-shock-to-the-world-economy-g20-leaders-tell-george-osborne-a6900036.html.

——— (2016c), 'EU referendum letter: 1280 business leaders sign letter backing Remain', 23 June 2016, available at http://www.independent.co.uk/news/business/news/eu-referendum-brexit-letter-remain-barclays-anglo-american-a7094811.html.

——— (2016d), 'EU referendum: workers' rights will be watered downed if Britain leaves the EU, claims TUC', 3 May 2016, available at http://www.independent.co.uk/news/uk/politics/workers-rights-will-be-watered-down-if-britain-leaves-eu-claims-tuc-a7010381.html.

——— (2016e), 'Jeremy Corbyn faces calls to resign from Labour MPs over disastrous referendum campaign', 24 June 2016, available at http://www.independent.co.uk/news/uk/politics/jeremy-corbyn-resign-brexit-eu-referendum-labour-leader-a7100446.html.

——— (2016f), 'Wales has changed its minds over Brexit and would now vote to stay in the EU, poll finds', 5 July 2016, available at http://www.independent.co.uk/news/uk/politics/wales-has-changed-its-mind-over-brexit-and-would-now-vote-to-stay-in-the-eu-poll-finds-a7120246.html.

*The New York Times* (2016a), 'The Brexit spillover', 28 June 2016, available at http://www.nytimes.com/2016/06/28/opinion/the-brexit-spillover.html.

——— (2016b), '"Brexit": Explaining Britain's vote on European Union membership', 21 June 2016, available at http://www.nytimes.com/interactive/2016/world/europe/britain-european-union-brexit.html?_r=0.

——— (2016c), 'Editorial board: Britain leaves on a cry of anger and frustration', 24 June 2016, available at http://www.nytimes.com/2016/06/25/opinion/britain-leaves-on-a-cry-of-anger-and-frustration.html.

*The Telegraph* (2016), 'EU referendum: Nato chiefs warn Brexit will "give succour to the West's enemies"', 20 June 2016, available at http://www.telegraph.co.uk/news/2016/05/09/eu-referendum-nato-chiefs-warn-brexit-will-give-succour-to-the-w/.

*The Wall Street Journal*, 'IMF issues fresh warning on "Brexit" consequences', 17 June 2016, http://www.wsj.com/articles/imf-issues-fresh-warning-on-brexit-consequences-1466204404.

CHAPTER 6

# There *IS* an Alternative: The Danish Formula of Inclusive Capitalism

## 1 Background and Rationales

The world has witnessed sea changes in the EU politics in the last decade, from the continuing rise of populist right parties (PRPs) in a number of EU countries since 2014 to the unexpected results of the Brexit referendum. In essence, the EU politics has entered into a watershed period, departing from the conventional consensus on politico-economic liberalization, in the form of European single market and single currency, to the anti-establishment and anti-EU, in the form of trade protectionism and populist nationalism. Despite their individual differences in national contexts, all these events shared a common striking characteristic—it was those left behind and economically disadvantaged voters who delivered such results. The phenomenon, as Goodwin (2017) indicates, was a 'working-class revolt', and with workers becoming the 'core clientele' of these populist movements, they have formed a 'new type of working-class politics'.

The fact that PRPs voters versus non-PRPs voters and Brexit voters versus non-Brexit voters were divided along with the lines of winners and losers of European integration and globalization highlights the significance and imperative of addressing economic inequality and distributive justice.

The concise version of this chapter was first published by *Asia Europe Journal* (2019) Vol. 17 on 21 February 2019 at https://doi.org/10.1007/s10308-019-00538-2



C.-M. Luo, *The EU's Crisis Decade*,
https://doi.org/10.1007/978-981-13-6565-2_6

According to the latest surveys, as many as 65–70% of households in advanced economies faced either stagnant or declining incomes during 2005–2014 (Munich Security Conference, 2017: 9). The wealth inequality was even worse, twice the income inequality in Europe and the US (Hutton, 2015: 103). The top 1% of wealth holders increased their share of all household wealth from 45.5% in 2000 to 50.1% in 2013. Together with the top decile, they achieved the record high of owning 87.8% of the world's wealth. Meanwhile, the median wealth per adult, an indicator of reflecting the economic life of an average person, was below the level of 2007 in all regions, except China (Credit Suisse Research Institute, 2017: 16–17). In the UK, only 10% of overall income growth went to the bottom half of the income distribution between 1979 and 2012 (Institute for Public Policy Research, 2017: 2), while in the US, the incomes of the top 1% grew by 31% and the incomes of the remaining 99% grew less than 0.5% between 2009 and 2012 (World Economic Forum, 2017: 23). The Institute for Public Policy Research (IPPR) (2017: 15) even contends that, from 2008 to 2021, the UK economy would enter into the longest period of earnings stagnation for 150 years since the 1860s. Jacobs and Mazzucato (2016: 1) therefore argue that economic inequality has grown to 'levels not seen since the 19th century'.

## 2 The Significance of Economic Inequality

When economic growth no longer translates into the higher earnings and improvements of living standards for a majority of working population,[1] disillusion in mainstream parties and free-market system were the natural answers delivered from voters in one election or referendum to another. Political backlashes, revealing in the Brexit referendum and in the latest general elections in the UK, the Netherlands, France, Austria, Germany, and Italy, were then understandable. A survey conducted by McKinsey Global Institute (2016: 6) found that citizens who held the most negative views on free trade and immigration were the same group who felt their incomes were stagnant or falling and were more likely to support PRPs.

[1] Due to the decoupling of economic growth from income growth, economists, such as Stiglitz et al. (2009: 12–18) and Coyle (2017: 19), call for designing a better indicator than the current one—gross domestic product (GDP)—to measure economic welfare so as to reflect the distribution of income, consumption, and wealth more correctly. Hay and Payne (2015: 26) propose a hybrid measurement of social, environmental, and developmental index (SED) to replace the index of GDP, while the OECD proposes the 'Better Life Index' and the World Economic Forum proposes the UN's 'Human Development Index' as the alternative (World Economic Forum, 2017: 10).

Commentators (IMF, 2017a: xvii; World Economic Forum, 2017: vii; Jacobs and Mazzucato, 2016: 5–10; Hutton, 2015: 9 & 101–2) were further concerned that, despite the world economy returned to growth from the global financial crisis since 2008, the recovery, in terms of growth rate and labour productivity, was slowest in modern times. This has led some economists to question whether Western capitalism has entered into the so-called secular stagnation as the 'new normal', in which structural weakness of investment and demands resulted in low and chronic growth. The root of such low growth was argued to be the stagnant living standards and rising inequality.

## 3 Effects on the Economy

Economic inequality influences economic performance, but how the two interrelate with each other was inconclusive among theoretical economists. In the past, most economists, such as Lazear and Rosen (1981: 841–64), Bourguignon (1981: 1469–75), and Barro (2000: 5–32), believed that economic inequality was inevitable in the early stage of economic developments, but it should be short-lived as growth would gradually 'trickle down' through the layers of society from the rich to the poor, the so-called trickle-down economics. By contrast, Galor and Moav (2004: 1006–26), Aghion et al. (1999: 1615–60), Perotti (1996: 149–87), and Stiglitz (2013: 115–30) contend that economic inequality is negative to growth, as it would deprive the poor from having access to better health and education opportunities, lower public investment, and distort resource allocation through rent seeking of the rich in law and regulation.

Empirical evidences from recent studies support the view that inequality impedes growth, at least for the medium term. Cross-country studies by Berg et al. (2012: 150–65) and Ostry et al. (2014: 15–26) found that income distribution was strongly related to growth duration. More equal societies tended to support growth longer and more durable. An increase in Gini (a measurement of income inequality) by 1% was estimated to result in lowering the growth duration by 11–15%. Kumhof et al. (2012: 5–27) found that income inequality, compounded with financial liberalization, has led to global current account imbalances between developing and developed countries. Stockhammer (2015: 935–54) further points to economic inequality as the major cause of the global financial crisis, as working-class households had to rely on mortgage debt to keep up with consumption in the face of stagnant or falling wages, while rich households had greater propensity to speculate on financial assets.

Official reports from international organizations also hold similar views. In its annual survey, the IMF (2017b: 1) indicates that some inequality is inevitable in a market economy as a result of differences in talent, effort, and luck, but excessive inequality would lower economic growth. A joint report from International Labour Organization (ILO) and OECD (2015: 2–12) indicates that the decline in labour share on private consumption would result in the decline in private investment and then induce economies to rely on more credit/household debts or net exports in order to maintain aggregate demand. This would ultimately lead to the instability and imbalances of the world economy. Oxfam (2014: 9–10) points out that extreme economic inequality not just prevented the growth from lasting but also undermined the future growth. It was the missing link explaining why the same growth rate would result in different rates of poverty reduction. Berg and Ostry (2011: 13–18) from the IMF estimate that 10% decrease in inequality could increase the growth duration by 50%, while countries with more structural inequality tend to grow more slowly. Reports from the OECD propose that rising inequality between 1985 and 2005 might knock more than 4% off growth between 1990 and 2010 in half of OECD countries due to under-investment in human capital (2017a: 37–8). By contrast, a reduction in inequality by 1 Gini point could translate in an increase in cumulative growth of 0.8% in the following 5 years, or, on a 25-year horizon, it could lead to a cumulative gain in GDP of 3% (Cingano, 2014: 17–18).

## 4 Effects on Politics and Society

Additionally, economic inequality has wider social and political implications. In societal terms, the IMF (2017b: 1) points out that economic inequality would erode social cohesion and bring social division, leading to political polarization. A survey by IPPR (2017: 29) found that high levels of economic inequality were correlated with physical and mental illness, crime, social trust, and education attainment. Wilkinson and Pickett (2009: 11–44, 2017: 11–20) found that economic inequality eroded social trust, increased anxiety and illness, and encouraged excessive consumption. Social and health problems were found irrelevant to the levels of incomes but relevant to that of economic inequality. By contrast, more equal societies enjoyed higher levels of interpersonal trust, mutual support, and lower level of violence.

In political terms, economic inequality endowed economic elites the excessive influence over politics, media, and public debates. An empirical research on 2000 policy debates in the US over 20 years found that economic elites and business interests had substantial impacts on US government policies, while the public had little or no influence. Similarly, financial institutions were reported spending more than €120 million per year on influencing EU policy-making. Economic inequality thus translated into political inequality (Oxfam, 2014: 59–60). Accordingly, Stiglitz (2013: 158–64) argues that such economic and political inequalities undermined the public trust in politics and, in the long run, 'democracy would be in peril' (Ibid.: 181).

It is then understandable why in the Eurobarometer survey social inequality and unemployment were perceived by Europeans being surveyed as the most important challenges that the EU faced (European Commission, 2017). Another survey on ten EU countries (Raines et al., 2017: 2–3) reports that only 34% of the public felt they have benefited from the EU, compared with 71% of the elite, highlighting the public perceptions of uneven distribution between the elite and the public of gains produced from European market and monetary integration. In the light of its wide-ranging negative effects on economic, societal, and political well-beings, Pope Francis regards economic inequality as 'the root of social ills' (quoted from Lagarde, 2014), while the then US president, Barack Obama (2014), admits the rising inequality as the 'defining challenge of our time'.

## 5 Economic Inequality in an AI Era

The need of addressing economic inequality has become even more imperative as the world economy has been moving into the Fourth Industrial Revolution. Although the exact impact of automation was uncertain, McKinsey (2017: 27–35) estimates that automation technology, such as machines, robots, and artificial intelligence (AI), had the potential impact to nearly half, 49%, of the global workforce. It would push distribution of income more favourable to capital owners relative to workers and thus increase income inequality. McKinsey Global Institute (2016: 18) projects that some 30–40% of the population may experience stagnant or falling market income as automation technology accelerates. What caused commentators (Ostry, 2017: 1; IPPR, 2017: 66–7; Aoun, 2018: 2; Sundararajan, 2017: 7) most concerned was that automation would not just replace labour for capital[2] but also change the power relations between capital and labour. Labours would be harder to bargain with employers for any pay rise, while the return to capital would rise as a result of automation growth. These would therefore accentuate the existing trend of economic inequality.

If not addressing the challenges of economic inequality in time, Piketty (2014: 571) warns that the consequences are 'potentially terrifying', because, in history, it took war and depression to arrest inequality. Streeck (2014: 63–4) accordingly predicts that capitalism was in critical condition and the world economy risked the possibility of breakdown on the scale of the 1930s. The World Economic Forum (2017: 6–11 & 23 & 31–2) accordingly asked for reforming market capitalism right immediately. 'To save globalization, its benefits must be shared more broadly'. Otherwise, 'rising income and wealth disparity' would be the biggest risk for the global economy in the next ten years.

## 6 Worldwide Consensus Is Forming, But Divided on Causes and Diagnoses

A worldwide consensus was forming on the need of reforming capitalism and searching for a new model that can be shared by the majority of population—the so-called inclusive growth model or inclusive capitalism.[3] Decision-makers in both public and private sectors, such as the EU (2017), OECD (2017a), IMF (2017b), and World Economic Forum (2017: vii & xii), have been actively engaged in related discussions. However, commentators were divisive on the origins of economic inequality. For some, such as Piketty (2014: 25–7), Jacobs and Mazzucato (2016: 11), and Hutton (2015: 12), economic inequalities are the symptoms of the failings and dysfunctions of Western capitalism and they are structural. As Piketty explains (2014: 25–7), this is because the average rate of return on capital $r$ is always larger than the average rate of economic growth $g$ ($r > g$), fundamental in capitalism.

[2] However, David Author (2015: 3–30) from MIT contends that such worries of 'automation anxiety' (2015: 4) were overdue, because most automated systems lack flexibility. He predicts that middle-skill jobs combining specific vocational skills with middle level of 'literacy, numeracy, adaptability, problem-solving, and common sense', the so-called 'new middle skill jobs', will be growing in coming decades (2015: 27).

[3] Hay and Payne (2015: 3–50) term it as 'civic capitalism' and Hutton (2015) terms it as 'stakeholder capitalism'.

The IMF (2007: 161–92, 2017a: 125), OECD (Bassanini and Manfredi, 2012), and McKinsey Global Institute (2017: 7–10), in line with arguments of populist right parties, attribute economic inequality to technological changes and globalization over the past 40 years. The former was estimated to account for around half of this trend, while the latter contributed to a quarter, especially in reducing labour income shares in tradable sectors in advanced economies (IPPR, 2017: 31). But in their latest reports, both IMF (2017b: 4) and OECD (2017a: 28–34) recognize economic inequality as a compound outcome produced by both global forces and country-specific policies.

However, Onaran and Guschanski (2017: 60 & 155–62) disagree with this perspective that technology and globalization could benefit both the rich and the poor and their effects were intermediated through policies. Oxfam (2014: 14 & 21) also argue that economic inequality was not inevitable in market capitalism, neither was it a necessary outcome of globalization and technological progress. It was 'the result of deliberate policy choices'. The World Economic Forum (2017: xii) also regards economic inequality as 'largely endogenous rather than exogenous', not 'an iron law of capitalism'. Hutton (2015: 4) attributes the worsening economic inequality largely to the dismantling of the social security system in the name of 'rolling back the state', rather than the interaction of globalization and new technologies. Resolution Foundation's report (Corlett, 2016: 8–9) equally contends that, given the fact that there was a large variation of economic inequality between countries, it was not inevitable and domestic policies do play a key role.

To distinguish which factors were more deterministic of causing economic inequality was unrealistic, if not possible. Market capitalism did not exist in vacuum. Neither did globalization and technological changes. They were embedded in socio-political systems which national policies have shaped and directed. Their effects, whatsoever, have interacted with, as well as being channelled through, national policies. As Stiglitz (2013: xliii & 35 & 100) points out, 'markets often lead to high levels of inequality'. 'But it was not market forces alone'. 'At different times, different forces have played different roles'.

Different diagnoses on the origins of economic inequality, accordingly, have led to different prescriptions. For those who held the global forces accountable for rising economic inequality, economic protectionism and trade defence policies were the policy responses to tackle economic inequality, as can be seen in the US Trump administration's trade policies and the EU's trade defence measures. International organizations, such as IMF (2017b) and OECD (2017a), suggest internal rather than external policy approaches, such as progressive income taxes, universal basic income, quality public schooling and healthcare, active labour market policies, and sufficient unemployment benefits. Some initiatives were even tried in some areas, for example, Ontario's trial on universal basic income and Microsoft's trial on affordable internet access in some developing countries (*The Guardian*, 24 April 2017).

These policy suggestions, based on their different diagnoses on the causes of the issue and with their different prescriptions to policy dimensions, were rather one-sided than comprehensive, rather partial than systematic, and rather patchy than holistic, depending on the business functions of individual proposers. What the right policy combination is remains unclear. As the World Economic Forum (2017: vii) observes, 'inclusive growth remains more a discussion topic than an action agenda'. Moran (2015: 98–100) thus reminds that 'the big problem…is turning vision into reality' and to specify 'how that economy might in day-to-day fashion be steered'. The IMF (2017b: 6) and OECD (2017a: 73) therefore suggest that in-depth studies at individual country level were needed in order to embody the substance and operation of inclusive capitalism so as to provide practical policy lessons.

## 7 Research Questions and Aims: Inclusive Capitalism in Action

This research is an attempt to fill in this gap—to translate the aspiration for inclusive capitalism into policy practices by studying an indicative country: Denmark. A country-study approach was chosen because, as Putnam (2015: 243) points out, pursing an inclusive growth model must be cost-effective. It must learn 'from practical experience what works where' and from 'best available evidence' that it has promises. Based on such criteria, Denmark was selected as an appropriate case for the following reasons. First, this research defines an inclusive growth model in a literal and straight manner as an economy able to be equitable to be 'inclusive' and able to be competitive to 'grow' simultaneously. In the able-to-grow sense, Denmark has been ranked as one of the top ten countries of the IMD World Competitiveness Ranking for several years and one of the top five countries in the IMD World Digital Competitiveness

Ranking in 2017 (International Institute for Management and Development, 2017). Second, in the equitable and inclusive sense, Denmark was ranked as the second best EU country on the Inclusive Development Index (IDI) of the World Economic Forum (2017: x & 48) and the best EU country on the Social Justice Index of Bertelsmann Stiftung, a German think-tank, in 2017 (Schraad-Tischler et al., 2017: 6–10). It was also the only country in the EU that had no any system barriers to social mobility during early years, school years, and working age (Eurofound, 2017: 49, Table 9). Social mobility has become a reference for observing the fairness and inclusiveness of societies, especially after the Brexit vote was delivered in a time when the UK society was experiencing downward social mobility (Social Mobility Commission, 2017: 1; Eurofound, 2017: 38). Third, Denmark, along with Norway, was the least unequal country across the life course among OECD countries (OECD, 2017b: 19, Table 1) and also one of the very few OECD countries that has not witnessed the rise of economic inequality since the mid-1990s (OECD, 2017b: 10). Measuring by Gini coefficient, household disposable income inequality was the lowest in Denmark among OECD countries (Causa et al., 2016: 7 & 20–1). In terms of cross-generational equity, the intergenerational income inequality in Denmark was also the world's lowest, only 15%. In the US, nearly half of children born to low-income parents would become low-income adults. 'American dream', therefore, was believed as a myth in the US and was realized in Denmark (Oxfam, 2014: 48; Stiglitz, 2013: xlv). In a latest survey using economic, political, and social index, it was ranked among the happiest countries in the world (Helliwell et al., 2018: 21).

## 8 Analytical Framework

This research will adopt a systematic, whole-of-government/holistic approach to exploring Denmark's inclusive capitalism in order to identify the right policy combination that underpins the whole economic system. It will resort to the Inclusive Development Index (IDI), compiled by the World Economic Forum (2017: viii), as the analytical framework (see Fig. 6.1). It is composed of seven policy pillars: education and skills, basic services and infrastructure, corruptions and rents, financial intermediation of real economy investment, asset building and entrepreneurship, employment and labour compensation, and fiscal transfers.

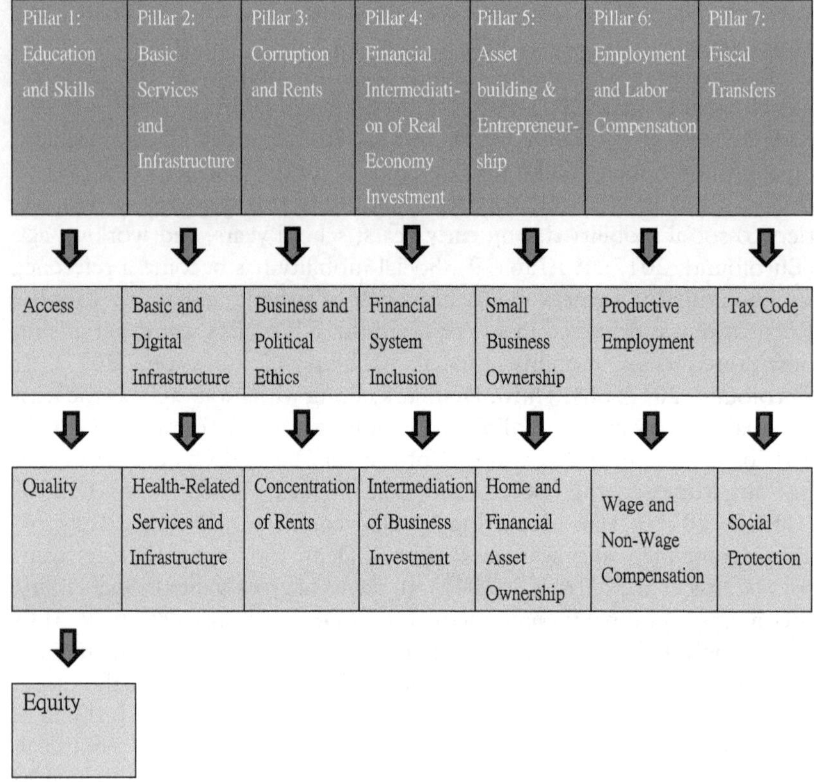


**Fig. 6.1** Inclusive Development Index (IDI). Source: World Economic Forum (2017: viii)

## 9 The Danish Formula of Practising Inclusive Capitalism

According to the analytical framework of IDI, seven policy domains in Denmark will be briefly reviewed individually.

### *9.1 Pillar 1: Education and Skills*

Education is the foundation of human development. As the IMF (2017b: 22) indicates, public education not only can reduce economic inequality across generations but also can lead to an improvement in economic efficiency, because education resources are allocated on the basis of individual's capability rather than of their family socio-economic backgrounds. Different from other policies, education has potential to promote economic equity and growth simultaneously.

In terms of economic equity, as job competition tends to favour those with better qualifications, it simply explains the critical importance of a fair and equal education system. Economic equity and social mobility were found to be maximized in the least elitist system of public education, whereas liberal free-market approach to education often serves those who can afford desirable educational choices and thus, in private schooling system, intergenerational social mobility was significantly reduced (Eurofound, 2017: 51). Empirical surveys on different types of European welfare regimes found that origin-destination association was weaker for those with highest level of education, and therefore education is identified as one of the most important factors in reducing poverty and securing acceptable living conditions (Ibid.: 8–9 & 44).

In terms of economic efficiency, educational inequality would slow growth because it prevents economically disadvantaged people from fully developing their capacity. On the contrary, even expensive investment in early çhildhood education could produce real return rates, about 6–10%, outperforming long-term stock market returns in the US (Putnam, 2015: 231–3). Evidences from OECD countries suggest that education investment, from early childhood to adulthood, was found to produce strong returns for government tax revenue, as skill-upgrading was positively associated with wage rises (OECD, 2017a: 47). Rasmussen (2005: 54) and Hemerijck (2013: 272–3 & 277) therefore contend that in a world of knowledge-based competition, investment at all levels of education and throughout the life course becomes paramount. Inadequate schooling today may put individuals at risks of becoming insecure workers tomorrow.

In providing equal opportunities of education for children and young people, Denmark was the best country in the EU and had the least elitist model of public education (Schraad-Tischler et al., 2017: 99; Eurofound, 2017: 51). Denmark's public expenditure on education, exceeded 8% of its GDP, was the highest among OECD countries (Hemerijck, 2013: 277–81). Education at all levels, from kindergartens to universities, was free, seen not as a privilege, but a right and duty (Rasmussen, 2005: 54).

Denmark's emphasis on education started from early childhood education and care (ECEC) and continued to lifelong learning and vocational training in adulthood. In terms of ECEC, ECEC in Denmark was seen not only as a major arrangement to further female employment but also as key to later personal development because of its lasting effects on cognitive abilities. It was perceived as the first pillar of human capability formation. Inequality in ECEC, therefore, would result in growing income and wealth inequality in adulthood, perpetuating a vicious cycle (OECD, 2017a: 18 & 42–4; Eurofound, 2017: 50). In Denmark, ECEC has emphasized both the availability and quality. Moreover, as high as 94.1% of children over 3 and 72.7% under 3 were taken care of by these facilities. The facts that the high enrolment of ECEC showed low differences by income groups and that Denmark had a relatively high fertility rate, between 1.7 and 1.9, and female employment rate explain the success of its ECEC provision (Hemerijck, 2013: 269–72). ECEC in Denmark emphasized the curriculum quality with focus on learning since 2004 for ages 0–5 years on the one hand and improving involvement of mandatory preschool and preventing social exclusion on the other. The former has produced positive outcomes for both children and ECEC staff, who have been equipped with new methods of working. The latter has been addressed by a large programme for 2014–2017, called 'Early Effort—Lifelong Effect', particularly for disadvantaged children to look at their development and learning (Eurofound, 2017: 56).

In primary and secondary education, public school reforms were introduced in 2013 in Denmark that aimed to reduce the effects of social background in relation to academic results and to strengthen trust with the public school system. The concrete measures were to provide help for students with homework as such assistance would not be available at home for disadvantageous students. Longer school days were thus introduced with longer teaching and activity hours (Eurofound, 2017: 56). Early school leavers in Denmark, 7.2%, were low compared to other EU countries, with an average of 10.7% (Randall and Karlsdottir, 2018: 88–90). Denmark's heavy investment in education yielded good results in educational outcomes. Denmark was the best performer on the index of skill acquisition among advanced economies and has been performing well in the results of OECD's Programme for International Student Assessment (PISA), especially in mathematics, with lesser disparity between 5th percentile and 95th percentile scores in literary (Randall and Karlsdottir, 2018: 88–90; Nelson and Stephens, 2012: 216–17). The facts explain the equity and quality of public education in Denmark.

Higher education was another important area for social mobility. Increased access to higher education could lower the overall origin-destination association and thus help reduce economic inequality. But financial constraints may hold back a family's decision to invest in higher education. Recently, there were concerns in many advanced countries about diminishing benefits of higher education as occupational returns have been declining. Yet, it was the prestige of educational establishment from which job applicants graduated, along with other skills, that counts (Eurofound, 2017: 8–9 & 72–3). Empirical studies by Brezis (2018: 203–8) further found that a higher elitist higher education regime was positively related to a higher wage gap and skill differential, as well as a higher Gini index, through the channels of higher competitiveness in the selection process and the gaps in budgets. Higher education in Denmark, while not compulsory, was free of charge. It also displayed lower levels of elitism and lower levels of inequality. It was worth noticing that unlike Sweden and Finland, students in Denmark were more evenly split between academic and vocational pathways (Randall and Karlsdottir, 2018: 92; Brezis, 2018: 203).

Denmark's emphasis on education continued to adulthood. Denmark had a very high level of firm-based training, with 76% of workers receiving some training from their employers (OECD, 2017d). Vocational training, work-based learning, and skill upkeep were the most obvious methods of improving skills on a systematic and targeted basis and key to form a competitive and dynamic workforce. Denmark established 13 guidance centres in 2010, called 'VEU centres' and described as 'one-stop entrance', for adult education and training. VEU centres provided free one-on-one career guidance, various educational programmes, and technical skill training. Some centres also provided second-opportunity programmes for adults who were early school leavers (OECD, 2017a: 45–6). Denmark also had very high rates of lifelong learning, the second highest country in the EU, with 35% of its population involved (Hemerijck, 2013: 280–3).

The economic returns to heavy investment in extensive education reflect in the good competitiveness and productivity of the Danish economy and its adaptability in times of changes. Nelson and Stephens (2012: 221–3 & 226) point out that ECEC and active labour market policies spending on vocational training were the most effective variables on increasing the overall levels of employment, whereas ECEC and education attainment were found to be the most effective variables on knowledge-intensive service employment, regarded as high-quality employment. They conclude that 'investing in people' (education) increased both the quantity and quality of employment. Manufacturing jobs in Denmark were among the most ICT-intensive in OECD countries. ICT equipment and knowledge-based capital were estimated to contribute 11% of labour productivity growth in Denmark from 2000 to 2014. Denmark was also the only OECD country that has witnessed the greatest increase in the influence of ICT services sector in domestic production networks over the period of 1995–2011 (OECD, 2017d).

## 9.2 Pillar 2: Basic Services and Infrastructure

Public services, as Oxfam (2014: 90) rightly points out, were the 'virtual income' for people and can mitigate income and wealth inequality. They were estimated to reduce income inequality by 20% in average. Public services range widely, and in order to have a focused discussion, this research will look into two specific policy areas that single out in the IDI analytical framework—digital infrastructure and health-related services.

As the world economy has been changing by advances in technology and such changes were expected to accelerate in an AI era, access to an open digital infrastructure has become an important component of making an inclusive economy. Both citizens and business could benefit greatly from public investment in and provision of digital infrastructure to improve their market competitiveness, and therefore can contribute to social inclusion and economic growth. Access to fast broadband service was an essential condition to digital services (Johnsen et al., 2018: 160–1).

Denmark has been a top performer in providing public digital services. It was ranked as the world's third best country on the index of ICT infrastructure in the survey of the Global Talent Competitiveness Index (Lanvin and Evans, 2018: 140). Digitalization has long been on the national agenda and the current Digitalization Strategy 2016–2020 was the fifth of this kind, marking a continuation of 15-year policy efforts on digitalization. Denmark's digital strategy, as Johnsen et al. (2018: 162 & 167–8) explain, had dual aims—to provide good conditions for economic growth on the one hand and to reduce administrative burden and economic inequality on the other. These policies have effectively promoted the widespread and quality of public digital services in Denmark. For example, Next Generation Access (NGA) networks, which offered speed above 30 Mbps, have been set by the EU as a policy target to achieve by 2020. Denmark has completed 93% of household coverage by NGA networks in 2016, ahead of most EU countries. Good NGA coverage did not automatically translate into the internet usage by all people (Johnsen et al., 2018: 167–8). But

Danish people were frequent internet users, with more than 1.2 subscriptions per person to mobile broadband in 2016, and 97% of people aged 16–74 were internet users (OECD, 2017d). Denmark was also the leading EU country in the public use of digital public services, with 73% of individuals having submitted completed forms to public authorities over the internet in 2016 (Johnsen et al., 2018: 167–8).

In terms of health services, narrowing health outcome gaps can help reduce inequality. Empirical evidences found that there was a strong positive association between lower inequality in health coverage and average life expectancy. Also, good health was an asset for everyone and the society, as it can improve school attendance and education outcomes and thus contribute to better employment and earnings. Public healthcare thus contains a distributional impact through financial protection. Universal health coverage (UHC) from public financing was found to drive down economic inequality. Public healthcare, together with public education, was seen as a powerful instrument that the government can address to reducing inequality (IMF, 2017b: 26–7; OECD, 2017a: 47; Oxfam, 2014: 90 & 97 & 99). Therefore, Kohler (2015: 30) contends that public healthcare, together with public education, should be a right-based approach to human development.

A healthy workforce was seen as foundation of the welfare model in Denmark. Health services have been provided by the government and were viewed as an approach to reducing social and spatial inequalities in access to healthcare (Rehn-Mendoza and Weber, 2018: 170 & 180). Denmark's public spending on healthcare in relation to GDP, 8.6%, was the highest in the EU. Most of healthcare services were free and out-of-pocket payments (OPP) were limited, only accounting for 13.7% of total health spending, well below the OECD average (nearly 20%). One characteristic of public healthcare in Denmark was its very high spending on residential care/home-help services for the elderly, the highest among OECD countries. Municipalities had legal obligation to offer free long-term care to the elderly in need (Eurostat, 2018a; Klein and Hansen, 2016: 7; Hemerijck, 2013: 268–9). High investment in public healthcare has resulted in good quality and wide coverage of health services. According to the Euro Health Consumer Index, Denmark scored highly for its good health system outcomes, short waiting time, and wide reach of health services (Schraad-Tischler et al., 2017: 100). With the help of widespread digital infrastructure, Denmark also had the highest share of people using internet to access health services among Nordic countries (Rehn-Mendoza and Weber, 2018: 180).

### 9.3 *Pillar 3: Corruption and Rents*

The government, being the most authoritative allocator of resources, plays a unique, commanding high role in the economy. From a liberal economic perspective, it has been seen as a negative force to market function and should be limited to a minimum level. As Crouch (2015: 66–7) questions: 'how can we trust the government to defend collective and public goods when it was captured by the powerful interest groups?' Inclusive capitalism thus needs a 'civic state' (Kelly and D'Arcy, 2015: 88–9). By contrast, corruption is 'the cancer in the system'. Systemic corruption in the government would distort governments' decisions, weakening governments' regulating functions, discouraging investment, and lowering the public trust in the government, which would lead to tax evasion (Hagan, 2018). Empirical studies confirm that corruption hit the poorest hardest not just because the poor heavily rely on the public services, but because it was much easier for the elites to capture public resources to enrich themselves through 'crony contracting'. Corruption and favouritism with nepotistic hiring and promotion resulted in economic and social inequality and thus undermine the inclusive growth (Eurofound, 2017: 45; Oxfam, 2014: 62).

Good governments therefore, as Schubert and Martens (2005: 15) suggest, should deliver transparency, accountability, and value for money. In terms of transparency, it was recognized by policy practitioners as a very effective tool to anti-corruption (Hagan, 2018). In the survey of Transparency International (2018), Denmark was ranked as the world's second best country on the index of corruption perception and even the world's best country on the index of corruption of Global Talent Competitiveness Index survey (Lanvin et al., 2018: 23). In terms of accountability and value for money, indeed, people evaluate the quality of public services on the basis of their personal experiences and the perceived responsiveness of public services affected people's trust in the government most than other factors. According to a survey on OECD countries, a 10% increase in people's satisfaction with public services would raise their trust in the government by 4.5% (OECD, 2017a: 69). Morel et al. (2012: 365–7) contend that the success of governance depends on its delivery quality. Without quality services, any public investment in education, labour market policy, and social welfare cannot be qualified as investment but rather as pure spending. Public governance in Denmark received strong credibility because of its high transparency and good delivery results. Public trust in government and public administration was high

(Laursen et al., 2016: 2). Denmark's public expenditure in relation to GDP, 53.6%, was among the highest in the EU, but there was a wide acceptance of high level of public expenditure and taxation. One major reason, as Schubert and Martens (2005: 17) explain, was the good quality and delivery of public services.

In short, the large public sector in Denmark was proved not a liability to but an asset of its competitiveness because its quality and uncorrupted services enabled business and individuals to develop. As Levitas (2015: 93) argues, the size of the government should not be a concern; the concern should be how it can be a force for common good in a capitalist economy.

## 9.4 Pillar 4: Financial Intermediation on Real Economy Investment

The financial sector was a key mediator between capital and industry as it could allocate capital into productive activities. But the role that it has played in the real economy has been questioned since the outbreak of the global financial crisis in 2008. According to the OECD report (2017a: 34–6), recent developments in this sector, mainly in the form of expansion of bank credit and stock markets, have been correlated with increasing economic inequality in the OECD. The expansion of bank credit, particularly for financing real estate, was found associated with slower household income growth due to bust in housing markets, and these negative effects hit people at the bottom of income distribution most. Stock market expansion, on the other hand, was found linked with stronger household income growth at the top of income distribution because stock holdings were concentrated in the hands of high-income people. In the eurozone, stock market wealth was four times more unequally distributed than household income. High holding concentration caused the expansion of stock markets, which delivered more dividends and capital gains, to only benefit high-income people and thus aggravated income inequality.

Furthermore, the expansion of the financial sector did not contribute to stronger growth in most OECD countries, but crowded out long-term investment. Short-termism and high trading frequency of stock markets reduced the willingness of business to invest and changed corporate investment behaviours (OECD, 2017a: 63; Jacobs and Mazzucato, 2016: 13). Therefore, the OECD (2017a: 63) reminds governments to promote more equitable financial markets that serve the real economy and channel capital into productive activities.

National financial systems can be roughly distinguished into two kinds: stock market-based or bank-based. The former is argued to be conducive to financing new start-up firms, especially in the cutting-edge technology sector, but may be harmful to industrial development in the long run due to its short-termism. The latter is believed to establish the long-term financial relationship mainly with established firms but is less helpful to supporting new start-ups. The Danish financial system was primarily bank-based. Commercial banks and mortgage banks dominated the financial system and accounted for two-thirds of financial sector assets, equivalent to about 400% of its GDP. By contrast, the Danish equity market was medium-sized by international standards, composed of vast majority of small- and medium-sized enterprises (SMEs), and its turnover has been low. The relatively large size of the Danish banking system in part reflected the high level of domestic interconnectedness (Lundvall, 2002: 87–8; Berg, 2017; IMF, 2014: 8–9, 2006: 24).

The other characteristic of the Danish banking sector was its unique mortgage financing model, which was once described as 'most sophisticated mortgage systems in the world' (Haldrup, 2017: 2). According to Danish law, all mortgages were granted by mortgage credit institutions (MCIs) to home-buyers and should be supported by 'equivalent bond with maturity', with cash flow being matched with underlying loans perfectly, the so-called balance principle. Loan-to-value ratios (LTVs), 80% at maximum, and valuation principles were also legally regulated. All mortgage-covered bonds were secured by associated 'collateral pools' of underlying properties, and MCIs were in principle non-profit organizations. These key elements—the balance principle of securitization, safety margins of LTVs, conservative valuation standards, diverse and sizeable collateral pools—of the Danish mortgage financing system resulted in a market-determined and transparent property market with public access to rich information on properties and affordable credit for those without large prior savings (Haldrup, 2017: 4–27). The mortgage-covered bond market was at the heart of the Danish financial system (see Fig. 6.2). In terms of GDP share, it was the largest in the world, accounting for 150% of Denmark's GDP; in terms of monetary value, it was the second largest in Europe (IMF, 2014: 5–8 & 16; Chong, 2010: 372). Under such a system, MCIs faced little market and refinancing risks, and 'there has never been an incident of default on a Danish mortgage bond' (Chong, 2010: 373). Even during the global financial crisis, the Danish mortgage bond market was still unscratched and continued functioning. Berg and Bentzen

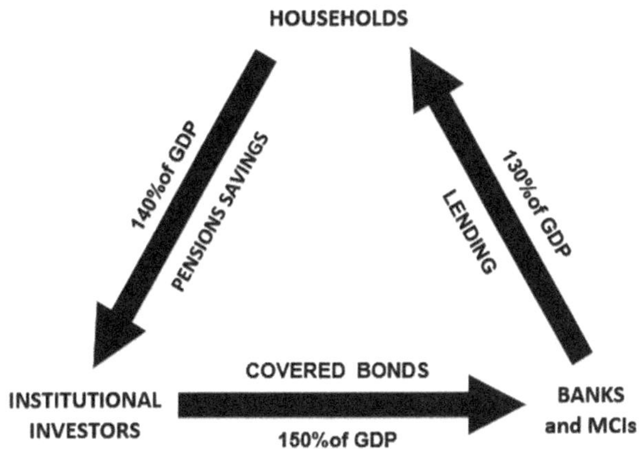


**Fig. 6.2** The Danish mortgage financing system. Source: Quote form IMF 'Denmark: financial system stability assessment', 2014, p. 9

(2014: 59–63), Gyntelberg et al. (2012: 64–6), Chong (2010: 397), and Haldrup (2017: 8) all attribute such exceptional performance to the good design of the mortgage finance system because the balance principle provided flexibility and transparency for borrowers and confidence and security for investors.

Nevertheless, it does not mean the Danish financial system was flawless and immune from financial crises. In fact, the Danish banking sector was seriously hit by the 2008 global financial crisis, and the number of banks decreased almost by half, down from 145 in 2007 to 74 in 2017. The reasons for such great losses of the Danish banking sector were common with those in other countries: high growth in bad-quality loans, misjudgement of credit risks, heavy concentration, and exposure to risky industries (Berg, 2017). The government had to rescue the sector with six bank packages by capital injections, liquidity support, and government guarantees (OECD, 2014: 11). It was widely believed that the collapse of the Danish banking sector was a result of the lack of control by both the banking executive management and financial authorities—Financial Supervisory Authority—for the two had close relationship with staff turnover. The corporate governance of Danish banks was further criticized for their unusual high remuneration of executive management and the male dominance at the top management level, which were found to be associated with excessive risk exposure to large customers and the construction sector (Rose, 2017: 168–93).

## 9.5 *Pillar 5: Asset Building and Entrepreneurship*

As the World Economic Forum (2017: 100) indicates, small business entrepreneurship and home ownership are usually the first means that working families can accumulate asset apart from savings and pensions. For most people, they provide a main ladder to the middle class. In terms of small business entrepreneurship, the degree of ease of starting and running a business in existing legal environments is critical for business and employment creation. Businesses are at the centre of supporting an inclusive economy, because as the OECD (2017a: 58–9) rightly contends, they are unique in creating and providing employment and in underpinning individual and collective welfares. In short, the sustainability of an inclusive economy replies on a thriving business sector. Regulatory clarity, fair cost for business financing, and flexibility in running business were found to be beneficial to inducing young companies. Young and small businesses were more affected by poorly designed regulations than larger and incumbent ones, which would limit their potential to grow and reduce the overall business dynamism.

Since the late 1990s, there has been a decline in business creation and dynamism. Against this world trend, business dynamism has been keeping very high in Denmark. Business birth rates and death rates were among the highest in European advanced economies (Eurostat, 2018b). In terms of business-friendly regulations, Denmark was ranked as the world's third best country on the ease of doing business index, only next to New Zealand and Singapore (Lanvin et al., 2018: 23 & 248). The industrial structure of Denmark was featured with many small- and medium-sized enterprises that excelled in pockets of high technology. SMEs accounted for 61% of Denmark's economic value added (EVA) and provided 65% of employment. One characteristic of Denmark's SMEs was its high productivity, 70% higher than the EU average, among which manufacturing and ICT sectors performed particularly well.

High business creation and dynamism could be partly attributed to Denmark's SMEs-friendly environment. Since 2008, the Danish government adopted 'Think Small First' principle in all policy- and law-making activities, and Denmark performed comparatively well than other EU countries on assisting SMEs in internationalization, skills and innovation, and responsive administration (European Commission, 2016: 1–5). Apart from these enabling functions, the Danish government has played little direct role in directing the economy beyond competition policy (Schubert and Martens, 2005: 28 & 40 & 44; Madsen, 2002: 262). High business creation and market dynamism helped to develop a competitive and innovative economy. Knowledge-intensive sectors have been the locomotive in facilitating innovation and economic growth, and eco-innovation was viewed as a key driver in Denmark's transition to a green economy. The Capital Region of Denmark—Region Hovedstaden—was one of the most innovative regions in the EU. The Global Innovation Index listed Denmark as the world's top ten most innovative country. On the Global Cleantech Innovation Index, it was ranked as the world's fifth best country. (Kristensen et al., 2018: 118–26 & 129).

In terms of home ownership, access to good and affordable housing is a fundamental human need and key to an inclusive economy. For most people, housing costs are the single largest household expenditure and represent a substantial financial burden. During the last decade, housing became less affordable and home ownership has been in sharp decline worldwide. The sharp increase in housing prices in relation to wages was one major reason of why wealth inequality has deteriorated much more than income inequality in OECD countries (OECD, 2017a: 13).

On housing equality, Denmark performed less well than most EU members. Less than half, 49.5%, of the total housing stock was owner-occupied, the second lowest in the EU. More than half of Danish people had to turn to the rental market, and entering the housing market has become difficult since 2010. The Danish government has provided a large amount of social housing and has solved 42% of overall rental needs. New policies aiming to increase social housing from 20% to 25% were also initiated by local governments; social housing, however, was far from meeting the growing demand. It was estimated that waiting list for social housing in Copenhagen has been growing to reach a 30-year delay. In addition, house price-to-income ratio was comparatively high in Denmark. Denmark's average housing costs compared to disposable income and the rate of housing overburden were the second highest in the EU, resulting in household debt in Denmark being the highest among advanced countries. With such high mortgage debt, surprisingly, Denmark had the very low share of people arrears on mortgage payment (Pittini et al., 2017: 20 & 28 & 60–1; IMF, 2014: 10), which was related to its unique mortgage finance system, as explained in Pillar 4.

## *9.6 Pillar 6: Employment and Labour Compensation*

A well-functioning labour market with high participation rate is the top priority for every country, not only because employment is a major source for financing welfare provision but also because quality employment prevents families and individuals from poverty and social exclusion (Hemerijck, 2013: 383). Denmark has been often cited by the OECD and EU as a role model for best practice in promoting labour market participation and quality employment. Unemployment, as a yardstick for observing the functioning of labour market, has been low in Denmark, less than 6%, since 2000, and its youth unemployment was also one of the lowest in the EU. Its employment rates, 77.4%, were among the top performers in the OECD, with high earnings quality, low labour market insecurity, and low long hours of working. High employment rate does not necessarily mean high productivity and welfare enhancement, as they may be achieved through low-paid jobs, temporary employment, and poor working conditions, which have been becoming a global phenomenon and referred to as 'the working poor'. Low-income rates in Denmark were the lowest among advanced EU economies as taking up low-paid jobs would entail an after-tax income loss. Denmark was also the only Nordic country where productivity per person employed has kept growing even during the global financial crisis between 2007 and 2015. The Danish labour market also provided equal opportunities for different groups as its gender income gap and employment gap for disadvantaged groups were the second lowest in the EU. (OECD, 2017a: 38; Norlen, 2018: 69–71; Karlsdottir et al., 2018: 74–7; Klein and Hansen, 2016: 12).

Many commentators attribute Denmark's outstanding performance on employment to its unique labour market system, the so-called flexicurity. It was a combination of flexibility and security and an outcome of serial labour market reforms since the 1990s. The need to introduce such a system, as Poul N. Rasmussen (2005: 52), the then Danish prime minister, explains, was for economic survival after the country experienced the sharp economic decline in the 1990s. Denmark, being an open economy, has well experienced the effects of globalization and adapting to it was a question of survival. Businesses needed flexibility to adapt to a fast-changing market competition and meet the challenges brought by globalization. On the other hand, more than one-tenth of jobs in Denmark were disappearing or outsourcing every year. Job changes became common for workers and lifelong learning and training were required for them to succeed in the job market and to avoid unemployment. 'Flexicurity' was a strategy to address these challenges faced by both employers and employees. It was composed of a 'golden triangle': first, flexible labour market which allowed employers to hire and fire easily; second, social security supported by generous unemployment benefits for unemployed workers;

and, third, active labour market policies (ALMPs) which aimed to enhance employability, with or without jobs (Bonoli, 2012: 196; Madsen, 2002: 243–58).

Under such a system, employers were endowed with external, internal, and functional flexibility and employees with employment and income security rather than job security. By international standards, job security in Denmark was very low and job mobility was very high, with 30% of job changes each year. There was no minimum wage protection in Denmark, either. Although Danish trade unions were powerful as they were entitled to one-third of the seats of company boards and working conditions were regulated through collective agreements, collective bargaining between employers and employees has been decentralized to a regional and company level in the last 20 years to tailor to local conditions. Legislation was generally controlling and procedural in order to allow more internal flexibility for production fluctuations and business cycles (Jensen and Larsen, 2005: 56–7 & 59; Deloitte, 2015: 27–9; Kvist et al., 2008: 253). Denmark was ranked as the world's best country on the index of easy hiring and redundancy and the world's fourth best country on labour-employer cooperation in the Global Talent Competitiveness Index survey (Lanvin and Evans, 2018: 140). Employees were compensated by the provision with employment security and income security to enable them in job transitions rather than fearing these changes. Employment security functioned through constant skill-upgrading and income security was realized by providing generous unemployment benefits at a high replacement rate of 90% of their previous income for one year (Rasmussen, 2005: 55; Madsen, 2002: 243–58).

ALMPs played a critical role in this 'flexicurity' system. Politically, they ensured that the welfare system would not be misused and justified the generous welfare provisions by gaining the public support as benefits receivers had the right and duty to participate in various activation schemes. Compared to other OECD countries, Denmark's ALMPs focused on 'activating' the unemployed, spending most on job training rather than direct job creation and employment assistance (Kvist et al., 2008: 237–41; Bonoli, 2012: 185–7). Economically, job training and education provided by ALMPs were proved to produce positive employment effects for the unemployed. Rasmussen (2005: 54) contends that ALMPs were more effective in getting the unemployed back to work than lowering unemployment benefits. The survey on participants of activation schemes found that the majority of them believed these schemes had positive effects on their lives and made them better qualified for job searching. Socially, ALMPs had a bigger vision of promoting an inclusive society. They were employed as policy tools to increasing social integration and reducing inequality. It is noteworthy that, despite its confirmed effectiveness, ALMPs had its limits. A significant minority, 24%, held a negative view on their employment effects. Also, the gap of employment rates between immigrants and natives still persisted across generations (Madsen, 2002: 243–58; Kvist et al., 2008: 222–4; Klein and Hansen, 2016: 8–9 & 11 & 18–19).

Under such design, ALMPs have turned the nature of Danish social welfare systems from passive compensation of unemployment risks to the active promotion of employability, and from dependency schemes to springboards for new opportunities, as they equipped the unemployed with new skills and better qualifications instead of simply repairing damages. ALMPs, which protected and enhanced the employability of the unemployed, were found to increase overall employment levels, particularly to quality jobs (Hemerijck, 2013: 165; Rasmussen, 2005: 54; Jensen and Larsen, 2005: 61–2; Nelson and Stephens, 2012: 206 & 211). This can explain why trade unions in Denmark were not concerned about job security, but about developing workers' competences. Jensen and Larsen (2005: 63–4), the then president of the Danish Confederation of Trade Union and director general of the Confederation of Danish Employers, respectively, jointly point out that from 1975 to 2000, employment in the textile industry fell by 80%, around 50,000 jobs, because of outsourcing, but two-thirds of unemployed workers managed to find new jobs within a year. Nearly 60% of Danish workers being surveyed thought it would be 'easy' or 'very easy' to find a new job. In other words, ALMPs have Danish workers well prepared for globalization and large-scale industrial readjustments.

Furthermore, ALMPs enhanced the competitiveness of Danish workers. Jobs can be distinguished into four types: discretionary learning, lean production, Taylorist organization, and traditional organization. Different types of jobs have different exposures to global competition, and discretionary learning jobs, involving complex problem-solving, were the least exposed to global competition. Empirical evidences found that the higher the expenditure on ALMPs, the more likely the discretionary learning patterns of work organizations would be (Lundvall and Lorenz, 2012: 239–41 & 245–8 & 254). Denmark's spending on ALMPs per head was the largest in the OECD, and its ratio of discretionary learning jobs was the second highest in EU-15 countries, only next to the Netherlands

(Hemerijck, 2013: 258–9; Lundvall and Lorenz, 2012: 239–41). In short, ALMPs enhanced employment security, justifying income security guaranteed by generous unemployment benefits and complementing flexibility for businesses to pursue competitiveness. Denmark's flexicurity therefore reconciled two seemingly incompatible objectives—flexibility for employers and security for employees—promising that there will be no left behinds or losers in economic changes.

## 9.7 Pillar 7: Fiscal Transfer

As many commentators suggest, fiscal policies, if properly designed, can simultaneously promote social inclusion and economic growth. For the former, they were confirmed to be able to reduce economic inequality by about one-third directly through progressive taxation and indirectly through transfer spending on education and health (IMF, 2017b: 6–7; McKinsey Global Institute, 2016: 14; OECD, 2017a: 49–51; Oxfam, 2014: 120). For the latter, redistribution policies on education, childcare, health, labour market participation, and unemployment benefits were confirmed to be associated with higher growth (Cingano, 2014: 20; Crouch, 2015: 65). On the contrary, if badly designed, fiscal policies could exacerbate economic inequality (Oxfam, 2014: 81–2). Fiscal policies, indeed, were powerful policy tools to address the rising economic inequality, but their design depended on social preferences, administrative capacity, and fiscal sustainability on the one hand and fiscal sovereignty has been constrained by growing financial globalization on the other (IMF, 2017b: 27–8; OECD, 2017a: 28). One characteristic of fiscal policies in advanced economies in the last three decades was the introduction of neoliberal tax reforms, in which corporate income tax and personal income tax were lowered in order to attract investment, thus shifting tax bases from progressive income tax (PIT) regime towards regressive tax structures. These trends have been argued to contribute to the rising economic inequality (Kohler, 2015: 17; IMF, 2017b: 28; OECD, 2017a: 26).

Denmark was different from other advanced economies in tax regime, tax revenues, and public spending. In terms of tax regime, similar with other advanced economies, its personal income tax rates have been reduced after several reforms in the last decades, ranging from 38% to 55.8%, but Denmark still maintained the PIT structure. It still had one of the highest personal income tax rates in the OECD. By contrast, Denmark's tax rates on business were relatively modest by international standards. Its corporate tax rates, used to be as high as 50% in the 1990s, had been reduced to 22% from 2016 after several tax reforms, below the OECD average level. Similarly, Denmark taxed capital gains for individuals at progressive rates from 27% to 42%, but for companies, the rates were reduced to the range of 0–23.5%. Denmark had no wealth tax (Deloitte, 2015: 9–12 & 22–5; OECD, 2006: 12; Copenhagen Capacity, 2018).

In terms of tax revenues, Denmark's tax-to-GDP ratio, 45.9%, was the highest among OECD countries. Unlike other OECD countries, Denmark's tax revenues came mainly from personal income tax (personal income, profits, and gains), much less from corporate income tax. The former accounted for 55.2% of the total revenue, much higher than the OECD average of 24.4%, while the latter accounted for only 5.6% of its total revenues, well below the OECD average of 8.9%. Also, unlike most OECD countries, Denmark almost had no revenue, only 0.1%, from social security contribution. Its revenue from property taxes, value-added taxes (VAT), and other consumption taxes was at the similar level with the OECD average (OECD, 2017b: 3, 2017c: 1–2).

In terms of public spending, Denmark's public spending in relation to GDP, 53.6%, was the third highest in the EU, next to Finland and France. The characteristic of its public spending was that it spent most of its tax revenue on education, health, and social protection (such as unemployment benefits and social assistance). The former two were the highest in the EU, while the latter one was the third highest in terms of the ratio of GDP. These three policies altogether accounted for 72.6% of its total spending. By contrast, Denmark's spending on defence and public order and safety were relatively low compared to the EU average (Eurostat, 2018a).

Fiscal redistribution policies had asymmetrical effects: they benefited people at the bottom of the social class pyramid more as their disadvantages associated with lower social class origins have largely disappeared. Fiscal transfer has effectively reduced market income inequality in Denmark, measured by Gini coefficient, by 35% (Eurofound, 2017: 8–9; OECD, 2017a: 260). For example, rising housing prices once deteriorated economic equality in the early 2000s in Denmark, but it was partially offset by progressive taxation. The share of taxable income held by the top 1% was around 5% in Denmark, and the share of households living in relative poverty, measured by living below 50% of the median disposable income, was among the lowest in the OECD. Such performance has been stable in the last decades and was exceptional among OECD countries, as income inequality has worsened in most OECD economies (Causa et al.,

2016: 7 & 19–21). In terms of income distribution, Denmark was the most equitable country in the EU (Lindberg and Rispling, 2018: 110–1). Such relative economic equality was found to be helpful to shaping Denmark's economic pattern. Economic equality promoted social trust between employers and employees and enhanced employees' willingness to job training and learning. Denmark was the best country on organizational learning (in)equality in EU-15 countries, characterizing it as a learning economy, good at learning by doing and by using and interacting, rather than in large-scale intensive science-based sectors (Lundvall and Lorenz, 2012: 249–50 & 252–3).

In short, Denmark had a relatively large public sector. Its fiscal transfers were financed by general tax revenue, mainly from personal income tax, based on progressive tax structure, and spending most revenues on enabling and equalizing policies such as education, health, and social protection.

## 10 Characterizing the Danish Formula of Inclusive Capitalism

Evaluating by the above seven pillars, Denmark did not perform all that well in all criteria. It has performed particularly well in education and skills, basic services, corruption and rents, employment and labour policies, as well as fiscal transfers, but much less well in financial intermediation and asset building, mainly housing equality. More precisely, what Denmark has performed well was in areas involving capability developing for labour, from childhood to adulthood, and in areas involving market competition for capital, from business creation to operation. The Danish model could be 'socially inclusive' because it maximized the chances for everyone in their life course (through public education and health) and in the labour market (through ALMPs). It could be 'economically productive' because it provided sufficient flexibility, skilled labours, quality infrastructure, and friendly corporate taxes for business to compete in the world market. The Danish formula could be seen as successful as its strong competitiveness shows the success of education and labour market policies, leading to an innovative and learning economy and its good adaptability to global competition. Its high employment rates represent the success of ALMPs and public childcare policies. Its low-income inequality and sustainable economic growth show the success of public governance and taxation. The Danish model has proved to be a triple-win formula:

pro-business (because of high flexibility and ease of doing business), pro-labour (because of income equality and social protection), and pro-government (because of fiscal sustainability), resulting in an outcome of 'triad of high employment, distributive justice and decent levels of economic growth' (Hemerijck, 2013: 289). Inclusive capitalism thus embodied in a day-to-day reality in Denmark; not just existed in academic and media discussions.

Looking further, quality public services in education, health, ALMPs, digital infrastructure, and public administration all originate from one common source: the government staging at the centre as a big investor and enabler. Without right policy-making, heavy public investments could be counter-productive. Equally, without reliable and uncorrupted public governance, progressive and heavy taxation could not be accepted and be effectively collected, and all meaningful public investments would collapse as a result. The Danish formula thus formed a self-producing organism: governance as the generator of driving inclusive capitalism by enabling individuals through public education, public health services, ALMPs, and social protection, so as to provide quality and skilled labours for businesses. Businesses were enabled by high flexibility, uncorrupted governance, and quality infrastructure. High business creation and dynamism, accompanied with lifelong learning workforce, resulted in a competitive and innovative economy. A growing and competitive economy further underpinned sustainable fiscal transfers through high and progressive taxation, which directed most public spending back to education, health, and social protection (see Fig. 6.3).

In short, right thinking behind policy-making and effective governance held the key to the success of the Danish formula. At the policy-making level, the right thinking behind policy-making—treating economic policies also as social policies, and vice versa—reconciled economic growth and equality simultaneously. Public policies, indeed, reflect the values and preferences of a society, and they differed from country to country. Hemerijck (2013: 156 & 164) argues that a variety of egalitarian policies in Denmark derived from its ideological roots in Lutheranism and its corresponding ethos of public responsibility. However, such arguments neglected a fact that the Danish model has been transforming since the 1990s. It was not a priori assumption, but rather posterior practices. Also, as economic inequality has become a global risk and seeking equal chances to good living is a common need for all humankind, implementing inclusive capitalism was a universal call and should transcend national preferences

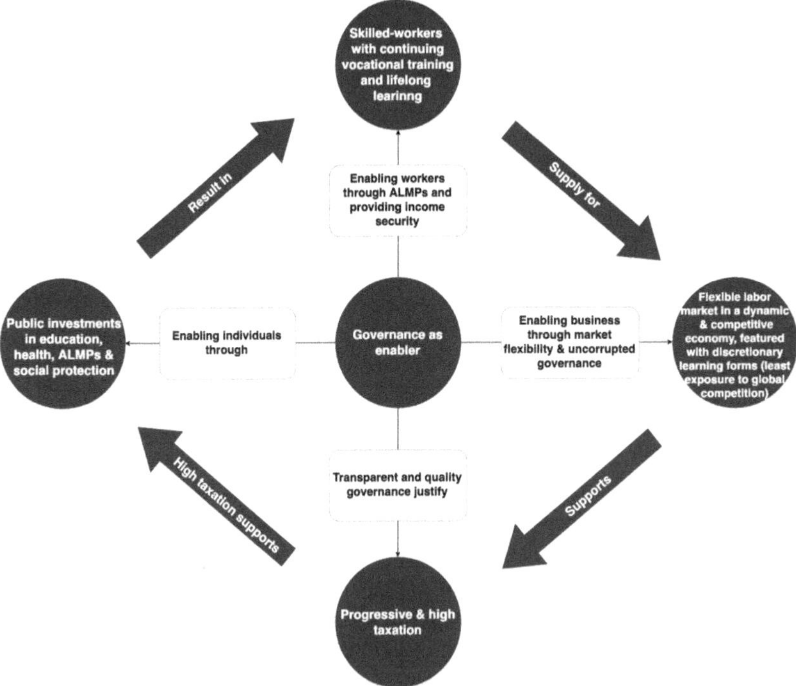


**Fig. 6.3** The Danish formula of inclusive capitalism

to different values and ideologies. At the policy implementing level, to what extent administration capacity in Denmark could deliver quality services, while being responsive and uncorrupted, determined whether and how the Danish formula could be successful or not. The administration was the interface between the state and the people, translating static policies into real, concrete services. That was an interesting mystery beyond the scope of this chapter and required further investigation.

## 11 Conclusion

Inclusive capitalism, as World Economic Forum (2017: ix) indicates, cannot be achieved by single policy solely; it is 'an integrated system'. As Madsen (2002: 262) warns, taking isolated policy within this specific combination and transferring to other social-economic-political environments may run high risk of being unsuccessful. While having its limits and deficiencies, the Danish formula largely embodied inclusive capitalism as a policy eco-system, composed of a wide range of policies surrounding acquired equal opportunities. At the core, it was more about the right thinking behind policy-making and effective governance than the policy constellation it presented. For effective governance, good policies and best practices can be emulated relatively easily, but the institutional capacity of delivering good governance could not be built up just overnight. The role of state was rediscovered and re-emphasized in the Danish formula.

What was more challenging, however, was the thinking behind policy-making. The Danish formula highlighted a simple fact that policies related directly to personal development, such as education, health, and labour market policies, were the most critical ones as they could address economic growth and inequality simultaneously. They constituted the organic body of producing an inclusive economy. For a very long time, the world has been embracing the neo-liberal ideology, believing that economic growth and justice were a trade-off and cannot co-exist. Market liberalization policies promoted by the EU and 'Washington Consensus' in the last decades embodied such an ideological orthodoxy. Yet, the Danish formula of inclusive capitalism has overcome such a dichotomy and provided a responsible answer to economic inequality other than trade protectionism and populist nationalism. It has proved that social investment in human capital was both an economic and a social strategy, and a large public sector, contrary to the neo-liberal arguments, can be productivity-enhancing and competitiveness-promoting. The Danish formula has shown that to get economics right (to be competitive and growing), it has to get policies right (to be enabling and inclusive). To get policies right, it has to get the thinking right. It turned out that it was not capitalism needed to reform. It was the prevailing liberalist orthodoxy that guided EU governance in desperate need of overhaul.

## References

Aoun, J. (2018), 'Robot-proof: How to protect jobs in an AI future', *Speech Transcript to the Royal Institute of International Affairs*, London, 22 January 2018.

Author, D. H. (2015), 'Why are there still so many jobs? The history and future of workplace automation', *Journal of Economic Perspectives*, Vol. 29 (3), pp. 3–30.

Aghion, P., E. Caroli and C. Garcia-Penalosa (1999), 'Inequality and economic growth: The perspective of the new growth theories', *Journal of Economic Literature*, Vol. 37 (4), pp. 1615–60.

Barro, R.J. (2000), 'Inequality and growth in a panel of countries', *Journal of Economic Growth*, Vol. 5(1), pp. 5–32.

Bassanini A. and T. Manfredi (2012), 'Capital grabbing hand? A cross-country/cross-industry analysis of the decline of the labor share', *OECD Social, Employment and Migration Working Papers*, No. 133.

Berg, J. (2017), 'Financial stability and financial sector policies in Denmark', *Speech of Director General of the Danish Financial Supervisory Authority at Special Event of Joint Vienna Institute*, 3 November 2017, Vienna.

Berg J. and C. S. Bentzen (2014), 'Mirror, mirror, who is the fairest of them all? Reflections on the design of and risk distribution in the mortgage systems of Denmark and the UK?', *National Institute Economic Review*, No. 230, November 2014, pp. 58–75.

Berg, A.G. and J.D. Ostry (2011), 'Inequality and unsustainable growth: Two sides of the same coin?', *IMF Staff Discussion Note*, SDN/11/08, Washington, DC: IMF.

Berg, A., J.D. Ostry and J. Zettelmeyer (2012), 'What makes growth sustained?', *Journal of Development Economics*, Vol. 98(2), pp. 149–66.

Bonoli, G. (2012), 'Active labor market policy and social investment: A changing relationship', in N. Morel, B. Palier and J. Palme eds., *Towards A Social Investment Welfare State? Ideas, Policies and Challenges*, Bristol: The Polity Press, pp. 181–204.

Bourguignon, F. (1981), 'Pareto superiority of unegalitarian equilibria in Stiglitz' model of wealth distribution with convex saving function, *Econometrica*, Vol. 49(6), pp. 1469–75.

Brezis, E. S. (2018), 'Elitism in higher education and inequality: Why are the Nordic countries so special?', *Intereconomics*, Vol. 53(4), pp. 201–8.

Causa, O., M. Hermansen, N. Ruiz, C. Klein and Z. Smidova (2016), 'Inequality in Denmark through the looking glass', *OECD Economics Department Working Papers No. 1341*, Paris: OECD.

Chong, J. H.W.C. (2010), 'Danish mortgage regulations—Structure, evolution, and crisis management', *Washington University Global Studies Law Review*, 9(2), pp. 371–98.

Cingano, F. (2014), 'Trend in income inequality and its impact on economic growth', *OECD Social, Employment and Migration Working Papers No. 165*, Paris: OECD.

Coyle (2017), 'Rethinking GDP', Finance and Development, March, pp. 17–9.

Copenhagen Capacity (2018), 'Taxation in Denmark', http://www.copcap.com/set-up-a-business/taxation (last viewed 30 April 2018).

Credit Suisse Research Institute (2017), *Growth Wealth Report 2017*, Zurich: Credit Suisse.

Corlett, A. (2016), *Examining an Elephant: Globalization and the Lower Class of the Rich World*, London: Resolution Foundation.

Crouch, C. (2015), 'The next step', in C. Hay and A. Payne eds., *Civic Capitalism*, Cambridge: Polity, pp. 62–9.

Deloitte (2015), Taxation and Investment in Denmark 2015, UK: Deloitte Network.

Eurofound (2017), *Social Mobility in the EU*, Luxembourg: Publications Office of the European Union.

European Commission (2016), *2016 SBA Fact Sheet: Denmark*, Brussels: European Commission.

——— (2017), 'Social summit for fair jobs and growth: Strengthening the EU's social dimension', Press Release on 16 November 2017.

Eurostat (2018a), 'Government expenditure by function—COFOG', 13 March 2018, http://ec.europa.eu/eurostat/statistics-explained/index.php/Government_expenditure_by_function_%E2%80%93_COFOG (accessed 14 March 2018).

——— (2018b), 'Structural business statistics overview', 5 February 2018, http://ec.europa.eu/eurostat/statistics-explained/index.php/Structural_business_statistics_overview (accessed 14 March 2018).

Galor, O, and O. Moav (2004), 'From physical to human capital accumulation: Inequality and the process of development', *Review of Economic Studies*, Vol. 71 (4), pp. 1001–26.

Goodwin, M. (2017), 'Labour faces the need to reconcile with working class Brexit', *Expert Comments of Chatham House*, London: Royal Institute of International Affairs (Chatham House).

Gyntelberg, J., K. Kjeldsen, M.B. Nielsen, and Ma. Persson (2012), 'The 2008 financial crisis and the Danish mortgage market', in A. Bardhan, R.H. Edelstein and C.A. Kroll eds., *Global Housing Market: Crises, Policies and Institutions*, New Jersey: John Wiley & Sons, pp. 53–67.

Hagan, S. (2018), 'Cancer in the system', *Chatham House Research Paper*, April 2018, https://www.chathamhouse.org/publications/twt/cancer-system-0 (accessed 9 April 2018).

Haldrup, K. (2017), 'On security of collateral in Danish mortgage finance: A formula of property rights, incentives and market mechanisms', *European Journal of Law and Economics*, 43(1), pp. 1–29.

Helliwell, J.F., R. Layard and J.D. Sachs (2018), *World Happiness Report*, New York: Sustainable Development Solutions Network.

Hemerijck, A. (2013), *Changing Welfare States*, Oxford: Oxford University Press.

Hutton, W. (2015), *How Good We Can Be: Ending the Mercenary Society and Building A Great Country*, London: Abacus.

Hay, C. and A. Payne (2015), 'Civic capitalism', in C. Hay and A. Payne eds., *Civic Capitalism*, Cambridge: Polity, pp. 3–50.

IMF (2006), *Denmark: Financial System Stability Assessment*, IMF Country Report No. 06/343, Washington, DC: IMF.

——— (2007), 'The globalization of labor', *World Economic Outlook*, April 2017, pp. 161–92.

——— (2014), *Denmark: Financial System Stability Assessment*, IMF Country Report No. 14/336, Washington, DC: IMF.

——— (2017a), *World Economic Outlook April 2017: Gaining Momentum?*, Washington, DC: IMF.

——— (2017b), *Fiscal Monitor: Tackling Inequality*, Washington, DC: IMF.

International Labour Organization and Organization for Economic Cooperation and Development (2015), *The Labour Share in G20 Economies*, Geneva and Paris: ILO & OECD.

International Institute for Management and Development (IMD) (2017), 'new competitive global elite emerges in IMD business school's latest world competitiveness ranking', News story, May 2017, Lausanne: IMD.

Institute for Public Policy Research (2017), *Time for Change: A New Vision for the British Economy*, London: IPPR.

Jacobs, M. and M. Mazzucato (2016), 'Rethinking capitalism: An introduction', in M. Jacobs and M. Mazzucato eds., *Rethinking Capitalism: Economics and Policy for Sustainable and Inclusive Growth*, Oxford: Wiley-Blackwell, pp. 1–27.

Jensen, H. and J. N. Larsen (2005), "The Nordic labour markets and the concept of flexicurity', in C. B. Schubert and H. Martens eds., *The Nordic Model: A Recipe for European Success?*, Brussels: European Policy Centre.

Johnsen, H.G., J. Grunfelder, M. F. Moller and T. Rinne (2018), 'Digitalisation for a more inclusive Nordic region', in J. Grunfelder, L. Rispling and G. Norlen eds., *The State of The Nordic Region*, Copenhagen: Nordic Council of Ministers, pp. 160–9.

Karlsdottir, A., L. Randall and G. Norlen (2018), 'Towards inclusive Nordic labor markets', in J. Grunfedler, L. Rispling and G. Norlen eds., *State of the Nordic Region*, pp. 74–86.

Kelly, C. and C. D'Arcy (2015), 'Putting the "civic" more into the mix', C. Hay and A. Payne eds., *Civic Capitalism*, Cambridge: Polity, pp. 84–9.

Klein, C. and L. A. Hansen (2016), 'Balancing inclusiveness, work incentives and sustainability in Denmark', *OECD Economics Department Working Papers No. 1338*, Paris: OECD.

Kohler, P. (2015), 'Redistribution policies for sustainable development: Looking at the role of assets and equity', DESA Working Paper No. 139, ST/ESA/2015/DWP/139, New York: Department of Economic and Social Affairs of United Nations.

Kumhof, M., C. Lebarz, R. Ranciere, A. W. Richter and N. A. Throckmorton (2012), 'Income inequality and current account imbalance', *IMF Working Paper*, WP/12/08, Washington: IMF.

Kvist, J., L. Pedersen, and P.A. Kohler (2008), 'Making all persons work: Modern Danish labour market policies', in W. Eichhorst, O. Kaufmann and R, Konle-Seidl eds., *Bringing the Jobless into Work? Experiences with Activation Schemes in Europe and the US*, Berlin: Springer, pp. 221–56.

Kristensen, I, J. Teras and M. Kull (2018), 'The Nordics: Europe's hotbed of innovation', in J. Grunfelder, L. Rispling and G. Norlen eds., *The State of The Nordic Region*, Copenhagen: Nordic Council of Ministers, pp. 118–30.

Lagarde, C. (2014), 'Economic inclusion and financial integrity', Speech by Christine Lagarde, Managing Director, International Monetary Fund, 27 May 2014, London.

Lazear, E.P. and S. Rosen (1981), 'Rank-order tournaments as optimum labor contracts', *Journal of Political Economy*, Vol. 89(5), pp. 841–64.

Lanvin, B. and P. Evans (2018), 'Country profiles', in B. Lavin and P. Evans eds., *The Global Talent Competitiveness Index: Diversity for Competitiveness*, Fontainebleau: INSEAD, pp. 111–233.

Lanvin, B., P. Evans, E. Rodriguez-Montemayor (2018), 'Diversity as a lever for talent competitiveness', in B. Lavin and P. Evans eds., *The Global Talent Competitiveness Index: Diversity for Competitiveness*, Fontainebleau: INSEAD, pp. 3–34.

Laursen, F., T. M. Andersen, and D. Jahn (2016), *Denmark Report: Sustainable Governance Indicators 2016*, Gutersloh: Bertelsmann Stiftung.

Levitas, R. (2015), 'Why not frighten the horses?', C. Hay and A. Payne eds., *Civic Capitalism*, Cambridge: Polity, pp. 90–6.

Lindberg, G. and L. Rispling (2018), 'Economic development', in J. Grunfelder, L. Rispling and G. Norlen eds., *The State of The Nordic Region*, Copenhagen: Nordic Council of Ministers, pp. 102–16.

Lundvall, B. (2002), *Innovation, Growth and Social Cohesion: The Danish Model*, Cheltenham, UK and Northampton, MA, USA: Edward Elgar.

Lundvall, B. and E. Lorenz (2012), 'Social investment in the globalizing learning economy: A European perspective', in N. Morel, B. Palier and J. Palme eds., *Towards A Social Investment Welfare State? Ideas, Policies and Challenges*, Bristol: The Polity Press, pp. 235–57.

Madsen, P.K. (2002), 'The Danish model of flexicurity: A paradise—with some snakes', in H. Sarfati and G. Bonoli eds., *Labour Market and Social Protection Reforms in International Perspective: Parallel or Converging Tracks?*, Hampshire: Ashgate, pp. 243–65.

McKinsey Global Institute (2016), *Power than Their Parents? Flat or Falling Incomes in Advanced Economies*, London, Mumbai, SF, Shanghai, Brussels, Paris and Silicon Valley: McKinsey & Company.

——— (2017), *Making It in America*, New York: McKinsey & Company.

McKinsey (2017), *A Future That Works: The Impact of Automation in Denmark*, Copenhagen: McKinsey.

Moran, M. (2015), 'It's the democratic politics, stupid', C. Hay and A. Payne eds., *Civic Capitalism*, Cambridge: Polity, pp. 97–103.

Morel, N., B. Palier and J. Palme (2012), 'Social investment: A paradigm in search of a new economic model and political mobilization', in N. Morel, B. Palier and J. Palme eds., *Towards A Social Investment Welfare State? Ideas, Policies and Challenges*, Bristol: The Polity Press, pp. 353–76.

Munich Security Conference (2017), Munich Security Report 2017: Post-Truth, Post-West, Post-Order?, Munich: Munich Security Conference.

Nelson, M and J. D. Stephens (2012), 'Do social investment policies produce more and better jobs?', in N. Morel, B. Palier and J. Palme eds., *Towards A Social Investment Welfare State? Ideas, Policies and Challenges*, Bristol: The Polity Press, pp. 205–34.

Norlen, G. (2018), 'Employment', in J. Grunfelder, L. Rispling and G. Norlen eds., *The State of The Nordic Region*, Copenhagen: Nordic Council of Ministers, pp. 62–86.

Onaran, O. and A. Guschanski (2017), 'Capital lessons: Labor, inequality and how to respond, *IPPR Progressive Review*, Vol. 24(2), pp. 153–62.

Ostry, J. (2017), 'To save globalization, its benefits need to be more broadly shared', Published by the World Economic Forum on 16 January 2017 at https://www.weforum.org/agenda/2017/01/to-save-globalization-its-benefits-need-to-be-more-broadly-shared/.

Ostry J. D., A. Berg and C.G.T. Tsangarides (2014), 'Redistribution, inequality, and growth', *IMF Staff Discussion Note*, SDN/14/02, IMF: Washington, DC.

OECD (2006), *Tax Policy Reforms in Denmark*, Paris: OECD.

——— (2014), *OECD Economic Surveys: Denmark*, Paris: OECD.

——— (2017a), *Bridging the Gap: Inclusive Growth 2017 Update Report*, Paris: OECD.

——— (2017b), *Revenue Statistics 2017: Tax Revenue Trends in the OECD*, Paris: OECD.

——— (2017c), *Revenue Statistics 2017 – Denmark*, Paris: OECD.

——— (2017d), *OECD Employment Outlook 2017*, Paris: OECD.

Oxfam (2014), *Even It Up: Time to End Extreme Inequality*, Oxford: Oxfam.

Obama, B. (2014), State of the Union Address, https://obamawhitehouse.archives.gov/the-press-office/2014/01/28/president-barack-obamas-state-union-address (accessed 12 December 2017).

Perotti, R. (1996), 'Growth, income distribution, and democracy: What the data say', *Journal of Economic Growth*, Vol. 1(2), pp. 149–87.

Piketty, T. (2014), *Capital in the Twenty-First Century*, translated by Arthur Goldhammer, Cambridge, MA USA: Harvard University Press.

Pittini, A, G. Koessl, J. Dijol, E. Lakatos and L. Ghekiere (2017), *The State of Housing in the EU 2017*, Brussels: Housing Europe.

Putnam, R. D. (2015), *Our Kids: The American Dream in Crisis*, NY and London: Simon & Schuster.

Raines, T., M. Goodwin and D. Cutts (2017), 'The future of Europe: Comparing public and elite attitudes', *Chatham House Research Paper*, issued on 20 June 2017, London: Royal Institute of International Affairs (Chatham House), pp. 1–48.

Randall, L. and A. Karlsdottir (2018), 'Education in an evolving economic landscape', in J. Grunfelder, L. Rispling and G. Norlen eds., *The State of The Nordic Region*, Copenhagen: Nordic Council of Ministers, pp. 88–99.

Rasmussen P. N. (2005), 'Learning from the North—Let's focus on best practice in all of Europe', in C.B. Schubert and H. Martens eds., The Nordic Model: A Recipe for European Success, *EPC Working Paper No. 20*, Brussels: European Policy Centre, pp. 50–5.

Rehn-Mendoza, N. and R. Weber (2018), 'Health and welfare', in J. Grunfelder, L. Rispling and G. Norlen eds., *The State of The Nordic Region*, Copenhagen: Nordic Council of Ministers, pp. 170–82.

Rose, C. (2017), 'The relationship between corporate governance characteristics and credit risk exposure in banks: Implications for financial regulation', *European Journal of Law and Economics*, Vol. 43(1), pp. 167–94.

Schubert, C.B. and H. Martens (2005), 'Introduction', in C.B. Schubert and H. Martens eds., The Nordic Model: A Recipe for European Success, *EPC Working Paper No. 20*, Brussels: European Policy Centre, pp. 8–28.

Schraad-Tischler, D., C. Schiller, S. M. Heller, and N. Siemer (2017), Social Justice in the EU—Index Report 2017, Gutersloh: Bertelsmann Stiftung.

Social Mobility Commission (2017), *Time for Change: An Assessment of Government Policies on Social Mobility 1997–2017*, London: Social Mobility Commission.

Stiglitz, J. E., Sen, A. and Fitoussi, J. (2009), *Report by the Commission on the Measure of Economic Performance and Social Progress*, Paris: CMEPSP.

Streeck, W. (2014), 'How will capitalism end?', *New Left Review*, Vol. 87, May–June, pp. 35–64.

Stiglitz, J. E. (2013), *The Price of Inequality*, NY and London: W.W. Norton & Company.

Stockhammer, E. (2015), 'Rising inequality as a cause of the present crisis', *Cambridge Journal of Economics*, Vol. 39, pp. 935–58.

Sundararajan, Arun (2017), 'The future of work: The digital economy will sharply erode the traditional employer-employee relationship', *Finance and Development*, June 2017, pp. 7–11.

*The Guardian*, 'Ontario plans to launch universal basic income trial run this summer', 24 April 2017, https://www.theguardian.com/world/2017/apr/24/canada-basic-income-trial-ontario-summer (accessed 15 December 2017).

Transparency International (2018), 'Corruption perceptions index 2017', 21 February 2018, https://www.transparency.org/news/feature/corruption_perceptions_index_2017 (accessed 14 March 2018).

World Economic Forum (2017), *The Global Risks Report 2017*, Switzerland: The Economic Forum.

Wilkinson, R. and K. E. Pickett (2009), *The Spiritual Level: Why Greater Equality Makes Societies Stronger*, NY and London: Bloomsbury Press.

——— (2017), 'The enemy between us: The psychological and social costs of inequality', *European Journal of Social Psychology*, Vol. 47, pp. 11–24.

CHAPTER 7

# Conclusion

At the beginning of the 2010s, the EU entered into a decade of crises. Preluded by the Greek sovereign debt crisis, a wider and larger-scale public finance crisis descended on a number of euro members, including the third and fourth largest economies of the eurozone. Despite the different causes and natures of the Portuguese, Irish, Spanish, and Italian crises, as explained in Chap. 2, EU leadership replied to these various crises with one common, inflexible recipe as its crisis management—austerity policies at the macroeconomic level on the one hand and labour market reforms, with reference to the German experiences, at the microeconomic level on the other. These neo-liberal policy responses, embodied the EU's long-held economic ideology, the so-called Brussels Doctrine, not just prolonged the crises but also aggravated the economic inequality and distributive injustice. A financial crisis, not surprisingly, turned into a political one—resulting in the continuing rise of populist, anti-EU right-wing parties (PRPs) in the EU politics since the European Parliament election in 2014 and culminating in the Brexit result of the UK referendum in 2016. There were, indeed, many plausible explanations for the electoral successes of PRPs and Brexit result. However, there were no more convincible arguments other than the simple fact that PRPs voters versus non-PRPs voters and Brexit voters versus non-Brexit voters were divided along with the lines of winners and losers of European integration. It was those left behind and economically disadvantaged workers from the European single market and single currency that formed the core clients for PRPs



C.-M. Luo, *The EU's Crisis Decade*,
https://doi.org/10.1007/978-981-13-6565-2_7

and Brexit votes. Crystal divisions among socio-economic classes highlight the seriousness of economic inequality and distributive injustice within the EU since the euro crisis.

Viewed from this perspective, the political crisis posed by the rise of PRPs and the Brexit referendum to the EU was the result of the economic mismanagement of EU leadership since the euro crisis. Austerity policies by EU leadership, along with quantitative easing by the European Central Bank, have worsened the economic inequality within the EU. It was the political prices that disillusioned voters asked from EU leadership to pay for their mismanagement. In essence, the crises that the EU has encountered in this decade—the euro crisis, the PRPs crisis, and the Brexit crisis—were not isolated events, but intertwined. More precisely, the latter two were the products of the former. They were self-induced by EU leadership.

What should be asked further is: Why would EU leadership resort to such a counter-productive policy answer to the euro crisis management, which led the EU to much larger, more inextricable crises? It was reported that, during the height of the global financial crisis, the UK Queen Elizabeth II asked distinguished economists at an LSE meeting why so many economists so badly misjudged such a critical risk within their profession (Oxenford, 2018). It was their firm belief in economic liberalism that market mechanism was omnipotent that has blinded their judgements. So was the same ideology that has misled the economic governance of EU leadership. Austerity policies and labour market reforms, as the EU's post-euro crisis economic management, imposed more market disciplines on EU member states and embodied such ideological orthodoxy. After all, it was the beliefs and ideas that have driven their governance and policies.

Regrettably and bizarrely, after encountering one crisis after another, there was no sign of any emerging alternative to the current neo-liberal orthodoxy among EU leadership. Reflections on economic liberalism did emerge among some policy-makers and commentators after the Brexit referendum. But very few European governments, if any, were intending seriously to address economic inequality and distributive injustice with any perceivable policy shifts other than protectionism and populism. Nor did they show any interest in exploring which policy areas that should start with first. Such ignorance and inaction of EU leadership to economic inequality, again, can only be understood from their long-held belief that 'there is no alternative' (TINA) to economic liberalism despite its imperfections. In fact, such a TINA belief was rather a political myth. It has never been a reality. As demonstrated in Chap. 6 on the Danish case, this book argues that there *is* an alternative to economic liberalism. Inclusive and fair capitalism does exist and functions well in practice for both economic growth and distributive justice.

What need to reform, therefore, is not only the economic orthodox held by EU leadership for long but also their misperceptions of capitalism. As Lagarde (2014) reminds, when 'the term "capitalism" is only used for the first time in 1854' by William Thackeray, 'he simply meant private ownership of money'. No more and no less. Capitalism is more about the concept of property ownership rather than that of economic liberalism. Economic growth/efficiency and distributive justice are not a trade-off assumed by capitalism; nor does it put any preference for one over another. With right policy combination, as the Danish case demonstrates, economic growth, market efficiency, and distributive justice can complement, rather than contradict, each other. In such contexts, capitalism, be it functioning through European market integration or globalization, is a win-win system, beneficial not just for the capital but for all economic actors and classes. For those who believe economic liberalism as the proper and the only realization of capitalism have made a serious epistemological fallacy.

Accordingly, market efficiency and economic justice is not a matter that capitalism predestines, but a matter of ideological preferences and policy choices. While EU leadership has been struggling between three competing visions for the EU's future—Germany's 'competitive Europe' (less Europe), France's 'protective Europe' (more Europe), and Hungary's 'anti-immigration, Christian Europe'—as Kundnani (2018) contends, none of these approaches addresses the roots of the EU's crisis decade: the economic thinking crisis. Without rightly recognizing the roots of this crisis decade, any vision of the EU forward may just repeat the same mistakes. What is more imperative for the EU's future, argued by this book, is an ideational revolution to EU leadership's entrenched neo-liberal economic ideology—its 'Brussels Doctrine'. Governing with such a doctrine, EU leadership has reduced European integration to a big economic project of marketization and liberalization since the 1990s, best represented as the European single market and currency. Market efficiency took precedence over economic justice, in the name of pursuing better competitiveness and greater growth, at the cost of dismantling social protection at the member-state level without equivalent replacements at the EU level. Such form of EU capitalism and governance has proved to result in an economically, politically, and socially divided EU.

Just as a divided house cannot be upheld for long nor can a divided EU. It should be reminded that European integration, like any other political and economic architecture by human designs, is not an aim itself. It is a means to enhancing the well-being of ordinary Europeans. Without a fair EU capitalism working for everyone and governance serving for most majorities' good, the EU's legitimacy and existence cannot be justified.

In a nutshell, the core of the EU's crisis decade lies in the misperceptions of EU leadership on market capitalism and embodied in their subsequent wrong economic governance and policy answers to these crises. The real danger to the EU, thus, is not the threats of ever-rising PRPs, not the intractable refugee crisis, not the loss of its third largest member after Brexit. These challenges were, indeed, significant, but not fatal. What constituted the EU's Achilles' heel was the misperceived economic ideology held by EU leadership, and it cast the real danger to the EU's future. Without an overhaul of its leadership's 'Brussels Doctrine', the increasing economic inequality cannot be corrected with much-needed policy changes, and public dissatisfaction and disillusion with the political establishment cannot be reversed accordingly. In such scenario, the EU cannot be guaranteed to be immune from the next, self-induced crisis by its economic mismanagement, and the crisis decade that the EU has been experiencing during 2008–2018 may not be an exception, but a new normal in the years to come. The key to disengaging from such a crisis-ridden pattern is held in the way of EU leadership's thinking. As Hutton (2015: 11) rightly comments, 'above all, it is a crisis of ideas'. If there was any lesson that was painfully learnt from this crisis decade for the EU and beyond, it was that: all rights and wrongs start with the ideas.

## References

Hutton, W. (2015), *How Good We Can Be: Ending the Mercenary Society and Building A Great Country*, London: Abacus.

Kundnani, H. (2018), 'Competing visions of Europe are threatening to tear the Union apart', 1 July 2018, *The Guardian*, available at https://www.theguardian.com/commentisfree/2018/jul/01/three-competing-visions-of-europe-threatening-to-tear-union-apart (accessed 27 July 2018).

Lagarde, C. (2014), 'Economic inclusion and financial integrity', Speech by Christine Lagarde, Managing Director, International Monetary Fund, 27 May 2014, London.

Oxenford, M. (2018), 'The lasting effects of the financial crisis have yet to be felt', *Chatham House Expert Comment*, 12 January 2018, available at https://www.chathamhouse.org/expert/comment/lasting-effects-financial-crisis-have-yet-be-felt (accessed 6 March 2018).

# Index[1]



[1] Note: Page numbers followed by 'n' refer to notes.


C.-M. Luo, *The EU's Crisis Decade*,
https://doi.org/10.1007/978-981-13-6565-2

W

Zeitfracht Medien GmbH
Ferdinand-Jühlke-Straße 7
99095 Erfurt, Deutschland
produktsicherheit@kolibri360.de